T0352625

Best Outdoor Adventures
ASHEVILLE

. . . .

A Guide to the Region's Greatest
Hiking, Cycling, and Paddling

. . . .

JOHNNY MOLLOY

GUILFORD, CONNECTICUT

FALCONGUIDES®

An imprint of The Rowman & Littlefield Publishing Group, Inc.
4501 Forbes Blvd., Ste. 200
Lanham, MD 20706
www.rowman.com
Falcon and FalconGuides are registered trademarks and Make Adventure Your
Story is a trademark of The Rowman & Littlefield Publishing Group, Inc.

Distributed by NATIONAL BOOK NETWORK

Photos by Johnny Molloy
Maps by Melissa Baker

British Library Cataloguing-in-Publication Information available

Library of Congress Control Number: 2020941236

ISBN 978-1-4930-4801-4 (paper : alk. paper)
ISBN 978-1-4930-4802-1 (electronic)

∞™ The paper used in this publication meets the minimum requirements of
American National Standard for Information Sciences—Permanence of Paper
for Printed Library Materials, ANSI/NISO Z39.48-1992.

**The author and The Rowman & Littlefield Publishing Group, Inc.
assume no liability for accidents happening to, or injuries sustained
by, readers who engage in the activities described in this book.**

Contents

Overview

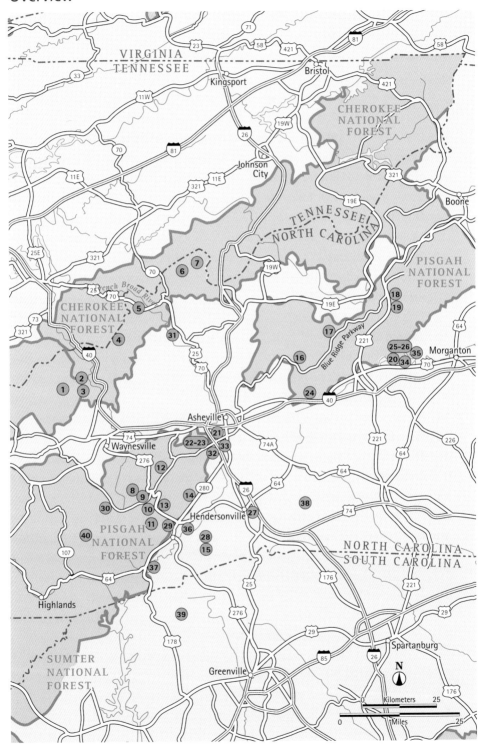

Introduction

Asheville, North Carolina, and its surrounding environs have deservingly gained a reputation as an outdoors haven, a mountain mecca, with opportunities to hike, pedal, and paddle found right in town and stretching outward from the French Broad River to the majestic highlands stretching in all directions. It's one thing to have an alluring mountainscape—after all, Asheville is known as the Land of the Sky—but yet another to have attractive lands under public domain, preserved as parks and forests, overlain with hiking trails, biking trails, and boat landings, as well as places to camp, destinations where we can execute outdoor adventures. Greater Asheville is blessed with getaways in and near town, from well-loved French Broad River Park to Lake Jordan to Bent Creek to the North Carolina Arboretum. Radiating outward, the Blue Ridge Parkway, Mount Mitchell State Park, and Pisgah National Forest present adventure opportunities among crashing streams and soaring peaks. Great Smoky Mountains National Park provides still more adventure possibilities. Places like Lake James State Park afford kayaking, mountain biking, hiking, and camping prospects. Visit wild waterfalls, bicycle or hike at DuPont State Forest; the destinations go on—federally designated wildernesses, inviting greenways, and winding rivers.

All this spells paradise for the outdoor adventurer. Let's start with hiking—the most accessible of activities. In this guide you can find hiking adventures representing a mosaic of the opportunities found in these parts. You can make a rocky, rugged trek in Linville Gorge to a breathtaking view or walk the inspiring bluffs above the French Broad River at Hot Springs. Perhaps you prefer exploring a secluded mountain valley with everywhere-you-look beauty on Bradley Creek. You could enjoy a historic hike to Little Cataloochee Church. Waterfalls are found all around the Asheville sphere—view the tall shower of Crabtree Falls on the Blue Ridge Parkway, the secluded cataracts at Hickey Fork, the delicate spillers that compose Twin Falls, or the remote spiller on the Jerry Miller Trail. Perhaps instead you want to grab a first-rate panorama at Mount Pisgah or Looking Glass Rock or Mount Sterling Tower.

Mountain bikers and greenway riders can also find a variety of rewarding adventures within easy striking distance of Asheville. You can tackle the challenging trails at Bent Creek Experimental Forest or ride the speedy Wimba Loops. Sometimes we just want to roll down a greenway or cruise with our family. In that case, this guide has got you covered. Roll down the Ocklawaha Greenway through Hendersonville, or ride the French Broad River Greenway. Ride through history on the Point Lookout Trail. Combine mountain scenery and urban greenway near Brevard on the Estatoe Greenway.

The paddling adventure opportunities are varied and rewarding as well. Tackle segments of the French Broad River Paddling Trail, from the narrow and splashy upriver sections near Rosman to the brawling, boulder-strewn lower French Broad near Marshall. Looking for a flatwater paddle? This guide offers several paddling adventures of that sort. Paddle the shoreline on convenient Lake Jordan. Head to a roaring 100-plus-foot waterfall while exploring Bear Creek Lake. Visit unheralded Lake Adger, discovering its many coves. Soak in superlative mountain vistas while paddling Lake Oolenoy. Cruise along the protected park shores at Lake James, enjoying yet more mountain landscapes.

The camping section details five nearby car camping destinations where you can not only camp for the sake of camping and relaxing but also as a base camp for many of the hiking, paddling, and bicycling adventures detailed in this guide. I stayed at every one of these campgrounds while assimilating information for *Best Outdoor Adventures Asheville*. The campground information includes an overview of the camping locale, when to go there, and what activities are available.

No matter what specific activity you choose, the important thing is to get out there, have some adventures, and make some memories. May this guide help you reach that goal.

Weather

Asheville, Hendersonville, and the mountains enveloping them experience all four seasons in their entirety—sometimes all at once when you take into account the elevation variations of the region, ranging from a little above 1,300 feet along the French Broad River at Hot Springs to 6,684 feet at Mount Mitchell. Summer can be warm with a few hot spells, though cool breezes can always be found along mountain streams and in the high country. Morning hikers can avoid the common afternoon thunderstorms that arise in the mountains. Electronic devices equipped with internet access allow hikers to monitor storms as they come up, though coverage can be spotty in remote national forest lands. Hikers increase in number when the first northerly fronts of fall sweep cool clear air across the Southern Appalachians. Crisp mornings, great for vigorous treks, give way to warm afternoons, more conducive to family strolls. Fall is drier than

Eastward view from Mount Sterling Tower
(adventure 2)

summer. Winter brings subfreezing days and chilling rains, and copious amounts of snow in the high country. We are talking more than 60 inches annually at 5,000 feet, though the city of Asheville averages 14 inches per year. Winter also brings fewer hours of daylight. However, a brisk hiking pace and wise time management will keep you warm and walking. Each cold month has a few days of mild weather. Make the most of them, and seek out lower-elevation hikes. Spring will be more variable. A mild day can be followed by a cold one. Extensive spring rains bring regrowth, but also keep many hikers indoors. March can bring heavy snows. However, avid hikers will find more good hiking days than they will have time to hike in spring and every other season. A good way to plan your hiking is to check monthly averages of high and low temperatures and average rainfall for each month in Asheville. This will give you a good idea of what to expect each month. However, remember that temperatures can be significantly cooler and precipitation higher in the adjacent highlands.

Month	Average High (°F)	Average Low (°F)	Precipitation (inches)
January	47	28	2.9
February	50	31	3.2
March	58	37	3.3
April	67	45	3.0
May	75	53	3.3
June	82	61	3.4
July	85	65	3.3
August	84	64	3.4
September	77	57	3.3
October	68	46	2.1
November	58	38	2.9
December	49	30	2.8

Flora and Fauna

The landscape of greater Asheville varies greatly, from the deep valley of the French Broad River and other lowland waterways to high peaks extending in every direction. Widespread public lands create large swaths for wildlife to roam. At the top of the food chain stands the black bear. You can run into one anywhere in the region and on any trail included in this guide. Although attacks

Elk roam the forests and fields of Cataloochee in Great Smoky Mountains National Park (adventure 1).

by black bears are very rare, they have occurred in the Southern Appalachians. Seeing a bear is an exciting yet potentially scary experience. If you meet a bear while hiking, stay calm and don't run. Make loud noises to scare off the bear and back away slowly. Remain aware and alert. Don't turn your back on the bear and, again, don't run. In addition to bruins, a wide variety of wildlife calls these landscapes home. Deer are the animal you're most likely to see along area trails. They can be found throughout western Carolina. A quiet hiker may also witness turkeys, raccoons, or even a coyote. Do not be surprised to observe a beaver, muskrat, or playful otter along mountain streams. If you feel uncomfortable when encountering any critter, keep your distance and they will generally keep theirs.

Overhead, many raptors will be plying the skies for food, including hawks, falcons, and owls. Depending on your location, other birds you may spot include kingfishers and woodpeckers. Songbirds are abundant during the warm season, no matter the habitat.

The flora offers as much variety as you would expect with such elevational range. Moisture-dependent forests are found along the mountain streams and

Painted trillium is but one of many wildflowers to be found on Bradley Creek in spring (adventure 14).

waterways, places where rhododendron creates immense thickets below black birch, tulip trees, and maple. Here grow the incredible displays of wildflowers, reflecting a cornucopia of color—purple dwarf crested iris, white trilliums, pink phlox, and red cardinal flower. On drier slopes rise hickory, oak, and mountain laurel. Cedars and pines thrive on rocky, sun-burnished slopes. Northern hardwood forests of yellow birch, beech, and cherry appear as you head higher in the mountains. Higher still are the rare spruce-fir forests that thrive above 5,000 feet, where northern red squirrels chatter and Turk's cap lilies color the late summer. It all adds up to vegetational variety of the first order that can be seen and experienced as spring climbs the mountains and fall descends back to the valleys.

Wilderness Restrictions/Regulations

The best outdoor adventures near Asheville take place on the federal lands of Pisgah National Forest, the Blue Ridge Parkway, and, to a lesser extent, Great Smoky Mountains National Park, as well as DuPont State Forest, Mount Mitchell State Park, Lake James State Park, and urban park property. Entrance to the area's federal lands is mostly free. Users of the national forest and national parks are expected to monitor their own behavior in backcountry areas, though you may see a ranger in designated wildernesses. Developed recreation areas with campgrounds and trails will be more closely supervised.

Detailed trail and road maps are available of Pisgah National Forest, the Blue Ridge Parkway, and Great Smoky Mountains National Park. They come in handy in helping you get around. Backcountry camping is restricted to designated sites inside Great Smoky Mountains National Park but is generally more freewheeling in Pisgah National Forest. Backcountry camping opportunities are limited in Blue Ridge Parkway lands and prohibited in the state parks detailed in this guide.

Lakes and rivers will have designated public landings for ingress/egress, while greenways are generally city property. While traveling waterways, respect private property where applicable.

Getting Around

AREA CODE
The greater Asheville area code is 828.

ROADS
For the purposes of this guide, the best adventures near Asheville are confined to a 1-hour drive from the greater metro region, which includes Hendersonville. Northward this stretches to the state of Tennessee and west to Hot Springs and the easternmost North Carolina Smokies. Southward, hikes extend to the Brevard area. Adventures are located easterly as far as Lake James State Park near Nebo and as far south as Table Rock State Park, just over the state line in South Carolina.

Two major interstates converge in the greater Asheville region. Directions to trailheads are given from these arteries. They include interstates I-40, I-26, and I-240—the alternate interstate through Asheville. Other major roads are US 74A, US 25, and US 70. The Blue Ridge Parkway is an important route to hikes in this guide.

BY AIR
Asheville Regional Airport (AVL) is located off NC 280, roughly halfway between Asheville and Hendersonville. To book reservations online, check out your favorite airline's website or search one of the following travel sites for the best price: cheaptickets.com, expedia.com, orbitz.com, priceline.com, travelocity.com, or trip.com—to name just a few.

BY BUS
Asheville Redefines Transportation (known as "ART") operates bus service throughout Asheville, though it won't do you much good for this book, since the best hikes near Asheville are mostly in adjacent wild public lands not served by mass transit. Visit ashevillenc.gov or call (828) 253-5691. In addition to ART, Henderson County has Apple Country Transit. Greyhound serves many towns in the region; visit greyhound.com for more information.

VISITOR INFORMATION
For general information on the greater Asheville area, visit visitnc.com/asheville-the-foothills or call (800) VISITNC (800-847-4862). This site links you to various western Carolina community tourism sites.

The Davidson River flows alluringly through the first part of the John Rock hike (adventure 11).

How to Use This Guide

This guide contains just about everything you will ever need to choose, plan for, enjoy, and survive an outdoor adventure near Asheville. Stuffed with useful area information, *Best Outdoor Adventures Asheville* features forty mapped and cued outdoor adventures, twenty hikes, ten bicycle rides, and ten paddles, as well as informative narratives on car camping. The adventures are grouped by activity.

Each section begins with an introduction to the hiking, bicycling, or paddling adventure in which you are given a sweeping look of what lies ahead. Each individual adventure narrative starts with a short **summary** of the adventure's highlights. These quick overviews give you a taste of the adventure to follow.

Following the overview you will find the **specs** relevant to the activity: quick, nitty-gritty details of the route. Most are self-explanatory, but here are some details:

Distance: This is the total distance of the recommended route—one-way for loop trips, round-trip for out-and-back or lollipop treks, point-to-point for a shuttle.

Hiking/Riding/Float time: The average time it will take to cover the route. For hike and bicycle routes, it is based on the total distance, elevation gain, and condition and difficulty of the trail. For paddles it also depends on the condition and difficulty of the water surface. Your fitness level will also affect your time.

Difficulty: Each adventure has been assigned a level of difficulty. The rating system was developed from several sources and personal experience. These levels are meant to be a guideline only, and adventures may prove easier or harder for different people depending on ability and physical fitness.

Trail surface: General information about what to expect underfoot.

Seasons: Best time of year for the activity.

Other trail users: Others you may encounter along the route, from equestrians to mountain bikers to motorboaters, depending on the activity.

Canine compatibility: Know the trail regulations before you take your dog with you.

Land status: National park, national forest, state forest, city park, etc.

Fees and permits: You may need to carry money with you for park entrance fees and permits.

Maps: A list of other maps to supplement the maps in this book. US Geological Survey (USGS) maps are the best source for accurate topographical information, but local park maps may show more recent trails. Use both.

Trail contacts: The location, phone number, and website URL for the local land and water managers in charge of all selected routes. Before you head out, get trail access information, or contact the land and/or water manager after your visit if you see damage or misuse.

Other considerations: Additional miscellaneous information to enhance your adventure.

Finding the trailhead: Dependable driving directions to where you will want to park.

The Hike/Ride/Paddle: The meat of the adventure, this is a detailed and honest, carefully researched impression of the route. It often includes area history, both natural and human.

Miles and Directions: The mileage cues identify all turns and trail name changes, as well as points of interest along the given route.

Paddling entries use additional, more relevant criteria, such as river/lake type, current, boats used, and the like.

Do not feel restricted to the routes mapped here. Be adventurous; use this guide as a platform to discover new routes for yourself. One of the simplest ways to begin is to tackle the route in reverse (though this may be difficult when paddling a river!). This way you get two adventures on one map. For your own purposes, you may wish to photograph the relevant pages from this guide on your device then take it with you on your adventure, or just take the book along. The important thing is to get out there on outdoor adventures and make some memories while doing them.

How to Use the Maps

Overview map: This map shows the location of each route in the area by route number.

Route map: This is your primary guide to each hike, pedal, or paddle. It shows all the accessible roads and trails, points of interest, water, landmarks, and geographical features. It also distinguishes trails from roads and paved roads from unpaved roads, or the proper water route from other creeks, channels, or parts of a given lake. The selected route is highlighted, and directional arrows point the way.

Map Legend

Municipal

≡(26)≡   Interstate Highway

≡(70)≡   US Highway

≡(212)≡   State Road

≡[465]≡   County/Local Road

Featured Local Road

Featured Unpaved Road

Unpaved Road

Railroad

Power/Pipe Line

State Border

Trails

Featured Trail

Trail

Paddle Route

Water Features

Body of Water

River/Creek

Intermittent Stream

Waterfall

Rapid

Symbols

Boat Launch

Bridge

Building/Point of Interest

Campground

Gate

Mileage

Overlook/Viewpoint

Parking

Pass

Picnic Area

Peak

Put-in/Takeout

Ranger Station

Restaurant

Tower

Trailhead

Visitor/Information Center

Land Management

National Park/Forest

State/County/City Park or Forest

Wilderness/National Monument

HIKING ADVENTURES

Of all the adventures presented in this guide, hiking is the most easily executed by the most people. It can be as simple as putting on your shoes then putting one foot in front of the other. Making it to the trailhead of your choice is another matter, though no matter where you live in greater Asheville, you can find a hiking adventure close by.

Here we present a collection of the best hikes in the greater Asheville region—a mosaic of foot-oriented adventures that vary in distance, difficulty, terrain, and highlights so you can sample the assortment of trail trekking experiences available in and around this scenic swath of western North Carolina. Grab a first-rate view from Looking Glass Rock. Walk the woodlands of Lake James State Park, or trek more-remote Linville Gorge. Check out the waterfalls of DuPont State Forest. Try new and different places—for these are the spices in the entree of the hiking life.

The French Broad River cuts through the Appalachians below Lovers Leap (adventure 5).

1 Big Fork Ridge Circuit

Old-growth trees highlight this loop hike that starts at lovely Cataloochee Valley in Great Smoky Mountains National Park. Add a visit to a pioneer homestead and you end up with a great day in the Smokies. The hike leaves Cataloochee on Rough Fork to see the Woody Place then rambles under old-growth trees, climbing up and over Big Fork Ridge to Caldwell Fork, a gorgeous stream. Visit the "Big Poplars," massive tulip trees worthy of national park protection, completing the circuit with a second climb of Big Fork Ridge.

Start: End of Cataloochee Road

Distance: 9.1-mile loop

Hiking time: About 5 hours

Difficulty: Moderate to difficult due to distance

Trail surface: Natural

Best season: Winter to best see the big trees

Other trail users: A few equestrians, some backpackers

Canine compatibility: Dogs prohibited

Land status: National park

Fees and permits: None for day hiking; fee and permit required for backpacking

Schedule: 24/7/365

Maps: USGS Bunches Bald, Dellwood; Great Smoky Mountains National Park

Trail contacts: Great Smoky Mountains National Park, 107 Park Headquarters Rd., Gatlinburg, TN 37738; (865) 436-1200; nps.gov/grsm

Finding the trailhead: From exit 20 on I-40 west of Asheville, head south a short distance on US 276. Turn right onto Cove Creek Road, which you follow nearly 6 miles to enter Great Smoky Mountains National Park. Two miles beyond the park boundary, turn left onto Cataloochee Road. Follow it to a dead end at the Rough Fork Trail, at the end of the parking area. GPS: N35° 36' 58.4" / W83° 07' 14.5"

The Hike

This is one of those hikes that makes you realize how special Great Smoky Mountains National Park is, and what a blessing for Ashevillians to have the Smokies in their own backyard. This hike combines superlative human and natural history into one scenic package. You start in the Cataloochee Valley, home to a preserved mountain community nestled among towering mountains, now

Admiring one of the giant tulip trees on this hike

complemented by wild elk. Here, pre-park pioneer homes ranging from log cabins to clapboard structures, along with churches and schools, have been preserved for all to see, set among woods and fields where families lived, loved, and died while calling the Cataloochee Valley home. This area is also home to crashing mountain streams, towering ridges, wild bears, and big woods, including massive old-growth tulip trees, some of which you will see on this circuit hike that explores two of the primary streams—Rough Fork and Caldwell Fork—flowing through Cataloochee.

Along the hike you will see the Woody Place, long the home of Cataloochee stalwarts. There is additional human history as well—the hike takes you by a pair of graves from the days when Civil War marauders on both sides crisscrossed this no-man's-land. The circuit hike does have challenges. It makes two climbs totaling approximately 2,000 feet of elevation change when looping from Rough Fork to Caldwell Fork and back again, surmounting Big Fork Ridge. Despite being along water much of the way, there are no wet-footed fords. Hiker bridges conveniently carry you across creeks. That fact makes it a good winter hike, when you can best see the old-growth trees and pioneer homesites, though the other seasons bring their delights too.

The circuit passes two fine designated backcountry campsites that can extend your adventure. A fee-based permit, accessible online, is required to camp overnight in the Smokies backcountry.

The route starts on the Rough Fork Trail at the end of Cataloochee Road, its fields sometimes harboring elk. The path traces crystalline Rough Fork as the watercourse dashes around rocks under groves of rhododendron and lush hardwoods. The Rough Fork Trail almost became a road in the 1960s. To alleviate anticipated traffic, park personnel wanted a route out of Cataloochee Valley instead of the existing one-way-in, one-way-out setup. And that was well before the arrival of the elk that have exponentially increased Cataloochee's popularity. Fortunately, the road was not built and we can walk up the still-wild Rough Fork valley.

Just 1.0 mile into the trek you can visit the Woody Place. By the way, the trip to the Woody Place makes a fine, short family-friendly out-and-back walk. Visit the wood clapboard structure fronted by a lone cedar in the front yard. The all-important springhouse stands nearby, while other outbuildings once dotted the locale. The garden was located in the level spot near the house. Pastures formerly extended well away from the structure.

Once inside the Woody Place, you will note the differing ceiling heights, giving away the fact that the home was built in stages over a long period, as most pioneer homes were back then. It started as a single-room log cabin, but they needed the extra room—fourteen kids lived here at once after Jonathan Woody wed a widow with her own children. Later, in the 1920s, when Cataloochee was discovered by tourists flocking to western North Carolina (as they have ever since), the Woody family hosted these visitors as they fished for trout and roamed the mountains. Steve Woody—Jonathan Woody's son—stocked Rough Fork with rainbow trout and charged anglers by the number of fish they caught and kept.

Old-growth forests begin not far beyond the Woody Place, dominated by red oaks and, sadly, the skeletons of deceased hemlock trees fallen prey to the hemlock woolly adelgid. Then you come to Big Hemlock backcountry campsite #40, where some of the evergreens have been preserved. The campsite, nestled between Hurricane Creek and Rough Fork, is heavily cloaked in rhododendron and dog hobble that form barriers between camps.

The hike then climbs a rocky, rooty path away from Hurricane Creek onto Little Ridge, shaded by big tulip trees as well as chestnut oak trees farther up. It is a little over 1,300 feet from the trailhead to the high point. The descent begins after the loop hike joins the Caldwell Fork Trail. Descend past the "Big Poplars," huge tulip trees, some of which take several people linking outstretched arms to encircle. Don't bypass the Big Poplars. Caldwell Fork backcountry campsite #41 is not far from the Big Poplars. This camp is set in a hardwood flat along its namesake stream.

The circuit next passes a trail intersection, then comes to a spur trail leading to the Civil War graves of three former Union soldiers, buried in two graves. They were killed just before the end of the Civil War by some fellow Northerners who were terrorizing local residents in the wartime chaos. It isn't long before the second and final climb of the hike—gaining a little over 600 feet—leads you over Big Fork Ridge on a path carved out by Cataloochee residents and subsequently improved by the National Park Service. After crossing Big Fork Ridge, the path descends past more pioneer homesites and the site of an elk enclosure where the animals were acclimated before being released into the wilds, where they have thrived ever since. Hopefully you will see some of these critters while in Cataloochee Valley.

Big Fork Ridge Circuit

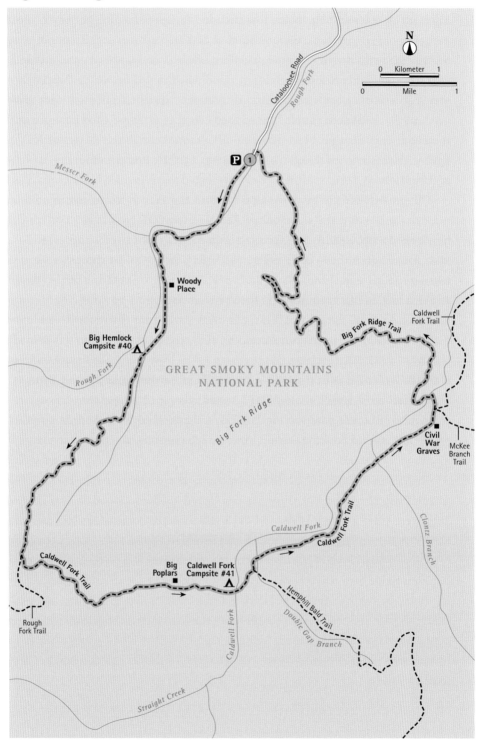

Miles and Directions

0.0   Start on the Rough Fork Trail as it leaves the uppermost end of Cataloochee Valley. Cruise a wide, nearly level track shaded by yellow birch, maple, and white pine. The valley shortly closes in. Span Rough Fork on a wooden hiker bridge; cross the waterway again on a second hiker bridge. Walk a wet section of path before bridging Rough Fork a third time.

1.0   Come to the Steve Woody Place after reaching a clearing.

1.5   Reach Big Hemlock backcountry campsite #40 after crossing Hurricane Creek. Climb to Little Ridge beyond the campsite.

3.0   Come to a trail intersection. Turn left, joining the Caldwell Fork Trail, now heading downhill under more old-growth forest of northern hardwoods such as cherry and buckeye.

4.1   Intersect the short spur trail to the Big Poplars, old-growth tulip trees (not poplars, as they were formerly known).

4.4   Come to Caldwell Fork backcountry campsite #41, situated in a flat along Caldwell Fork. Cross Caldwell Fork on a hiker bridge then pass a homesite on your right, now foresting over.

4.5   Pass the Hemphill Bald Trail. Stay straight down the Caldwell Fork valley, often traversing a hillside well above the stream.

5.9   Reach a side trail leading right to a gravesite. Up the spur are two graves where three Union soldiers are interred. Meet the McKee Branch Trail not far beyond here. Keep straight, still on the Caldwell Fork Trail, through former farmland, now being reclaimed by fire cherry, locust, and tulip trees.

6.0   Turn left on the Big Fork Ridge Trail. Span Caldwell Fork on a wooden hiker bridge then climb a pioneer-originated path through hardwoods. Soon make a big switchback, working up Rabbit Ridge.

7.5   Bisect a gap in Big Fork Ridge. Your climb is over and the rest of the hike is downhill as you reenter the Rough Fork valley.

9.1   Cross Rough Fork on a footbridge then arrive back at the trailhead.

2   Mount Sterling Tower

This Great Smoky Mountains National Park hike begins at high and historic Mount Sterling Gap then climbs higher to enter the rare spruce-fir forest that cloaks only the highest mantles of the Southern Appalachians. The ascent tops out at 5,842-foot Mount Sterling, where a preserved metal fire tower delivers unparalleled 360-degree views of the Smokies in the near and range after range in North Carolina and Tennessee.

Start: Mount Sterling Gap

Distance: 5.4 miles out and back

Hiking time: About 3 hours

Difficulty: Moderate; does have steep sections

Trail surface: Natural

Best season: Whenever the skies are clear

Other trail users: A few backpackers, an occasional equestrian

Canine compatibility: Dogs prohibited

Land status: National park

Fees and permits: None for day hiking; fee and permit required for backpacking

Schedule: 24/7/365

Maps: USGS Cove Creek Gap; Great Smoky Mountains National Park

Trail contacts: Great Smoky Mountains National Park, 107 Park Headquarters Rd., Gatlinburg, TN 37738; (865) 436–1200; nps.gov/grsm

Finding the trailhead: From Asheville, take I-40 west to exit 451, just west of the North Carolina state line in Tennessee. Take the paved road and cross the Pigeon River. After the bridge, turn left to follow the Pigeon upstream. Come to an intersection 2.3 miles after crossing the Pigeon. Turn left here onto old NC 284 and follow it 6.7 winding miles to Mount Sterling Gap. The trail starts on the west side of the gap. GPS: N35° 41' 59.9" / W83° 05' 50.9"

The Hike

This is a problematic hike to rate for difficulty. The hike is not long—5.4 miles. However, it is fairly steep; you gain a little over 1,900 feet in 2.7 miles. Yet the trail is well graded and in good shape. Though sustained, the uptick does not stretch for miles and miles like some other Smokies treks, so I give it a moderate rating—with an asterisk. The extraordinary view is worth the effort, no matter

Looking down from Mount Sterling on hikers below and mountains beyond

the rating. The preserved metal tower stands at 5,842 feet, purportedly the highest elevation true fire tower still standing east of the Mississippi River.

Originally constructed in 1935 by the Civilian Conservation Corps, the tower was designed for fire watching. A small cabin and outhouse were also constructed for the person manning the tower. Firewatchers generally stayed up here for two-week stints during the spring and fall fire seasons. The tower was decommissioned in the mid-1960s when airplanes began to be used for fire watching; the firewatcher's cabin was left to deteriorate until the 1980s. Since then the fire tower has been stabilized and its heights used as a communications tower for Great Smoky Mountains National Park. This is one of two metal fire towers preserved in the Smokies, the other being Shuckstack Tower at the other—western—end of the park.

Mount Sterling Gap, at an elevation 3,890 feet, lets you start high and get higher. Long before I-40 and the roads we have today, Mountain Sterling Gap was a point of passage for travelers between North Carolina and Tennessee. During the Civil War, the remote mountains around the state line became a no-man's-land, neither Confederate nor Union, loyal only to whomever controlled passes such as Mount Sterling Gap. Conscription agents from both armies sought deserters and draft dodgers to fill their respective ranks—or eliminate from the ranks of the opposition's armies. Conflicts occurred regularly.

The snowy crest of the Smokies
as seen from Mount Sterling

On April 10, 1865, Albert Teague, a member of the local Confederate home guard, intercepted three Union sympathizers at the gap and marched them along to the fiddle tunes played by one Harry Grooms. Grooms was carrying the fiddle and bow with him when he was captured along with his brother George and his brother-in-law Mitchell Caldwell. Teague shot Harry Grooms and the two others after one final song, allegedly "Bonaparte's Retreat," subsequently known also as "Grooms Tune." The three Union partisans were buried by Harry's wife, thrown into a common grave in the community of Mount Sterling by Big Creek. The headstone above the freshly mounded dirt stated one word: "Murdered."

Though Mount Sterling is known for its spruce-fir forest, the hike begins among hardwoods—primarily oaks—cloaking the east–west ridge linking Mount Sterling and Mount Sterling Gap. When the leaves are off the trees, you can view the mantle of evergreens on the crown of Mount Sterling. You are hiking the south side of the ridge, where galax and mountain laurel belie the increasing elevation. Eventually the path rises enough—and curves around to the north side of the ridge—to enter the spruce-fir zone, starting with the red spruce then accompanied by fellow cool-climate specialists yellow birch and beech. Demonstrating the influence of exposure, mountain laurel, pines, and oaks are seen again when the trail enters southern exposure.

After angling onto the reaches of Mount Sterling Ridge, breaking 5,000 feet, the spruce-fir ecosystem takes over. Here, red spruce rise thick and high, creating a shady, moist environment where springs trickle cool across the trail—a forest floor rich with mosses and an understory of Fraser fir.

Once atop Mount Sterling Ridge, you will see thickets of Fraser fir trees along with a few grasses, remnants of the days when this ridge was grazed by cattle. The path is mostly level before rising to reach a little-used horse hitching post a little ways from the Mount Sterling summit. Just ahead, open onto a clearing and the top of Mount Sterling. This is also the location of backcountry campsite #38, also named Mount Sterling.

The tower stands at the very crest of the summit, where a USGS benchmark denotes the actual high point. Woe to those who reach the tower via the Baxter Creek Trail—a very tough 6-mile climb from Big Creek Ranger Station. A few backpackers make their way here via Mount Sterling Ridge Trail; however, the vast majority of tower visitors come via Mount Sterling Gap.

The park's eastern swath is the featured view from the tower. The main crest of the Smokies runs to your north and west, mostly covered in spruce and fir as well. I-40 and its road cut in the Pigeon River gorge are easy to spot to the

Mount Sterling Tower

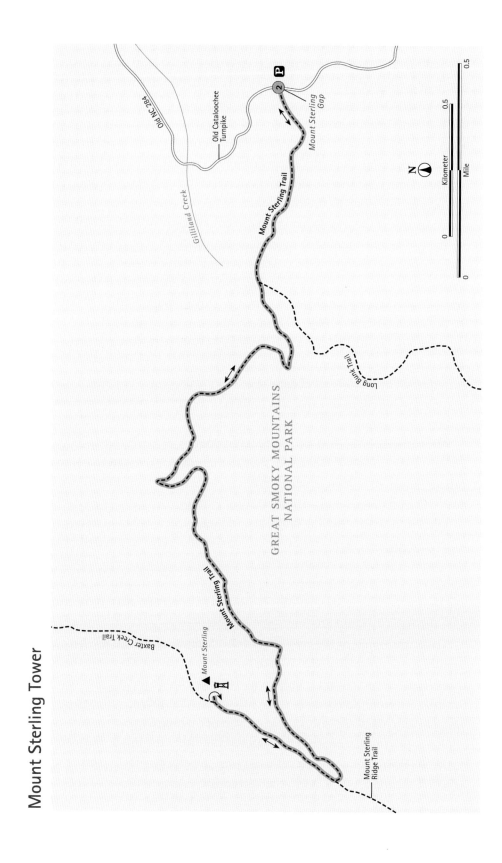

east. Look east also for the meadow of Max Patch. A hike there is also detailed in this guide. The hills of East Tennessee stretch to the west. At night, the lights of Newport, Tennessee, and Waynesville, North Carolina, are easily spotted. Backpackers overnighting at the campsite here climb the tower for nocturnal vistas.

Mount Sterling backcountry campsite #38 is a desired site. The most popular camp spot is in the grassy area immediately below the tower. The campsite's claim to fame is being the highest backcountry campsite in the Smokies without a trail shelter. Other private wooded individual camps are set in the adjacent woods, especially desirable when the wind is howling. Looking for water? A spring is located 0.5 mile down the Baxter Creek Trail. Back during the firewatcher days, those manning the tower would use this spring as well as capture water from the cabin roof into a cistern.

Miles and Directions

0.0   Start on the Mount Sterling Trail as it ascends westerly from Mount Sterling Gap as a wide trail. Walk around a pole gate and waste no time climbing on the jeep road, built to haul men and materials up to the peak to construct the tower and cabin.

0.5   Level out and meet the Long Bunk Trail, which heads left for 3.6 miles to meet the Little Cataloochee Trail to the south. Our hike keeps straight, aiming ever higher.

0.7   The Mount Sterling Trail makes a sharp switchback to the right, leaving the southern exposure.

1.3   Switchback left, curving back into what is left of the oaks at this high elevation.

2.3   Meet the Mount Sterling Ridge Trail after cresting out on Mount Sterling Ridge. The Mount Sterling Ridge Trail leaves left for 1.4 miles to Pretty Hollow Gap. We go right on the Mount Sterling Ridge Trail, heading northeast for the peak of Mount Sterling on one of the more level segments of this hike.

2.7   Emerge onto the clearing atop Mountain Sterling. You will see Mount Sterling Tower rising from the high point as well as the main camping area for campsite #38. Climb the tower for spectacular views. Return the way you came.

5.4   Arrive back at Mount Sterling Gap.

3   Little Cataloochee Historic Hike

This secluded hike to Little Cataloochee Church, nestled in Great Smoky Mountains National Park, is a trip back in time. Start at a remote trailhead, tracing an old road. Pass a preserved historic cabin on your undulating trek into the Little Cataloochee Valley, where the pioneer community of Ola once stood. Explore Ola to see home-sites and evidence of the past. Finally, climb a hill to bucolic Little Cataloochee Church, built in the 1800s and still maintained.

Start: Old NC 284

Distance: 4.0 miles out and back

Hiking time: About 2 hours

Difficulty: Easy–moderate

Trail surface: Natural

Best season: Year-round; summer growth may make historic sights less visible.

Other trail users: A few equestrians

Canine compatibility: Dogs prohibited

Land status: National park

Fees and permits: No fees or permits required

Schedule: 24/7/365

Maps: USGS Cove Creek Gap; Great Smoky Mountains National Park

Trail contacts: Great Smoky Mountains National Park, 107 Park Headquarters Rd., Gatlinburg, TN 37738; (865) 436–1200; nps.gov/grsm

Finding the trailhead: From exit 20 on I-40 west of Asheville, take NC 276 south a short distance to Cove Creek Road. Turn right on Cove Creek Road and follow it nearly 6 miles to enter the park. Two miles beyond the park boundary, reach paved Cataloochee Road. However, keep straight, looking for a sign for "Big Creek, Cosby," joining gravel Old NC 284. Follow it for 2.1 miles then come to a split. Stay right, still on gravel Old NC 284, and continue 3.5 miles to the Little Cataloochee Trail, on your left. *Note:* Do not block the gate at the trailhead. GPS: N35° 40' 32.1" / W83° 05' 13.5"

The Hike

Many parts of what later became Great Smoky Mountains National Park were settled and owned by ancestors of the first pioneers, who cleared off fertile valleys in this back of beyond then established communities and cultivated a way

A view of historic Little Cataloochee Church from its graveyard

of life that has long since faded away. However, the very establishment of the national park that threw these people off their land preserved relics of this North Carolina pioneer past. And in very few places is that past better preserved than in the Smokies. This network of valleys draining mile-high mountains was first settled in the 1830s. The primary community that sprang up was known as Cataloochee. Not long after families named Caldwell, Hannah, and Palmer moved in and offspring were born, Cataloochee already seemed a mite crowded for some. Pioneers being the way they are, some of the offspring got a little restless and

Little Cataloochee Church is set on a hill in the Great Smoky Mountains.

moved on. A fellow named Dan Cook led the way to this settlement a few ridges over on Little Cataloochee Creek, building his log cabin in the 1850s.

But things really got going when one Will Messer married Dan Cook's daughter Rachael and bought 100 acres on Little Cataloochee Creek. There, Messer established Ola, named for his daughter Viola. Messer built the all-encompassing general store, a post office bearing the name Ola, and a blacksmith shop along with his own rangy eleven-room house.

Others followed, and Ola began to thrive. John Hannah built his cabin in 1864, even using bricks in his chimney, a very unusual thing in this place at that time. This hike takes you past the John Hannah cabin and through Ola; however, the highlight of the hike is the visit to Little Cataloochee Church. This white church sitting atop a hill is a vivid reminder of the simplicity of those days gone by. Also known as Ola Baptist Church, the rectangular structure was built in 1889; the belfry you see was added in 1914. Even today, a rope connects to the bell and visitors to Little Cataloochee Church toll the bell much as they did more than a century back. A well-maintained, fenced cemetery filled with residents of Ola who attended this church stretches out on a hillside below the white chapel. Inside, the whitewashed walls brighten sunlit wooden floors, where simple bench pews and a pulpit stand in wait. An old-fashioned wood stove sits in the center of the house of worship.

Being very difficult to access from the outside, the community of Ola and Little Cataloochee Church were served by a circuit-riding preacher, who visited various country churches on a rotating basis. He came about one Sunday a month, spending the night with different church member families. On the other Sundays, weekly gatherings were still held at the church. Members would have Sunday school and praise music. Other gatherings, including weddings and funerals, were held at hilltop Little Cataloochee Church.

When someone in the Ola community passed away, the 400-pound church bell was tolled to let residents within earshot know. The bell would be rung several times, followed by extended silence. The bell toller would then ring the bell once for each year of the person's life. Locals would count the tolls to identify the deceased.

In late fall, after the crops had been harvested, Little Cataloochee Church would host a weeklong camp meeting and revival. Long services alternated with group meals and fellowship. The men would head in and out of the services, gathering outside to chew tobacco and shoot the breeze. To this day, descendants of those who lived in Cataloochee annually meet at the preserved church to worship, maintain the graves of their ancestors, and share a meal and stories of the past, perhaps to see and appreciate the beauty of their ancestral home.

Life in Little Cataloochee happily crawled along as the world moved on. It came as a great surprise when the residents heard the "Feds" wanted to turn their quiet isolated valley into a national park. Some were glad to go, but most left their homeland with heavy hearts, uprooted and bought out by the government using eminent domain. Today we can see the evidence of those days gone by.

I recommend making this hike from late fall through early spring, when the leaves are off the trees and you can best see the homesites, rock walls, and other evidence of pre-park settlers. You will also enjoy seclusion. This trek begins at a remote trailhead for the Smokies, and the few people who hike to Little Cataloochee Church usually start at more-popular Cataloochee Valley. Be forewarned: The trail to Little Cataloochee Church has lots of ups and downs, though the undulations are never too long or too precipitous. However, the hike follows a roadbed, making it foot-friendly. After spanning Correll Branch, the Little Cataloochee Trail curves into the Little Cataloochee Creek valley on a hillside well above the stream. The wide track travels under pines and oaks then intersects the lesser-used Long Bunk Trail. Shortly after the junction, come to the John Hannah Cabin, built in the 1860s and since restored by the park service. The

Little Cataloochee Historic Hike

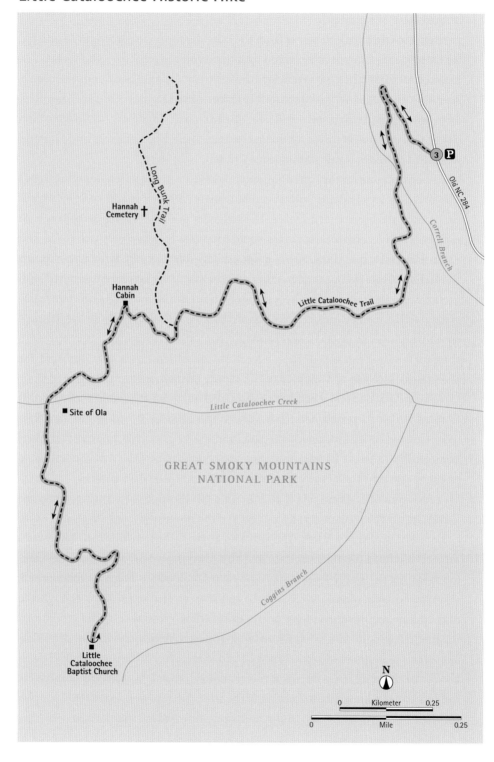

Long Bunk Trail

Hannah
Cemetery †

Hannah
Cabin

Little Cataloochee Trail

3 P

Old NC 284

Correll Branch

■ Site of Ola

Little Cataloochee Creek

GREAT SMOKY MOUNTAINS
NATIONAL PARK

Coggins Branch

■ Little
Cataloochee
Baptist Church

N

| 0 | Kilometer | 0.25 |

| 0 | Mile | 0.25 |

distinctive redbrick chimney adds color to the wood cabin, showing the effects of time. Explore uphill from the cabin to find rock piles in fields that were once striped with rows of corn and now adorned with gray, straight-trunked tulip trees. While you are at it, imagine grassy hillsides dotted with the apple trees Hannah harvested.

It isn't long before you cross Little Cataloochee Creek on a bridge, arriving at Will Messer's community of Ola. Scan the area for relic apple trees. Ample evidence of homesites is scattered throughout the flats on the creek's south side. Any remains you find are part of Great Smoky Mountains National Park. Explore, enjoy—then leave the artifacts behind.

From there the trail leads up a ridge where Little Cataloochee Church stands atop a hill separating Little Cataloochee Creek from Coggins Branch. The fine, well-maintained, sturdy white sanctuary astonishes even more after seeing the older, rustic cabin of John Hannah and other remnants of Ola in various stages of disrepair.

Miles and Directions

0.0 Start at the Old NC 284 trailhead on a wide roadbed that is the Little Cataloochee Trail. (It is maintained this way to allow Little Cataloochee descendants auto access to the church and family graves.) Drop to span Correll Branch beneath a thick forest canopy.

1.0 Intersect the Long Bunk Trail after meandering through pine-oak woods with an understory of mountain laurel. It heads right and climbs toward Mount Sterling Gap. Our hike stays straight with the wide Little Cataloochee Trail.

1.2 Meet the spur trail to the Hannah Cabin. Turn right here and soon come to the hillside cabin, notable for its brick "chimbley." After visiting the cabin, continue on the Little Cataloochee Church Trail.

1.4 Bridge Little Cataloochee Creek. You are now in the heart of what once was the community of Ola. Explorers can spot evidence of pre-park settlement, but be sure to leave all artifacts behind for others to discover.

2.0 Reach Little Cataloochee Baptist Church after topping the ridge dividing Little Cataloochee Creek and Coggins Branch. Respectfully explore the church and its grounds then return the way you came.

4.0 Arrive back at the trailhead.

4 Max Patch Loop

Make an easy circuit through and around this former mountaintop pasture, now a protected meadow with superlative views known as the "Grandstand of the Smokies." First take the Max Patch Loop Trail, traversing the western slopes opening into Tennessee. Take the short side trip to the 4,629-foot summit of Max Patch, soaking in 360-degree panoramas. Trace the Appalachian Trail northbound into highland forests. Return to the trailhead in a mélange of field and forest, soaking in more highland panoramas.

Start: Trailhead on Max Patch Road

Distance: 2.7-mile loop with spur

Hiking time: About 1.3 hours

Difficulty: Easy–moderate

Trail surface: Natural

Best season: Year-round when skies are clear

Other trail users: None

Canine compatibility: Leashed dogs allowed

Land status: National forest

Fees and permits: No fees or permits required

Schedule: 24/7/365

Maps: USGS Lemon Gap; National Geographic #782: French Broad & Nolichucky Rivers [Cherokee and Pisgah National Forests]

Trail contacts: Pisgah National Forest, Appalachian Ranger District, 632 Manor Rd., Mars Hill, NC 28754; (828) 689-9694; fs.usda.gov/nfsnc

Finding the trailhead: From exit 7 (Harmon Den) on I-40 west of Asheville, take Cold Springs Creek Road (FR 148) right for 6.3 miles to reach a T intersection. Turn left here onto NC 1182 (Max Patch Road). Continue for 2 miles to the Max Patch parking area, on your right. GPS: N35° 47' 47.3" / W82° 57' 45.0"

The Hike

Max Patch is one of those venerated places people speak of in hushed, almost reverential tones. Traversed by the Appalachian Trail as it straddles the North Carolina–Tennessee state line, the meadows of Max Patch are not only a great place to see but also a great place from which to view the surrounding magnificence of the Southern Appalachians. Often dubbed the "Grandstand of the

Hikers trek the Appalachian Trail as it crosses Max Patch.

Smokies," the open fields of Max Patch deliver an unobstructed panorama of the most visited national park in the country, a park in which Ashevillians and residents throughout western North Carolina take pride. This view of Great Smoky Mountains National Park is close enough that on a clear day, you can stand there with the naked eye and point out specific mountains lying within the boundaries of the national park as well as many a highland ridge beyond. You can also see Mount Mitchell—much farther than the Smokies—to the east.

Max Patch is about more than distant panoramas. The near beauty and lure are strong too, whether you are picking fruit-heavy blackberry bushes in late summer against a backdrop of tall wildflowers, traipsing through wind-tossed tawny grasses, or crossing a white carpet of snow as chill winds blow across winter skies so clear that the mountains seem close enough to touch. And then there is the rising greenery of spring climbing the mountains as Appalachian Trail thru-hikers cross the open bald.

However, there are the times when Max Patch is obscured in fog, rain, or clouds—or storms. And storms atop this grassy peak can be dangerous, for Max

Meadows and mountains stretch to the horizon from Max Patch.

Patch was the site of a tragic event in 2010. A couple had come from Knoxville, Tennessee, to hike the bald. Bethany Lott had raved about Max Patch and finally brought her boyfriend, Richard Butler. Unbeknownst to Bethany, Richard had brought an engagement ring, planning to propose to her atop Max Patch, the place she loved above all the rest. Shortly after Richard and Bethany set out, a June thunderstorm descended quickly on the mountain. Just as the skies were darkening, flashes of lightning shot down from the sky onto Max Patch, striking the pair! Bethany had been walking in the lead and was a bit higher up the meadow when the bolt hit them, the third in a quick series of lightning strikes according to Richard's later recounting of the accident. Bethany died atop her beloved Max Patch despite the efforts of a debilitated Richard to seek help. The lightning had affected Richard as well, going through his legs and coming out his shoes, temporarily compromising his ability to run. By force of will, Richard got off Max Patch and sought help. But it was too late. He later slipped the engagement ring on Bethany's finger after paramedics' vain attempts to resuscitate her.

Try to come here on a clear day and you will be well rewarded and out of danger. It is an ideal walk for novice mountain hikers, since the views are so rewarding. Not only does the Appalachian Trail cross Max Patch's 300-plus acres of grasses, but additional paths can be used to make a loop hike. Still other trails provide shortcuts if necessary. The recommended loop hike climbs less than 500 feet.

The name Max Patch is almost certainly a corruption of its original name: Mac's Patch. Cattle and sheep grazed here in the 1800s. Before that, no one knows for sure if Max Patch was one of those unexplained natural Southern Appalachian balds or cleared by farmers down in the valleys for summertime grazing lands. Later, Max Patch became an airstrip that claimed (probably correctly) to be the highest landing strip in the East. Air shows were held here in the 1920s and 1930s, drawing crowds from western North Carolina and East Tennessee. At one time, there were even crude cabins set up for tourists. In 1982 Max Patch was purchased by the government and became part of Pisgah National Forest rather than a ski resort, which it almost became. Today the bald is kept mown by the USDA Forest Service.

A trail with no name once led from the parking area straight up the bald, but it has been closed due to the erosion it caused. Instead of that path, I recommend making the circuit hike using the Max Patch Loop Trail. It leads left on an old grassy roadbed, roughly tracing the North Carolina–Tennessee state line. Views into the Volunteer State extend westerly. The loop trail, bordered by berry bushes and a few trees, leaves the state line to enter forest. After passing a spring box left over from cattle grazing days, the loop trail reenters grasses then meets the Appalachian Trail (AT). A side walk up the AT takes you on a must-do trip to the tiptop of Max Patch. From this spot, 4,629 feet as reckoned by the USGS survey marker, you can gaze upon Great Smoky Mountains National Park. At 4,928 feet, Mount Cammerer is the easiest peak to spot; look for the flattish top, squat tower, and sharp drop to the right. Mount Sterling, standing at 5,843 feet, is easy to find too; look for the metal tower atop its peak. And there is more—wave upon wave of mountains near and far. It makes you grateful to be alive and in the Southern Appalachians!

Backtrack on the Appalachian Trail, heading northbound. The AT is marked with wooden trailside posts through the meadows. These posts make the trail easier to find in the often foggy/cloudy weather atop Max Patch. The fields are traded first for tall hardwoods then rhododendron thickets before you rejoin the Max Patch Loop Trail. The next segment of the hike wanders through a mosaic

Max Patch Loop

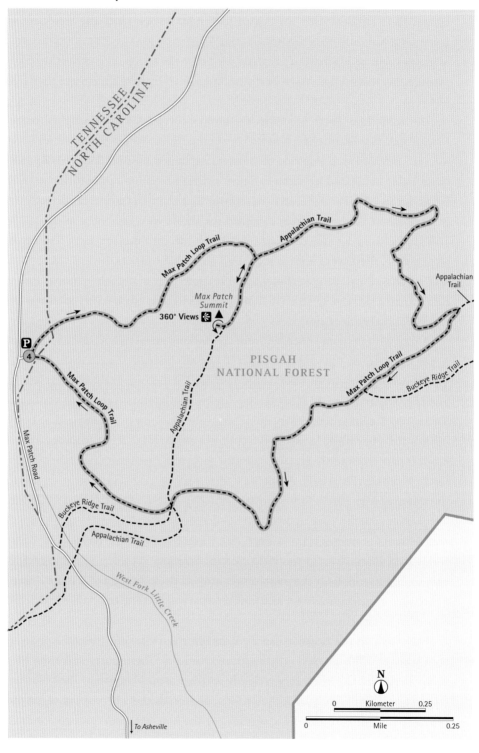

TENNESSEE
NORTH CAROLINA

Appalachian Trail

Max Patch Loop Trail

Appalachian Trail

Max Patch
Summit

360° Views

P
4

PISGAH
NATIONAL FOREST

Max Patch Loop Trail

Buckeye Ridge Trail

Max Patch Loop Trail

Appalachian Trail

Max Patch Road

Buckeye Ridge Trail

Appalachian Trail

West Fork Little Creek

To Asheville

N

Kilometer
0   0.25

Mile
0   0.25

of woods, bushes, and grasses. Buckeye Ridge rises to your left. The grassy crown of Max Patch soars to your right. The Max Patch Loop Trail continues circling the bald, crossing the AT a second time before returning to the trailhead. Somewhere along the way, find a relaxing spot and soak in the highland serenity that is Max Patch.

Miles and Directions

0.0 Start from the main parking area and head left on the Max Patch Loop Trail, a signed doubletrack path. Do not take the closed path heading straight up the meadow, now blocked by a fence. Views open west into Tennessee and the lower French Broad River valley.

0.2 Leave the grasses and walk through a hardwood forest. The fields of Max Patch rise uphill.

0.3 A spur trail leads left to a spring box for cattle, which formerly grazed Max Patch.

0.5 Open onto a meadow then meet the Appalachian Trail. Turn right (southbound) on the AT and soon reach the top of Max Patch, delineated by a USGS survey marker. Backtrack, now heading northbound on the AT, passing the junction where you picked up the AT earlier.

1.0 The trail leads into the woods. Continue descending.

1.4 Come to a fenced-in spring and small campsite. Leave the woods and bisect thickly growing patches of rhododendron.

1.5 Reach a trail intersection. Turn right here, leaving the AT to rejoin the Max Patch Loop Trail.

1.7 Keep straight as the equestrian-friendly Buckeye Ridge Trail enters on your left. The Max Patch Loop and Buckeye Ridge Trails run in conjunction here on a roadbed, leading over a pair of wooded streamlets.

2.3 Come to a four-way trail intersection. Here the Appalachian Trail goes right (uphill) and left (downhill), while the Buckeye Ridge Trail continues to follow the old roadbed. Keep straight with the grassy Max Patch Loop Trail as it cuts through brush, grass, and trees. Enjoy more views as you aim for the trailhead.

2.7 Arrive back at the trailhead.

5   Lovers Leap

This hike leaves the trail town of Hot Springs and makes a loop, passing cliffs above the French Broad River where you can soak in a historic view from Lovers Leap. First trek along a narrow mountain stream where spring flowers rise. Meet the famed Appalachian Trail then join Lovers Leap Ridge. Trace the AT atop this narrow spine as the brawny French Broad flows hundreds of feet below. As you near Hot Springs, come to a stone promontory affording views of the town below and the mountains rising above the French Broad River valley. Enjoy an encore vista from the actual Lovers Leap before leaving the AT and returning to the parking area.

Start: Silvermine trailhead
Distance: 4.1-mile loop
Hiking time: About 2.2 hours
Difficulty: Moderate
Trail surface: Natural, gravel

Looking down on the mud-stained
French Broad River as it flows
through Hot Springs

Best season: Year-round; good in winter

Other trail users: None

Canine compatibility: Leashed dogs allowed

Land status: National forest

Fees and permits: No fees or permits required

Schedule: 24/7/365

Maps: USGS Hot Springs; National Geographic #782: French Broad & Nolichucky Rivers [Cherokee and Pisgah National Forests]

Trail contacts: Pisgah National Forest, Appalachian Ranger District, 632 Manor Rd., Mars Hill, NC 28754; (828) 689-9694; fs.usda.gov/nfsnc

Finding the trailhead: From Asheville, take I-26 North to exit 19A (Marshall). Join US 25 N/US 70 W and continue 21 miles to Hot Springs. Immediately before crossing the bridge over the French Broad River, just east of Hot Springs, turn right on River Road. Drive a very short distance to the river; turn left on paved Silvermine Creek Road, following it under the US 25/US 70 bridge. Stay left again as the road curves up Silvermine Creek past houses. Reach the signed Silvermine parking area, on your left, 0.3 mile from US 25/US 70. GPS: N35° 53' 33.0" / W82° 49' 05.6"

The Hike

You can combine this fun trek with a trip to the trail town of Hot Springs, hemmed in by mountains on all sides save for where the French Broad River fights its way west into Tennessee. This hike is just across the river from the town built around and named for the hot springs, a highlight among other area attractions such as rafting, kayaking, camping, and hiking.

And did I mention eating? One of the perks of hiking is eating a calorie-laden—and guilt-free—meal after your hike. Hot Springs has dining options aplenty, especially compared with your average trailhead. The outdoorsy tourist town is worth a day trip.

The Cherokee had found and used the thermal springs along the French Broad long before colonial settlers made their way to these mineral waters that some believed had healing properties. By the time the United States had come to be, sick folk were soaking in the 100°F waters in an attempt to get better.

William Nelson saw this as an economic opportunity. He bought the springs and established a "resort" here, the first in what became a long line of hotels based around the springs. Back in those days, roads were rough and getting across the mountains wasn't easy. However, by 1828 the Buncombe Turnpike was routed along the French Broad River and passed beside the springs, raising the profile of the area for thousands of passersby who made their way from North Carolina into Tennessee and vice versa on the road.

The grand age of the springs began when Asheville's James Patten built a 350-room hotel in 1831. Times were good, and for the next eight decades the springs and the hotels beside them thrived. In 1882 a hot spring was discovered, and the town of Warm Springs became Hot Springs. Despite the hotter water, the tourist trade declined until, in 1917, the town's main hotel housed German merchant sailors at the height of World War I rather than tourists seeking the healing hot aqua. This last hotel burned down after the war. Only recently, with the rise in popularity of the Appalachian Trail in particular and outdoor tourism in general, has Hot Springs regained its swagger as a tourist destination.

Not only the hot springs make Hot Springs but also the French Broad River. It has already flowed through Asheville on its journey to reach the mountain-rimmed trail town. You will look down from Lovers Leap on the wide French Broad as it flows in shoals and sweeps its way through the hamlet. Even though this is a hike with a view, the trek is low elevation—a little over 2,400 at its highest point—and therefore a good winter choice. However, it is not so low as to be hot and thus can be enjoyed year-round.

The hike starts at the Silvermine parking area. Here the Pump Gap Loop Trail leads you up the hollow of Silvermine Creek, former site of Silvermine Group Camp. Traverse a wildflower-rich hollow pocked with rock outcroppings. Mosses and ferns are found in moist, shady spots.

The path keeps east, now heading up along Pump Branch. The valley narrows as you parallel the shrinking stream. The trail then leaves Pump Branch behind, climbing steeply, aiming for Pump Gap in rhododendron from which rises straight-trunked tulip trees.

After making Pump Gap and intersecting the Appalachian Trail, take the master path east along Lovers Leap Ridge, now in dry-situation hardwoods such as chestnut oak, black gum, and pine. Occasional views can be had through the trees as the trail leads up and down along the craggy boulders of south-facing pine-clad slopes. You will pass a large campsite where northbound AT thru-hikers—their packs heavy with goodies after resupplying in Hot Springs—gorge.

Ahead, find a spur trail that noses out on a rock spine for a fine view of the river valley for those who dare straddle the slender outcrop. Beyond this warm-up

Trees frame the vista of the French Broad from Lovers Leap.

view, the AT continues a downgrade along Lovers Leap Ridge. Then you come to a trail junction with the Lovers Leap Trail; briefly stay with the AT and come to Lovers Leap. From these heights you can see the river, the railroad, the rapids, the town below, and the mountains beyond from the spot where (according to legend) an Indian princess leapt to her demise after learning the love of her life had perished at the hands of an unwanted suitor. From here it is all downhill back to the Silvermine trailhead. Be careful on the steep slope above Silvermine Creek as you complete the circuit.

Miles and Directions

0.0 Start from the Silvermine parking area at a trail signboard and join a foot trail heading up the right slope of the hollow.

0.2 Reach a trail intersection. Head left on the Pump Gap Loop. Descend to an old road, passing a pair of long-disused concrete dynamite shacks.

Lovers Leap

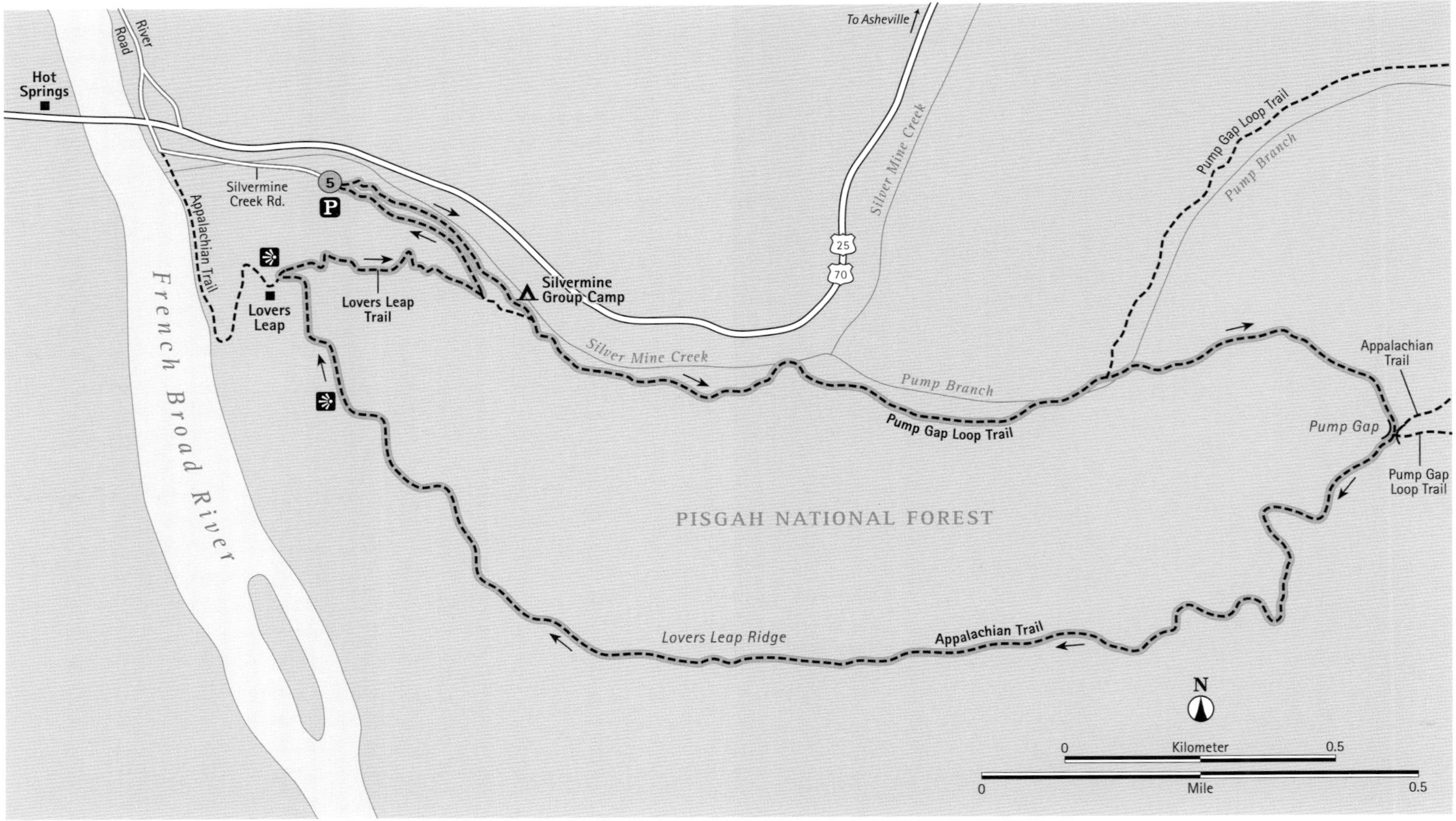

To Asheville

Silver Mine Creek

25 70

Pump Branch

Pump Gap Loop Trail

Appalachian Trail

Pump Gap

Pump Gap Loop Trail

Pump Gap Loop Trail

Pump Branch

Silver Mine Creek

PISGAH NATIONAL FOREST

Lovers Leap Ridge

Appalachian Trail

Silvermine Group Camp

Silvermine Creek Rd.

5 P

Lovers Leap Trail

Lovers Leap

Appalachian Trail

River Road

Hot Springs

French Broad River

N

Kilometer

Mile

0.5

0.5

0 0.5 0

0.4 The old road ends and becomes singletrack trail, squeezing past creekside boulders then crossing the creek via culvert. Ahead, the trail goes directly up along the braids of the creek.

1.0 An arm of the Pump Gap Loop Trail leaves left, also heading for the Appalachian Trail. Stay right toward the AT and Pump Gap.

1.5 The Pump Gap Loop Trail reaches Pump Gap and the Appalachian Trail. Turn right (southbound) on the Appalachian Trail. Climb a little as you head southwesterly, now on Lovers Leap Ridge.

2.1 Top out on Lovers Leap Ridge after winding through side slope drainages. Listen for the sounds of the cascading French Broad River as you trace the rocky AT.

2.8 Come near a large campsite on your left. Descend.

3.1 Look for a user-created path leading acutely left. Walk out and join a narrow, tan-colored rock ridge extending out toward the French Broad River. Stand alongside a gnarled pine and scope out the river below, Hot Springs downstream, and a host of mountains rising in the distance. Backtrack and rejoin the Appalachian Trail southbound.

3.4 Come to a trail junction. Your return route, the Lovers Leap Trail, leaves right. However, first follow the Appalachian Trail to two overlooks, the first just past the intersection with the Lovers Leap Trail and the second a little farther down the AT a switchback and an outcrop. This rock outcrop is Lovers Leap. Soak in the views then join the Lovers Leap Trail.

3.9 Make a sharp switchback left after heading steadily downhill on the Lovers Leap Trail. Return to the intersection with the Pump Gap Loop Trail and head left.

4.1 Arrive back at the Silvermine trailhead.

6 Falls of Hickey Fork

This challenging waterfall hike makes a loop through remote terrain near the North Carolina–Tennessee state line. Explore the upper Hickey Fork valley in Pisgah National Forest's Shelton Laurel Backcountry. Cross a log hiker bridge then turn up West Prong Hickey Fork, passing two significant waterfalls and other lesser spillers before rising to Seng Gap. A mountainside climb commences before you descend to East Prong Hickey Fork. Reach an often-gated forest road and easy hiking to close the loop. *Note:* There is a 1,800-foot elevation gain/loss, and the trails can be brushy and faint in places.

Start: Hickey Fork Road (FR 465) trailhead

Distance: 7.0-mile loop

Hiking time: About 4.5 hours

Difficulty: Moderate–difficult, rough trail in places

Trail surface: Natural

Best season: Year-round

Other trail users: None

Canine compatibility: Leashed dogs allowed

Land status: National forest

Fees and permits: No fees or permits required

Schedule: 24/7/365

Maps: USGS White Rock, Greystone; National Geographic #782: French Broad & Nolichucky Rivers [Cherokee and Pisgah National Forests]

Trail contacts: Pisgah National Forest, Appalachian Ranger District, 632 Manor Rd., Mars Hill, NC 28754; (828) 689-9694; fs.usda.gov/nfsnc

Finding the trailhead: From Asheville take I-26 North to exit 19A (Marshall). Follow US 25/70 for 21 miles. Turn right on NC 208 West and continue 3.4 miles to NC 212. Turn right on NC 212 East and follow it for 6.9 miles. Turn left on Hickey Fork Road at a sign for "Shelton Laurel Backcountry." Follow Hickey Fork Road, which becomes FR 465 in Pisgah National Forest, for 1.1 miles to a seasonally closed gate and parking area. GPS: N35° 59' 40.3" / W82° 42' 16.6"

The Hike

This hike takes place in Pisgah National Forest's Shelton Laurel Backcountry, a designated trail network banked against the North Carolina–Tennessee state line atop which runs the Appalachian Trail. The AT and the Shelton Laurel

Autumn sun shines on Hickey Fork Falls.

Backcountry trails also hook up to Bald Mountain Scenic Area and Rocky Fork trails of Tennessee's Cherokee National Forest. Together, a pathway complex of more than 100 miles adds myriad day hiking and backpacking possibilities. The Hickey Fork Loop is just one of the fine adventurous hikes in this far-flung portion of western North Carolina. The 7.0-mile circuit hike has wild waterfalls and almost guaranteed solitude. However, the path's infrequent use means a fainter, sometimes-obscure trailbed, overgrown sections, and occasional fallen trees across the path. This loop hike involves a 1,800-foot climb and subsequent descent, adding further challenge. However, the visual rewards and peaceful character of the loop overshadow the challenges.

The hike starts off in fun fashion as you cross East Prong Hickey Fork on a log bridge. Luckily it has handrails, minimizing potential peril. After spanning East Prong Hickey Fork, the narrow trail slithers through dog hobble, ferns, and rhododendron before meeting West Prong Hickey Fork on a seemingly convoluted route that keeps the path on national forest property. After crossing West Prong, you head up the narrow, thickly vegetated, and steep valley. The noisy falling waters of West Prong Hickey Fork testify to this steepness. Tiny tributaries cross over the trail, adding their waters to West Prong Hickey Fork.

The valley continues to narrow. Rock protrusions show their hard faces unobscured by scads of rhododendron. Ahead, the song of splashing water entices your ears—Hickey Fork Cascades. This first sizable faucet-style spiller drops more than 100 feet along a smooth, slender, mossy rock face flanked by rhododendron and shaded by hardwoods. Continue climbing past more spillers and come to Hickey Fork Falls. This waterfall is more of a classic curtain-type cataract, sloping over a rock ledge then diving down a tiered 35-foot-high stratified ledge. If this trail were busy at all, the path to the falls' base would be well beaten down.

The climb continues, becoming very steep after leaving West Prong Hickey Fork and ascending one of its tributaries. Here you huff and puff your way up 400 feet in a very steep 0.3 mile. Whew! Circle around an upland cove filled with tulip and magnolia trees.

You soon arrive at Seng Gap. "Seng" is mountain slang for "ginseng," a plant often extracted from the Southern Appalachians due to its purported medicinal properties. Our hike joins the Pounding Mill Trail as it climbs still more. Off-trail hiking enthusiasts have additional options: The no-longer-maintained portion of the Pounding Mill Trail leaves left down Pounding Mill Creek to NC 208, while the abandoned Little Laurel Trail descends along Little Laurel Creek to NC 208.

The hike leaves the Pounding Mill Trail for the White Oak Trail. The south-facing slope along which the White Oak Trail travels reveals winter views of nearby peaks and faraway ridges. You then cross the headwaters of West Branch Hickey Fork. Here, a very wide spring dribbles through a boulder field topped with trees. Trace the headwaters downstream on a slender trail.

Begin an easterly track on a lowering ridge that eventually leads you down to Big Rocky Branch and ultimately to FR 465. This seasonally closed forest road traces East Prong Hickey Fork downstream past its confluence with Little Prong and the trail connector to the Jerry Miller Trail. Walk with ease, bridging East Prong before completing the loop at the FR 465 gate and the trailhead parking area.

Falls of Hickey Fork

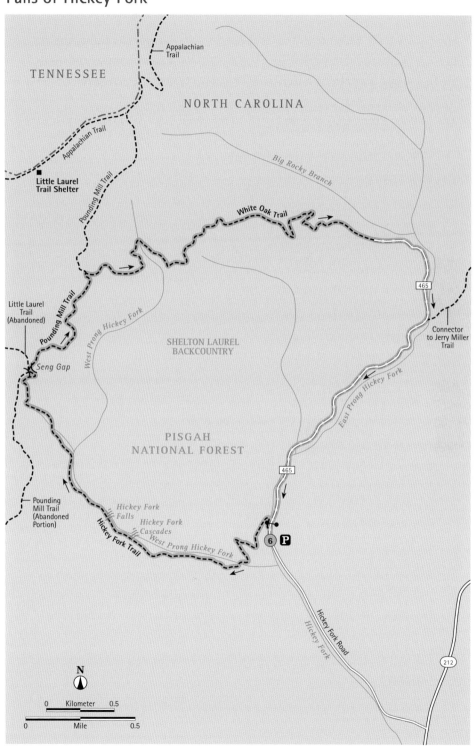

TENNESSEE

NORTH CAROLINA

Appalachian Trail

Appalachian Trail

Big Rocky Branch

Little Laurel Trail Shelter

Pounding Mill Trail

White Oak Trail

465

Little Laurel Trail (Abandoned)

Pounding Mill Trail

West Prong Hickey Fork

SHELTON LAUREL BACKCOUNTRY

Connector to Jerry Miller Trail

Seng Gap

East Prong Hickey Fork

PISGAH NATIONAL FOREST

465

Pounding Mill Trail (Abandoned Portion)

Hickey Fork Falls

Hickey Fork Cascades

West Prong Hickey Fork

Hickey Fork Trail

6 P

Hickey Fork Road

Hickey Fork

212

N

0 Kilometer 0.5

0 Mile 0.5

Miles and Directions

0.0 Start from the parking area at the seasonally closed gate on FR 465 and walk up FR 465, passing around the pole gate. Look left for the Hickey Fork Trail. Walk down stone steps, then cross East Prong Hickey Fork on a log bridge with handrails.

0.1 Turn away from East Prong Hickey Fork. Start curving around the nose of a ridge dividing East Prong from West Prong.

0.5 Come to then cross West Prong Hickey Fork.

0.9 The gradient steepens.

1.1 Reach the first visible cataract—Hickey Fork Cascades. This long, angled cascade dashes over a smooth, waterworn rock bed, spilling 100 feet or more. It is not easy to access but worth the trouble.

1.3 Reach Hickey Fork Falls, a 35-foot classic curtain-type waterfall. There is only a faint path to the base of this cataract.

1.7 The Hickey Fork Trail leaves West Prong Hickey Fork, ascending along a feeder stream. Begin a very steep segment, gaining 400 feet in 0.3 mile! The trail opens into a wide hardwood cove after the climb, leaving the rhododendron behind.

2.1 Follow the blazes on a sharp left as an old road tempts you to keep straight. Climb a ridge forested in pine, black gum, and mountain laurel. Turn into the Chimney Creek valley, striding under tunnels of rhododendron. Ascend.

2.3 Come to flat Seng Gap. Look closely before continuing. To your left, the abandoned portion of the Pounding Mill Trail leaves left for Pounding Mill Creek. Straight ahead, the abandoned Little Laurel Trail drops into the headwaters of Little Laurel Creek. This loop hike heads right on an old roadbed, joining the still-maintained segment of the Pounding Mill Trail. Ascend.

2.6 The Pounding Mill Trail passes through a gap. Keep climbing.

2.9 Reach a trail intersection. Here the Pounding Mill Trail climbs left along Seng Ridge about 1 mile to the Appalachian Trail and the Tennessee–North Carolina state line. The Hickey Fork Loop turns right, joining an old logging grade, now heading easterly on the White Oak Trail.

3.3 Turn into a hollow and abruptly leave right from the old logging grade you have been following.

3.4 Cross a wide, shallow spring branch, the headwaters of Hickey Fork. Descend.

Hickey Fork pours white over a leaf-littered rock face.

3.6 The White Oak Trail makes a sudden left turn, away from the headwaters. Begin cruising along the south-facing slope of piney Seng Ridge. Mountain laurel and chestnut oaks thrive here as well.

3.7 Step over a trickling stream that, when flowing well, forms a long ribbonlike slide over a slender yet steep rock face.

4.1 Join the nose of a ridge with drops-offs on both side of the trail. Look for the Baxter Cliffs through the trees. Descend on a pine-shaded, needle-carpeted trail.

4.4 Come to a gap. Pay attention as the White Oak Trail reaches a closed logging road. Don't be lured into following the wide logging road. Instead, the White Oak Trail makes a sharp left, diving toward Big Rocky Branch, still on singletrack, curving gently to reach the wider, lower valley of Big Rocky Branch.

4.7 Pick up a partly eroded logging grade in the Big Rocky Branch valley.

5.0 Emerge onto the end of FR 465. Begin descending FR 465 as it runs alongside East Prong Hickey Fork. The walking is easy on the gravel track.

5.8 An old concrete road bridge to the left crosses rocky Little Prong. An unofficial connector crosses the bridge and surmounts a gap to meet the Jerry Miller Trail. Stay on FR 465.

6.7 FR 465 bridges East Prong. You are now on the left bank, heading downstream.

7.0 Arrive back at the trailhead.

7   Jerry Miller Loop

This challenging circuit travels through Pisgah National Forest's Shelton Laurel Backcountry. The Jerry Miller Trail first leads past an impressive 100-foot waterfall then reaches the former meadow of Whiteoak Flats. A steady climb takes you near Baxter Cliff before joining the Appalachian Trail and Big Firescald Ridge, the protruding knife-edge rock rampart dividing North Carolina and Tennessee. Panoramic 360-degree views extend to distant horizons. The vistas continue for 0.5 mile before the AT enters wooded slopes. A final, very steep descent down Fork Ridge closes the loop.

Start: Jerry Miller trailhead on FR 111
Distance: 10.5-mile loop
Hiking time: About 6.5 hours
Difficulty: Difficult
Trail surface: Natural
Best season: Year-round
Other trail users: None

Peering into the Carolina mountains from the jagged crest of Big Firescald Ridge

Canine compatibility: Leashed dogs allowed

Land status: National forest

Fees and permits: No fees or permits required

Schedule: 24/7/365

Maps: USGS Greystone; National Geographic #782: French Broad & Nolichucky
  Rivers [Cherokee and Pisgah National Forests]

Trail contacts: Pisgah National Forest, Appalachian Ranger District, 632 Manor Rd.,
  Mars Hill, NC 28754; (828) 689-9694; fs.usda.gov/nfsnc

Finding the trailhead: From Asheville take I-26 North to exit 19A (Marshall). Follow US 25/70 for 21 miles. Turn right on NC 208 West and continue 3.4 miles to
  NC 212. Turn right on NC 212 East and follow it for 10.9 miles. Turn left on Big
  Creek Road at the Carmen Church of God and continue for 1.2 miles. The road
  seems to end near a barn. Here, angle left onto FR 111, taking the gravel road
  over a small creek. Enter the national forest. At 0.4 mile beyond the barn, veer
  left onto a short spur road to dead-end at the Jerry Miller trailhead. GPS: N36°
  01' 23.9" / W82° 39' 09.6"

The Hike

Named for a big-time hero of America's national forests, this is a hike of super-
latives—a big hike with big views from the ridgeline dividing North Carolina
and Tennessee, lending open perspectives in all directions with vistas continuing
unabated for more than 0.5 mile; a big 100-foot slide cascade waterfall; and big
wildflower displays from trillium in the creek bottoms to trout lilies up top. The
hike also has big climbs—it is more than 2,000 feet from low point to high point
on this circuit. You must go back down again, and during this downgrade you will
drop 1,000 feet in 1.0 mile! A part of the hike uses the most big-time path in the
East—the Appalachian Trail.

Furthermore, you can take side trips from this loop to attractions such as
Baxter Cliff, Whiterock Cliff, the Blackstack Cliffs (where I proposed to my wife),
and the Jerry Cabin trail shelter. Even without these side trips, the hike can be
long and arduous. Consider starting early to maximize the possibilities. I have
backpacked this loop on multiple occasions and consider it one of the best overnight circuits in western North Carolina.

Back in 1997, what was the Whiteoak Flats Trail was rerouted and renamed
the Jerry Miller Trail. The path was altered to keep it on national forest land,

Winter comes to the high country.

avoiding potential trespassing problems. It formerly started on the property of the Shelton family, who had occupied this parcel at the confluence of Whiteoak Flats Branch and Big Creek since the 1790s.

So what does that have to do with Jerry Miller and naming the trail for him? Well, Jerry Miller's mother was a Shelton from this very property. Miller was raised in both Madison and Buncombe Counties, becoming a US attorney for the Western District of North Carolina in the early 1980s. During his tenure, Miller prosecuted many a case arising from crimes perpetrated in the mountainous Pisgah and Nantahala National Forests.

It wasn't always so. Before Jerry Miller's tenure, the federal government didn't recognize federal jurisdiction in national forests, leaving enforcement to state and local authorities. National forests became havens for the lawless, threatening lawful forest users. The locals charged with enforcing the law were already strapped, trying to maintain order in the rural areas where national forests are typically found.

A drunk-driving case on the national forest prosecuted by Jerry Miller changed that. After many a legal tussle, the case went to the Supreme Court of the United States, where the robed ones recognized the federal government's role in patrolling, enforcing, and prosecuting the law in our national forests, adding a layer of protection for those who enjoy the millions of acres of wildlands throughout western North Carolina.

In appreciation of this change in law enforcement, the managers of Pisgah National Forest renamed the Whiteoak Flats Trail for Jerry Miller. At the trail's beginning stands a plaque memorializing this man who fought to keep the Carolina mountains safe for hikers like us.

The hike starts by bridging Big Creek then climbs a ridge to turn up the steep-sided hollow of Whiteoak Flats Branch. It isn't long before you come to 100-foot Whiteoak Flats Cascade. This significant slide plunges over a widening slope that steepens in a frothy climax into a shallow plunge pool. Boughs of rhododendron escort Whiteoak Flats Branch along this sightly spill.

The Whiteoak Flats Branch valley closes after the falls and you shortly enter the former meadow of Whiteoak Flats, now undergoing succession, with pines, tulip trees, and brush overtaking the former homesite. From there you rise via switchbacks toward the state line.

Come to the AT after bisecting Huckleberry Gap. The wild and stony ridgetop walk astounds once atop Big Firescald Knob. Views are nearly continuous into the mountains and valleys of Tennessee and North Carolina. It is my favorite spot on the AT in this area. If the leaves are off the trees, you can look down onto the Jerry Miller Trail you just climbed.

Marvel at the trail construction here as a slow-moving path works through the stone backbone amid gnarled brush and trees. Beyond the overlooks, you roll along the state-line ridge before turning back into North Carolina on the often-steep Fork Ridge Trail. Keep the brakes on as you dive for Big Creek and FR 111. The final part of the walk traces FR 111 back to the Jerry Miller trailhead and hike's end.

Miles and Directions

0.0 Start from the FR 111 parking area, where the Jerry Miller Trail memorial plaque is embedded in stone. Join the Jerry Miller Trail and bridge Big Creek. Turn downstream into a flat known for its spring wildflower displays. Switchback up a ridge dividing Big Creek from Whiteoak Flats Branch.

0.3 Enter the Whiteoak Flats Branch valley. Turn west in a thick forest on a steep slope.

0.9 The trail takes you by Whiteoak Flats Cascade, a 100-foot slide cataract. Continue up the narrowing valley.

1.2 Cross gurgling Whiteoak Flats Branch on a log bridge.

1.3 Step over a tributary then enter Whiteoak Flats.

1.6 Leave what's left of Whiteoak Flats meadow.

1.7 Cut through a second, smaller former clearing. Stay with the blazed trail. Watch for old roadbeds spurring off the correct route, including one heading left for the Hickey Fork valley.

2.1 Follow the blazes to make a sharp left as an old road tempts you to keep straight. Climb a ridge forested in pine, black gum, and mountain laurel. Turn into the Chimney Creek valley, striding through tunnels of rhododendron. Ascend.

4.0 Reach an intersection at grassy Huckleberry Gap. This is your first chance for a side trip. To your left, an unmarked trail surmounts a knob then drops sharply down to Baxter Cliff after 0.4 mile, presenting a view of Whiterock Cliff and the Hickey Fork watershed. Our hike keeps straight on the Jerry Miller Trail and then crosses uppermost East Prong Hickey Fork.

4.6 Intersect the Appalachian Trail. A left turn will take you to nearby Whiterock Cliff and the Blackstack Cliffs. This loop turns right (northbound) on the AT to quickly reach another trail junction. Here the old AT—the Big Firescald Bypass—stays left while you stay right on the official AT section. Snake over, around, and between whitish stone bluffs, boulders, and steps placed astride craggy windswept vegetation.

5.1 Top out on Big Firescald Knob and start relishing unobstructed views into Tennessee where a steep drop-off reveals wooded hills, farm fields, and rolling mountains. Waves of ridges extend into the Tar Heel State as far as the horizon allows. Ahead, pass the signed view at Howard's Rock.

5.6 A spur leads left off Big Firescald to the bypass. Stay with the AT, still in crags with views mixed with woods.

Jerry Miller Loop

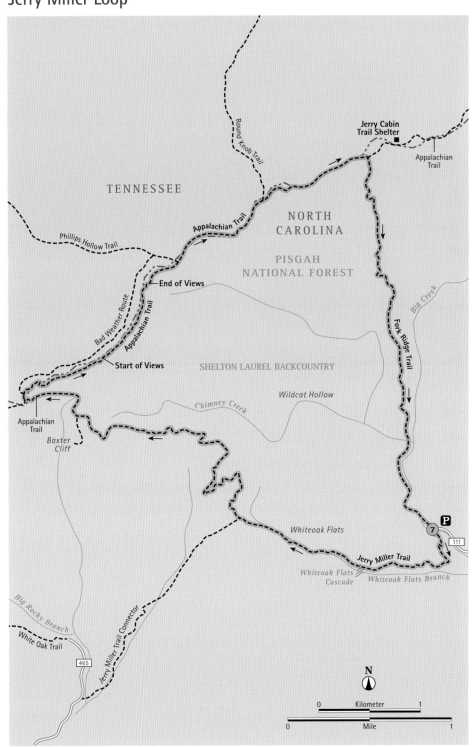

Round Knob Trail

Jerry Cabin
Trail Shelter

Appalachian
Trail

TENNESSEE

NORTH
CAROLINA

Phillips Hollow Trail

Appalachian Trail

PISGAH
NATIONAL FOREST

End of Views

Bad Weather Route

Appalachian Trail

Big Creek

Fork Ridge Trail

Start of Views

SHELTON LAUREL BACKCOUNTRY

Chimney Creek

Wildcat Hollow

Appalachian
Trail

Baxter
Cliff

P

7

111

Whiteoak Flats

Jerry Miller Trail

Whiteoak Flats
Cascade

Whiteoak Flats Branch

Big Rocky Branch

White Oak Trail

Jerry Miller Trail Connector

465

N

| 0 | Kilometer | 1 |

| 0 | Mile | 1 |

Peering into East Tennessee from Howard's Rock on the AT.

6.2 Intersect the Big Firescald Bypass. Keep straight in woods on the AT.

6.6 Drop to Licklog Gap and a campsite.

6.9 The Round Knob Trail leads left into Tennessee.

7.7 Come to the Fork Ridge Trail. The Jerry Cabin trail shelter is 0.25 mile north on the AT. This hike joins the Fork Ridge Trail. Descend more than 1,000 feet in the next 1.0 mile, despite a couple of short ascents.

9.7 Emerge at the Fork Ridge Trail parking area on FR 111.

9.8 Cross Chimney Creek at a road ford.

10.1 Cross Big Creek at another road ford.

10.5 Arrive back at the trailhead.

8 Art Loeb Trail Loop

The Art Loeb Trail is a Carolina icon. This hike traces the famed path through its most lofty heights while traversing Shining Rock Ledge within the Shining Rock Wilderness. Begin the loop on the Ivestor Gap Trail, traveling a level railroad grade for 4 miles through meadows and spruce-fir forest. Your return route takes the famed Art Loeb Trail through a series of ridgetop undulations where the panoramas are nearly non-stop, passing view after view from rocky points, grassy hillsides, and meadows. Expect heavy crowds on nice warm-season weekends, and just about any time the weather is decent. The hike can be cut for shorter loops should the distance become onerous.

Start: FR 816 Black Balsam trailhead off the Blue Ridge Parkway

Distance: 8.8-mile loop

Hiking time: About 5 hours

Difficulty: Moderate–difficult due to distance and navigation concerns

Trail surface: Natural

Best season: Fall and spring for best views; cold-weather weekdays for solitude

Other trail users: None

Canine compatibility: Leashed dogs allowed

Land status: National forest

Fees and permits: No fees or permits required

Schedule: 24/7/365

Maps: USGS Sam Knob, Shining Rock; National Geographic #780: Pisgah Ranger District

Trail contacts: Pisgah National Forest, Pisgah Ranger District, 1001 Pisgah Hwy., Pisgah Forest, NC 28768; (828) 877-3265; fs.usda.gov/nfsnc

Finding the trailhead: From the intersection of NC 280 and US 276 in Pisgah Forest, take US 276 North for 15 miles to the Blue Ridge Parkway. Follow the Parkway southbound for 8.4 miles to FR 816, on your right. Turn right on FR 816 and follow it for 1.2 miles to the dead end at the Black Balsam trailhead. GPS: N35° 19' 33.9" / W82° 52' 52.9"

The Hike

One of western North Carolina's most beautiful natural places, the open meadows of Shining Rock Wilderness are not as natural as they seem. This mile-high series of clearings along Shining Rock Ledge came about following the logging

A host of mountains await you on the Art Loeb Trail.

of the highlands that later became part of Pisgah National Forest and still later were designated as Shining Rock Wilderness.

A little over a century ago, Pisgah Ridge, Shining Rock Ledge, and much of this high country were cloaked in a lush green blanket of red spruce and Fraser fir. Logging companies from the North swooped down on these untouched stands, laid railroads to speed a complete stripping of the forests, then shipped the wood to be processed. The denuded hillsides became repositories for trunks, limbs, and brush that the loggers left to rot. However, before the refuse could decompose, it caught fire, spreading a conflagration that burned not only the logging remains but also stumps, roots, and soil down to bare rock. What soil remained was washed away by floods now flowing unchecked down the hillsides.

The high country was a wasteland, an earthly moonscape that contrasted greatly with the dense and ancient evergreen forests that existed before the loggers came. Nature always fills a void, and slowly grasses begin to grow where soil accumulated despite recurring fires. And so it has progressed—brush coming in where grass once grew, then small hardwoods rising, ultimately leading to a return of the evergreens.

However, much of the area remains open to this day. This accidental landscape is a huge attraction to hikers, who enjoy the views from its meadows and outcrops. The Shining Rock Wilderness encompasses more than 18,000 acres of this highland terrain from which views extend miles in all directions.

No wonder this place is so popular! However, don't let this status keep you from making a well-timed hike on the Art Loeb Trail. The 30-mile trail, named for a Brevard resident who helped this path come to be in 1969, starts down by Brevard at just above 2,300 feet then climbs Shut-in Ridge and continues along the crest, topping Chestnut and Pilot Mountains, among other peaks. A pair of trail shelters enhance this lower section. Ultimately, the path rises to Pisgah Ridge and crosses the Blue Ridge Parkway. Here, the Art Loeb Trail enters Shining Rock Wilderness, near where this hike begins. The path surmounts 6,000-foot-high knobs before nearing Cold Mountain. Finally the path drops to the Little East Fork of the Pigeon River, its other terminus. An end-to-end trek along the Art Loeb Trail is a backpacking adventure to remember. If overnighting is not for you, consider hiking the Art Loeb Trail in sections. It is worth the effort.

Our hike starts on the Ivestor Gap Trail, following an old railroad grade. Instant panoramas stretch down the Little East Fork Pigeon River to your left and up to Shining Rock Ledge on your right. The Ivestor Gap Trail makes an easy

Turk's cap lilies brighten the view of the Shining Rock high country.

ridge run along the west side of Shining Rock Ledge. It works around knobs, taking advantage of shortcut opportunities, and passes through Ivestor Gap.

The walking remains easy and scenic all the way to Shining Rock Gap, where you join the Art Loeb Trail, now southbound. The circuit hike continues on a railroad grade to Flower Gap. The Art Loeb Trail then ascends the crest of Shining Rock Ledge as a singletrack footpath, passing over knobs and through gaps. Views are extensive, culminating atop Tennent Mountain, elevation 6,046 feet. Keep rolling south to skirt the top of Black Balsam Knob. Vistas continue, and spur trails tempt you to explore the high point of Black Balsam Knob.

The Black Balsam Spur Trail takes you off Shining Rock Ledge and Black Balsam Knob via a series of switchbacks. Finally you return to the parking area, completing the hike.

Miles and Directions

0.0   Start at the Black Balsam trailhead, passing around a pole gate at the northeast end of the parking area on the Ivestor Gap Trail. Follow a wide railroad grade where trains and logs once traveled. Shortly pass a spring on your right. Additional springs flow across the path ahead. Willows, fire cherry, and rhododendron border the route.

1.2   Come to a gap between Tennent Mountain and Black Balsam Knob where a user-created spur trail leads right to the Art Loeb Trail. This is your first shortcut opportunity. Stay left with the Ivestor Gap Trail.

1.4   Bisect a ridge amid a nonnative red pine plantation.

1.7   Watch for the Fork Mountain Trail descending left for the Sunburst Campground trailhead.

1.8   Come to an unnamed gap, meeting the Art Loeb Trail and your second shortcut opportunity. The Ivestor Gap Trail splits left, still on the wide railroad grade, and stays on the west side of Shining Rock Ledge.

2.2   Reach Ivestor Gap and a five-way trail intersection. This is your third shortcut chance. The Art Loeb Trail heads north and south; the Grassy Cove Trail goes east. Stay left with the railroad bed and Ivestor Gap Trail on a narrower trail. More views lie ahead as you wind through open areas among springs, tree copses, and rhododendron thickets.

3.9   The Little East Fork Trail leaves left. Stay right, now easterly, toward Shining Rock Gap.

Art Loeb Trail Loop

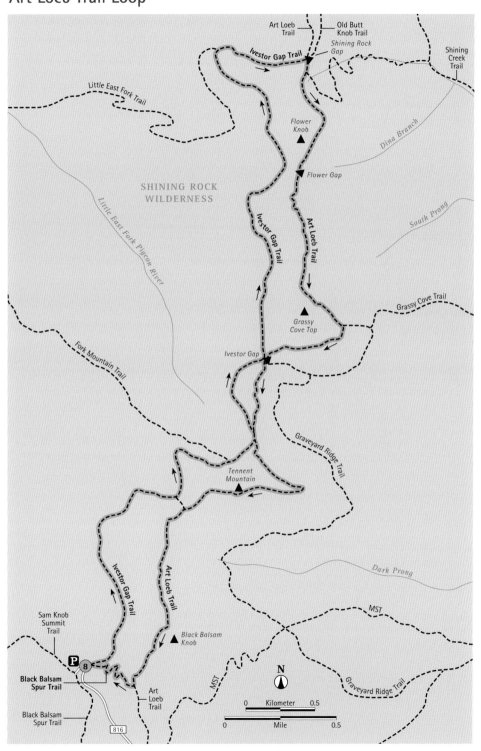

Art Loeb Trail
Old Butt Knob Trail
Shining Rock Gap
Shining Creek Trail
Ivestor Gap Trail
Little East Fork Trail
Dina Branch
Flower Knob
Flower Gap
SHINING ROCK WILDERNESS
Little East Fork Pigeon River
Ivestor Gap Trail
Art Loeb Trail
South Prong
Grassy Cove Trail
Grassy Cove Top
Ivestor Gap
Fork Mountain Trail
Graveyard Ridge Trail
Tennent Mountain
Dark Prong
MST
Ivestor Gap Trail
Art Loeb Trail
Sam Knob Summit Trail
Black Balsam Knob
P 8
Black Balsam Spur Trail
Graveyard Ridge Trail
Art Loeb Trail
MST
Black Balsam Spur Trail
816

N

0   Kilometer   0.5
0   Mile   0.5

4.3 Come to the small grassy flat of Shining Rock Gap and a nest of both user-created and official trails. Meet the Art Loeb Trail and turn right (southbound), avoiding those user-created paths and instead walking a wide railroad grade. Ahead, log steps leave left, indicating the Shining Creek Trail. Stay straight with the Art Loeb Trail.

4.9 Enter grassy Flower Gap. The Art Loeb Trail leaves the railroad grade and ascends the crest of Shining Rock Ledge as a singletrack trail. Wind-flagged trees rise above low-lying vegetation.

5.2 The Art Loeb Trail reaches an unnamed knob exceeding 6,000 feet. Views stretch in all directions. Beyond this knob, the Art Loeb Trail slips over to the east side of Grassy Cove Top.

5.7 Come to a trail junction. Here a spur trail leads left to the Grassy Cove Trail. Stay with the Art Loeb Trail.

6.1 Return to Ivestor Gap. Stay with the Art Loeb Trail as it cuts through a wooden stile, crosses a grassy clearing, and ascends into a stand of red pines. Tennent Mountain looms ahead as you work over a little knob.

6.5 Descend to a gap, briefly run in conjunction with the Ivestor Gap Trail, then split left, ascending on the rutted Art Loeb Trail.

7.2 Reach the peak of Tennent Mountain with its 360-degree landscapes and plaque. Look for landmarks in the near and waves of mountains extending as far as the clarity of the sky allows.

7.5 Drop off Tennent Mountain to reach a gap where a spur trail leaves right to the Ivestor Gap Trail. Climb the slope of Black Balsam, peering west above windblown vegetation. Watch out for user-created trails going to the top of Black Balsam. The official path is equipped with water-erosion bars and stays on the west side of Black Balsam Knob.

8.4 Turn right on the signed Black Balsam Spur Trail. Soak in some final views as you descend switchbacks.

8.8 Arrive back at the FR 816 Black Balsam trailhead.

9 Falls of Yellowstone Prong

This hike visits two waterfalls situated in the nearly mile-high Yellowstone Prong valley along the Blue Ridge Parkway. Each cataract exceeds 40 feet. Along the hike you will experience a medley of landscapes from meadows to hardwood forests to dense brush thickets to naked rock slabs. The busy and popular hike first leads to Lower Falls, accessed by stairs aplenty. From there you turn upstream, meandering through wetland bogs and meadows with views galore, along with woodland copses. Climb a bit to find Upper Falls, an impressive frothy ribbon dancing down a stone slope. After backtracking, pick up a new path, looping back to the trailhead.

Start: Graveyard Fields Overlook at Blue Ridge Parkway milepost 418.8

Distance: 3.2-mile loop

Hiking time: About 1.8 hours

Difficulty: Moderate

Trail surface: Natural

Best season: Year-round

Other trail users: None

Canine compatibility: Leashed dogs allowed

Land status: National forest

Fees and permits: No fees or permits required

Schedule: 24/7/365

Maps: USGS Shining Rock; National Geographic #780: Pisgah Ranger District

Trail contacts: Pisgah National Forest, Pisgah Ranger District, 1001 Pisgah Hwy., Pisgah Forest, NC 28768; (828) 877-3265; fs.usda.gov/nfsnc

Finding the trailhead: From the intersection of NC 280 and US 276 in Brevard, take US 276 North for 15 miles to the Blue Ridge Parkway. Follow the Blue Ridge Parkway 7 miles south to the Graveyard Fields Overlook, on your right at milepost 418.8. GPS: N35° 19' 13.2" / W82° 50' 49.3"

The Hike

The two cataracts on this hike—Lower Falls and Upper Falls—are part of the greater Graveyard Fields, a major attraction of the Pisgah National Forest just off the Blue Ridge Parkway. I think Upper Falls is the more impressive of the two cataracts. It is much less visited than Lower Falls, which is so close to the trailhead. Nevertheless, the entirety of the upper Yellowstone Prong valley is a continual visual cornucopia. The area is popular, but this is simply one of those "must-do" well-loved treks. Give this adventure a go—you will not be disappointed.

Situated where Yellowstone Prong and its tributaries flow down from 6,214-foot Black Balsam Knob, the waterfalls and the valley through which they flow present an array of highlights: the two falls, meadows delivering first-rate views, high-country hiking above 5,000 feet, and easy access. With such an array of upsides, it is not surprising that the hike is popular. The forty-space lot can fill on warm-weather weekend afternoons. If that's the case, move on to another adventure.

Avoiding the crowds is easy. Start early in the morning on a weekend, or arrive late in the afternoon. Things are always slower during the week. Spring is a good time to visit, although weekends can still be busy. However, the crowds are thick during the fall color season. Winter can be iffy, since access is dependent on the Blue Ridge Parkway (BRP) being open, especially at this high elevation. By the way, the BRP website offers real-time closure information, helping you avoid a wasted trip. Repeated bear encounters have permanently closed the Graveyard Fields area to camping.

The hike leaves Graveyard Fields Overlook and descends to Yellowstone Prong through rhododendron thickets. The clear highland stream flows below

An outdoor adventurer admires Lower Falls.

Upper Falls dances its way down a rock face.

the sturdy hiker bridge. Beyond the bridge, you head right for Lower Falls, avoiding unofficial, user-created paths that can confuse hikers.

An elaborate wooden tiered boardwalk with multiple steps leads to the base of Lower Falls. Here the wonderment of whitewater crashes more than 50 feet in stages, each stage presenting a different slope, delivering the froth of Yellowstone Prong in different ways. A substantial boulder pile jumbles at the falls' base. Waterfall fans use the boulders as impromptu seats.

From here, backtrack toward the trailhead, joining a new trail where you see a sign heading toward Upper Falls. Leaving most other hikers behind, you now enter fast-changing landscape—sometimes meadows, sometimes forest, sometimes upland bogs, sometimes gravel bars banked along the creek.

The nearly level trail continues up the Yellowstone Prong valley in a mosaic of growth—mountain laurel thickets, split-trunked maples, berry brambles, yellow birch copses, and plain ol' grass meadows. Watch for thick brush bordering highland bogs that reveal panoramas of the ridges surrounding Yellowstone Prong. Glance back toward the Graveyard Fields Overlook.

The last part of the trail climbs before reaching Upper Falls. Most hikers stop at a slide cascade below Upper Falls. This spiller runs over an open rock slab, usually along a channel to the right. Continue to 45-foot Upper Falls, a narrow cataract splashing on a tan rock base, widening out in fan fashion. But it is not over yet—Upper Falls next dives vertically, continuing over the wide rock slab then easing up. Explore the falls, but be careful traversing the naked rock slab astride Upper Falls.

After backtracking down the Yellowstone Prong valley, cross Yellowstone Prong on a trail bridge. Enjoy the view of Yellowstone Prong from the bridge. Willow and rhododendron border the rocky, clear waterway. From the bridge it is 0.5 mile back to the trailhead and Graveyard Fields Overlook on the Blue Ridge Parkway.

Miles and Directions

0.0 Start at the east side of the Graveyard Fields Overlook on stone steps, descending an asphalt trail. Enter Pisgah National Forest, winding through rhododendron thickets, black birch, and pin cherry, as well as fragrant galax.

0.1 Cross noisy Yellowstone Prong on a sturdy hiker bridge. Turn right beyond the bridge toward Lower Falls. The trail uses boardwalks to escort hikers over rivulets.

0.2 Come to a trail intersection. Here the Mountains-to-Sea Trail Connector leads left to the Mountains-to-Sea Trail. Keep straight to Lower Falls through spruce and maple. Watch for user-created trails leading down to the top of Lower Falls.

Falls of Yellowstone Prong

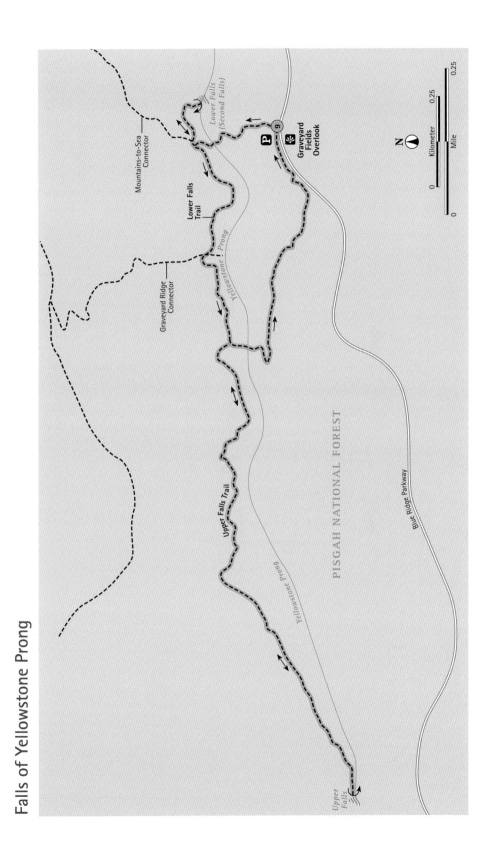

0.3 Reach the base of Lower Falls after following a multilevel boardwalk with multiple stairs. Lower Falls, labeled "Second Falls" on USGS maps, spills more than 50 feet down a broken rock slope into a pool. Backtrack after enjoying the cataract, heading back to the lowermost Yellowstone Prong trail bridge. This time, keep straight up the right-hand bank of Yellowstone Prong on the Lower Falls Trail in a mix of woods and meadows. Note how the trees are weather-beaten, despite being in a valley.

0.5 The terrain opens and you cross a boardwalk with views of Graveyard Ridge, Black Balsam, and Pisgah Ridge. Watch out for dead-end user-created trails.

0.9 Come to a trail junction. Your return route heads left to cross Yellowstone Prong; stay right, continuing up the Yellowstone Prong valley toward Upper Falls. Stay with the most heavily used trail. The official trails will have erosion bars and other structures to enhance or maintain the walking surface.

1.3 Step over the main tributary to Yellowstone Prong. Look for white quartz among the stones in the waterway.

1.5 Come along a hillside cloaked in yellow birch. Ascend along a stony slope.

1.7 The path splits. A trail leads left to a cataract. Many hikers think they have reached Upper Falls, but this is merely a warm-up slide cascade. After exploring this slide fall, return to the main trail and continue to climb on stone steps.

1.8 Reach Upper Falls. The 45-foot cataract dashes down a rock slope in myriad incarnations that change further under different flows. No matter the season, the falls are worth the walk. Backtrack from Upper Falls.

2.7 Return to the trail junction where you were earlier. Turn right and span Yellowstone Prong; head downstream, bordered by evergreens.

3.2 Arrive back at the Graveyard Fields Overlook after a final stretch of stone steps.

10 Looking Glass Rock

This hike leads to one of the area's most notable peaks—Looking Glass Rock. Here you can climb to a granite grandstand rising above the Davidson River valley where vistas of the Blue Ridge await. A first-rate but busy path switchbacks from the river through woods, passing occasional rock slabs before opening onto a colossal stone slab affording panoramas of the Blue Ridge rising in the distance as well as the greater Davidson River valley stretching out below.

Start: FR 475

Distance: 5.6 miles out and back

Hiking time: About 3.5 hours

Difficulty: Moderate–difficult due to ascent

Trail surface: Natural

Best season: Fall through spring for best views; weekdays for less traffic

Other trail users: None

Canine compatibility: Leashed dogs allowed

Land status: National forest

Fees and permits: No fees or permits required

Schedule: 24/7/365

Maps: USGS Shining Rock; National Geographic #780: Pisgah Ranger District

Trail contacts: Pisgah National Forest, Pisgah Ranger District, 1001 Pisgah Hwy., Pisgah Forest, NC 28768; (828) 877-3265; fs.usda.gov/nfsnc

Finding the trailhead: From the intersection of NC 280 and US 276 in Brevard, take US 276 North for 5.2 miles; turn left on FR 475 toward the Pisgah Center for Wildlife Education. Follow FR 475 for 0.3 mile; the trailhead will be on your right. GPS: N35° 17' 27.6" / W82° 46' 35.8"

The Hike

Spend any time in western North Carolina and you will hear about Looking Glass Rock. After seeing this unusual stone peak rising almost 2,000 feet above the Davidson River valley, you will agree it is a distinctive mountain. Standing proud at 3,969 feet with expansive, sheer granite walls curving around three sides, the dome is unmistakable. The open rock delivers vistas of the Blue Ridge Mountains rising to the west as well as nearby ridges and valleys. If you think there's a good view looking out from Looking Glass Rock, views of Looking Glass Rock are

The Blue Ridge rises high, majestic, and green above Looking Glass Rock.

rewarding as well, whether you see this signature peak from the Blue Ridge Parkway or John Rock, a nearby similar dome. Seeing the open rock faces of Looking Glass Rock reflecting the sun purportedly inspired the name. Others contend it was inspired by reflections off the thin sheets of ice that cover the exposed rock after freezing rains or, in some instances, where water dribbles from thin soils atop the rock then flows over the rock and freezes, creating a reflecting surface.

Open rock expanses this large are unusual in the eastern United States. The origin of Looking Glass Rock is volcanic. At one time, molten magma rose toward the earth's crust but did not quite break through before cooling, creating a dome. The dome never erupted and became a volcano. Instead, the resultant hardened granite formed what is known as a pluton, a body of rock below the surface of the earth. Eventually the body of rock was revealed following erosion of softer strata, leaving the exposed granite dome we see today.

Looking Glass Rock is an icon to not only hikers but also climbers. Known in climbing circles as "The Glass," climbers use six primary routes, with "The Nose" being the classic route. If you see intrepid athletes lurking around the mountain wearing those funny climbing shoes, draped in ropes and carabiners, they are likely using the routes that cloak Looking Glass Rock. The first ascent of The Nose was made in 1966, and ever since then climbers have flocked to this arguably best-known climbing peak in the entire Southeast, especially since Looking Glass Rock offers climbing routes to entertain novice, intermediate, and expert climbers, whether they are free climbing or using ropes.

Most of us adventurers use a trail to reach the top of Looking Glass Rock. Though not as dangerous or challenging as rock climbing, the hike to the peak is a nearly continuous ascent from the parking area. You gain almost 1,600 feet from bottom to top. However, due to the hike's popularity, the Looking Glass Rock Trail is a near-continual work in progress; its formerly steep gradient has been moderated by numerous switchbacks—enough of them, in fact, to practically make a hiker wobbly from the trail's back-and-forth turns.

When you reach the top, be very careful; do not take the open slopes for granted. If you fall, it is a long way down with nothing to stop you. Be especially careful after rains or in subfreezing conditions. Water seeps flowing over the rock can freeze, potentially making a minor slip a big deal.

Along parts of the trail you can find a tree known as Carolina hemlock. This is an often-compact, conical evergreen with needles spreading in all directions along its branches versus the needles of an eastern hemlock, which spread in two rows on either side of the branch. Carolina hemlock occurs—not surprisingly—in western North Carolina, as well as East Tennessee, Southwest Virginia, and in limited areas of Georgia and South Carolina. Unlike the moisture-loving eastern hemlock, it grows on dry slopes, usually between 2,000 and 4,000 feet, like those found on the slopes of Looking Glass Rock. Western North Carolina is the heart of the Carolina hemlock's range. The evergreen also seems to be less susceptible to the hemlock woolly adelgid, which is decimating eastern hemlocks throughout the Appalachians. However, since Carolina hemlocks are listed as rare in the wild, protective measures such as spraying a soapy insecticide for the hemlock woolly adelgid are undertaken in important and accessible stands of the trees.

The trek starts by climbing along a stream; then the Looking Glass Trail begins its switchback-athon. The higher you climb, the more frequent the switchbacks become. Once away from the lowlands, the trailside vegetation morphs to a more xeric variety—sourwood, pine, black gum, mountain laurel, and the unusual Carolina hemlock. Fragrant galax flanks the pathway. Eventually the trail leads to the ridge crest, but it keeps climbing. Look for views of adjacent mountains through the trees. Rock slabs start to appear along the sandy, rooty path, including a large one used as a helicopter pad. Stone and log steps aid your footing.

You reach a wooded high point a little before opening onto your destination—a huge sloped naked-granite slab bordered by tenacious cedars and pines gripping via shallow roots onto thin soils among cracks in the granite. Depending on recent rainfall, water may be seeping over the bare rock. The farther down you go, the steeper the granite slope becomes, until it is the domain of climbers only. Above you, the crest of the Blue Ridge towers more than 6,000 feet in places, with many mile-high peaks extending across the landscape. Scan for overlooks on the Blue Ridge Parkway, running along the crest of the mountains in front of you. To your left (southwest) layers of mountains stretch along the horizon to Georgia and South Carolina. This overlook on Looking Glass Rock is the most

Looking Glass Rock is an unmistakably unique mountain.

Looking Glass Rock

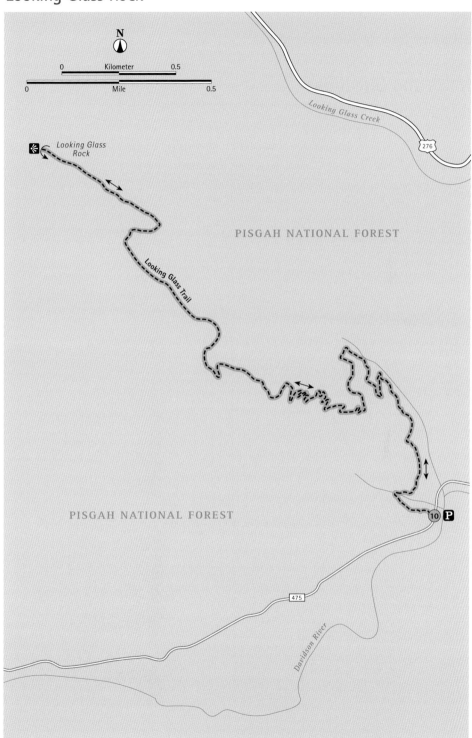

popular one on the mountain, but with a little searching you can find other vista points. It is worth the drive on the Blue Ridge Parkway to get views of Looking Glass Rock from the Parkway overlooks.

Miles and Directions

0.0　Start from the parking area on the Looking Glass Rock Trail, a wider-than-average hiker-only track designed for heavy traffic. Immediately bridge a little creek then ascend under magnolia, black birch, and tulip trees. Turn up an unnamed little streamlet flowing off the southeast side of Looking Glass Rock. Climb steadily above the spilling streamlet.

0.5　Make the first switchback. They come more frequently the higher you climb the mountain.

1.0　Reach the nose of the ridge atop Looking Glass Rock. If the leaves are off the trees, look southwest at the Art Loeb Trail wandering the ridge along Pilot Mountain among other peaks. Keep heading uphill.

1.5　Come along a small trickle of water then turn away. The uptick continues.

1.9　A few rock slabs are exposed among the trees.

2.1　Reach the first wide-open rock slab along the trail to your left. Head out onto it and look for the painted H, a helicopter landing pad. Return to the Looking Glass Rock Trail, keeping straight beyond the helicopter pad.

2.4　A short spur trail takes you to a large rock slab on your right. Here the main trail turns northwest, still atop the ridge crest. Watch for dead-end and user-created trails leading to campsites and harder-to-reach vistas.

2.7　Reach the high point of Looking Glass Rock, though you are in woods. Begin heading downhill under tree cover.

2.8　Open onto a huge sloped granite slab, your destination. The crest of the Blue Ridge extends across the horizon while lesser ridges and streams fall below. Explore, looking for other views. Return the way you came.

5.6　Arrive back at the trailhead.

11 John Rock Loop

This hike takes you to the top of John Rock, a granite dome rising above Pisgah National Forest. From John Rock you can see its more popular "big brother," Looking Glass Rock, and mountains beyond. Begin at an informative wildlife center and interesting fish hatchery, following the Davidson River. Turn up a tributary then begin an unbroken ascent to John Rock's naked top and a worthwhile panorama. The circuit drops off John Rock and descends along cascade-rich Cedar Rock Creek, where you can see the ribbon of Cedar Rock Creek Falls dancing down a stone slope, adding to this already geologically fascinating trek. After backtracking, pick up a new path, looping back to the trailhead.

Start: Pisgah Center for Wildlife Education
Distance: 5.6-mile loop
Hiking time: About 3.1 hours

Gazing down from John Rock on a foggy mountain morn

Difficulty: Moderate; does have 1,000-foot climb

Trail surface: Natural

Best season: Year-round; spring for bold cascades along Cedar Rock Creek

Other trail users: None

Canine compatibility: Leashed dogs allowed

Land status: National forest

Fees and permits: No fees or permits required

Schedule: 24/7/365

Maps: USGS Shining Rock; National Geographic #780: Pisgah Ranger District

Trail contacts: Pisgah National Forest, Pisgah Ranger District, 1001 Pisgah Hwy., Pisgah Forest, NC 28768; (828) 877-3265; fs.usda.gov/nfsnc

Finding the trailhead: From the intersection of NC 280 and US 276 in Brevard, take US 276 North for 5.2 miles; turn left on FR 475 toward the Pisgah Center for Wildlife Education. Follow FR 475 for 1.4 miles; turn left across the bridge over the Davidson River to the wildlife center and fish hatchery. The hike starts at the lower end of the parking area, away from the wildlife center. GPS: N35° 17' 03.2" / W82° 47' 26.2"

The Hike

John Rock is a worthy destination in its own right, but being literally in the shadow of one of the most famous mountains in the Southeast—Looking Glass Rock—makes it play second fiddle, despite the fact that it offers views similar to Looking Glass Rock and has a loop opportunity that also passes the cataracts of Cedar Rock Creek Falls.

My answer is to hike both, thus the two are included in this adventure guide. Asheville and greater western North Carolina residents almost have to hike Looking Glass Rock as a rite of passage. Avid hikers can then take on John Rock for its own deserving qualities and bragging rights. In addition to being a viewing point for Looking Glass Rock in the near and the Blue Ridge rising a mile high in the background, John Rock has fewer visitors. And then there are the drops of Cedar Rock Creek Falls. The trailhead is at the Pisgah Center for Wildlife Education, which focuses on North Carolina's mountain habitats and the wildlife within them. The educational opportunity can be bolstered by a visit to the adjacent fish hatchery, where trout are raised.

Crossing the stream coursing through Horse Cove

Because of its low elevation, this is a good winter hike, but dog owners should be aware that spring seeps atop John Rock, especially when frozen, have caused dogs to slip off the rock face. Pets have fallen even on the dry surface of the sloping rock. Keep Fido leashed up there!

Cedar Rock Falls makes a ledge dive.

After leaving the wildlife center, the hike wanders down the Davidson River, a popular angling venue, especially since it is regularly stocked with fish raised at the adjacent hatchery. Expect to see wader-clad anglers plying the pools and riffles of the translucent mountain stream. Cedar Rock Creek flows into the Davidson River, adding volume as you head downstream. Other streams that you bridge increase flow too. Pines grow thick.

The Cat Gap Loop leaves the Davidson River and turns up wide Horse Cove. This formerly settled and tilled terrain has reverted to forest dominated by tulip trees. After joining the John Rock Trail, the hike exchanges streamside scenes for granite, stunted pines, and eye-popping views. Of course you have to earn those views with a climb, but that is to be expected in these majestic highlands of western North Carolina. Gaze north across the Davidson River valley to see Looking Glass Rock showing off its own granite skin as the Blue Ridge forms a rolling rampart over a mile high in the yon. Below, the fish-filled raceways and buildings of the trout hatchery fill the streamside flats.

A second worthy view lies ahead; you then turn south along a ridge in classic hickory-oak woods. Beyond the high point, the trail descends to a gap and trail intersection. Here this loop turns right on the Cat Gap Bypass. **Option:** You can extend the trek about 0.4 mile by heading to Cat Gap and staying with the Cat Gap Loop Trail. This involves additional climbing, however.

The bypass wanders through richly vegetated coves before meeting the Cat Gap Loop. Here the circuit hike dives toward Cedar Rock Creek; switchbacks mitigate the steep ridge down which the trail travels. This ridge divides John Rock Branch from Cedar Rock Creek.

You then sidle alongside Cedar Rock Creek. As you descend, Cedar Rock Creek picks up steam until it is pouring off a pair of ledges—Cedar Rock Falls. These cataracts can be accessed from the main trail via a user-created pathway. The path then unexpectedly comes along the fish hatchery fence. The trail bridges Cedar Rock Creek twice before coming to the back of the wildlife center and trail's end.

Miles and Directions

0.0 Start from the lower end of the large trailhead parking area near a big sycamore tree, walking east on the Cat Gap Loop Trail. Hike along the Davidson River. Ahead, the official trail veers right and bridges Cedar Rock Creek, while an angler's access path continues downriver. Walk through wooded flats along the Davidson River after bridging Cedar Rock Creek amid dog hobble and rhododendron, where several big campsites lie.

0.3 Bridge a little tributary of the Davidson River; bridge another tributary 0.1 mile ahead.

0.5 The wide Cat Gap Loop Trail turns south up Horse Cove, through which flows an unnamed tributary of the Davidson River. In spring, wildflowers grow rich in Horse Cove.

0.8 The stream of Horse Cove comes into view as the trail comes along the foot of a little cascade.

0.9 Rock-hop the stream of Horse Cove where the valley narrows. The trail crosses gated old FR 475C. Continue working up a now steep-sided valley.

1.1 Bridge a tributary, continuing uphill.

1.2 Intersect the John Rock Trail. Turn right as the John Rock Trail curves around an upland cove. The Cat Gap Loop Trail keeps straight (you will rejoin it after climbing John Rock). The John Rock Trail alternates between small, rhododendron-choked rivulets in hollows and dry oak woods on ridges.

John Rock Loop

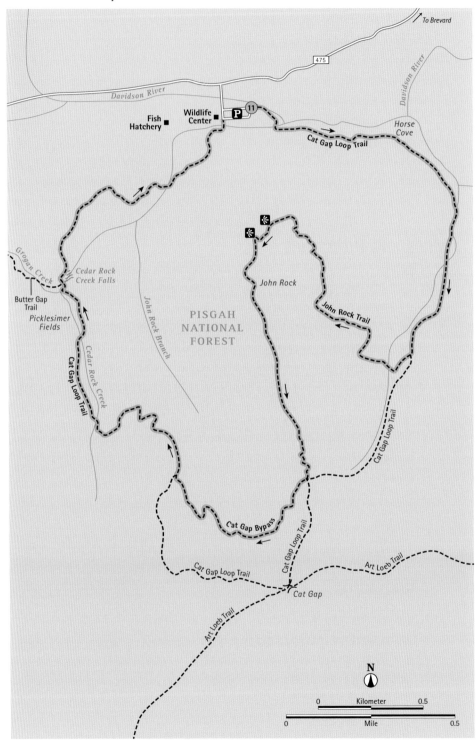

1.9 Level out on the crest of John Rock. Shrubby trees and mountain laurel form a tightly knit forest. Step over a little spring rivulet. Curve onto the north slope of John Rock, where the granite face extends forth. Hike among black gum, sourwood, and other dry-situation trees, along with leg-brushing blueberry bushes.

2.1 Turn right on a spur trail, heading onto the granite face of John Rock. Enjoy immediate and amazing vistas. First, find the fish hatchery below. The granite slab of Looking Glass Rock points north toward the Blue Ridge and the Blue Ridge Parkway. Be careful on the rock—water seeps over the granite, creating a slip hazard, especially when frozen.

2.2 A second spur trail heads to another granite slope and lookout. From there, turn south, away from the granite slope, ascending in the shade of classic hickory-oak woods.

2.8 Reach the high point of the hike. You are 1,000 feet above your starting point on the Davidson River. Drop sharply.

2.9 Come to a four-way trail intersection. Turn right here, picking up the Cat Gap Bypass Trail. The Cat Gap Loop Trail keeps straight for Cat Gap and an intersection with the Art Loeb Trail. The narrow bypass leads through holly- and magnolia-rich north-facing coves.

3.7 Reunite with the Cat Gap Loop after hopping over the upper reaches of John Rock Branch. Begin descending by switchbacks toward Cedar Rock Creek.

4.1 Rock-hop Cedar Rock Creek. Turn downstream beneath an evergreen canopy.

4.4 Cross over to the right-hand bank of Cedar Rock Creek after passing beneath a planted pine grove. Enter what remains of Picklesimer Fields.

4.7 Bridge Cedar Rock Creek and reach an intersection. Here the Butter Gap Trail heads left up along Grogan Creek, which adds significant flow to Cedar Rock Creek. User-created trails lead downstream to a series of cataracts below, highlighted by Cedar Rock Creek Falls. Stay right with the Cat Gap Loop Trail, descending.

5.3 Bridge Cedar Rock Creek again.

5.6 Finish the circuit after bridging Cedar Rock Creek a final time, arriving back at the rear of the wildlife center, itself worth a visit.

12 Mount Pisgah

This hike is the walking centerpiece of plentiful recreation opportunities along a lofty stretch of the Blue Ridge Parkway. From near the Parkway's Pisgah Inn, you will join a well-maintained trail past the headwaters of Pisgah Creek then work up the slope of Mount Pisgah on a rocky track, eventually reaching a platform and tower where a veritable land of milk and honey stretches out in all directions. Other trails spur from this locale, adding more hiking opportunities. You can also picnic, camp, or stay at the august Pisgah Inn.

Start: End of Buck Spring Overlook Road
Distance: 2.4 miles out and back
Hiking time: About 1.5 hours
Difficulty: Easy; does have a 700-foot ascent
Trail surface: Natural

Mount Pisgah as seen from the Blue Ridge Parkway

Best season: Whenever the skies are clear

Other trail users: None

Canine compatibility: Leashed dogs allowed

Land status: National park

Fees and permits: No fees or permits required

Schedule: 24/7/365

Maps: USGS Dunsmore Mountain, Cruso; National Geographic #780: Pisgah Ranger District

Trail contacts: Blue Ridge Parkway, 199 Hemphill Knob Rd., Asheville, NC 28803; (828) 348-3400; nps.gov/blri

Finding the trailhead: From exit 33 on I-26, south of downtown Asheville, take NC 191 South for 2.4 miles. Turn right onto the short, signed spur road to the Blue Ridge Parkway. Follow the Parkway right (southbound) for 13.9 miles to milepost 407.7, turning left at the sign for the Mount Pisgah parking area, which is Buck Spring Overlook Road. Follow Buck Spring Overlook Road for 0.3 mile to its dead end, passing the Buck Spring Overlook along the way. The Mount Pisgah Trail starts at the end of the road in a large parking area. GPS: N35° 25' 07.1" / W82° 44' 52.6"

The Hike

Taken from the Bible's book of Deuteronomy, Mount Pisgah is named for the mountain Moses climbed to view the Israelites' Promised Land—a "land of milk and honey." Fast-forward a few thousand years to 1776, when Griffith Rutherford—who lent his name to several North Carolina places—is battling the Cherokee for control of the French Broad River valley. Noting the richness of the valley where Asheville is located today, one of Rutherford's soldiers, a preacher by the name of John Hall, also thought the French Broad River valley a land of milk and honey and that a certain high peak with its commanding panoramas of this bountiful terrain should be named for the biblical crag upon which Moses had stood.

Thus, Mount Pisgah entered North Carolina history and lore, where it has remained ever since. Former North Carolina senator and Confederate general Thomas Clingman (for whom Great Smoky Mountains National Park's highest point, Clingmans Dome, is named) owned Mount Pisgah before selling off to George Vanderbilt, later to build the famous Biltmore Estate, along with its

A winter view of Mount Pisgah

125,000 adjacent acres, much of what later became today's Pisgah National Forest and Blue Ridge Parkway.

After selling Mount Pisgah to the USDA Forest Service, the Vanderbilt family kept a 400-acre parcel of land near the current trailhead for this hike, Buck Spring. Vanderbilt had constructed a hunting lodge on the property around 1900, starting a tradition of coming to this parcel of the Blue Ridge for rest, refurbishment, and recreation. The first Pisgah Inn followed in 1918, where wealthy patrons of the pre-air-conditioning South spent their summers. The current Pisgah Inn was built in 1964, after the state of North Carolina bought the land that once housed Vanderbilt's hunting lodge.

When the Blue Ridge Parkway became a reality, the park service made Mount Pisgah and its adjacent lands a recreation hub for the scenic road and the lands under its domain. They built trails, a campground, overlooks, picnic areas, and more. Today we can soak in the views from this storied mount and look out on our own promised land, and then enjoy the amenities of the Blue Ridge Parkway.

The hike leaves from near Buck Spring Overlook, a place with its own rewarding vistas, including a good look at Mount Pisgah and lands stretching to the east. Several trails emanate from the area, causing potential confusion for those looking for the proper trailhead. The Mount Pisgah Trail starts at the end of the spur road leading past Buck Springs Overlook. Interestingly, this spur road is routed atop the Buck Springs Tunnel, through which the Blue Ridge Parkway travels.

The trailhead is high, a shade under 5,000 feet. The heavily used but sturdy track circles a high south-facing cove from which emanates the headwater of Pisgah Creek (which feeds into the Pigeon River as opposed to the streams flowing east from the Blue Ridge feeding the promised land of the French Broad River Valley). It then starts to climb, reaching a gap separating Mount Pisgah from Little Pisgah Mountain, standing 5,270 feet in elevation. The Mount Pisgah Trail then straddles a narrow rocky ridge, where stone steps and naturally occurring rock guide you ever upward. Views begin to open through the trees of the Pisgah Inn, Buck Springs Gap, and the Blue Ridge Parkway, as well as mountains near and far.

Looking out on a land of milk and honey from Mount Pisgah

Mount Pisgah

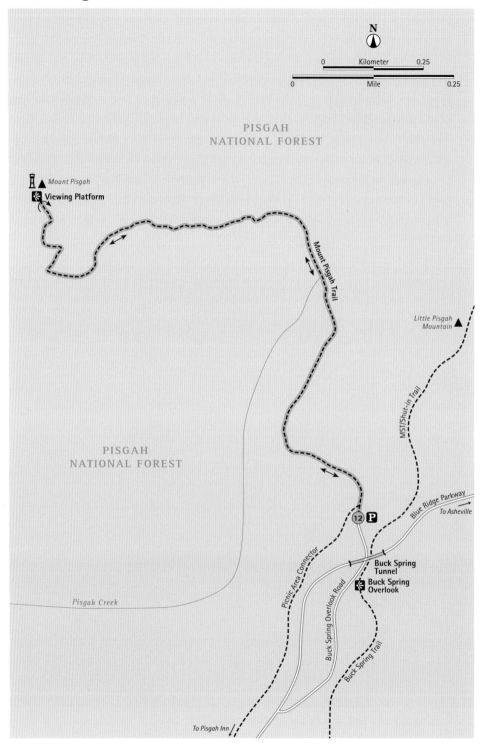

Trailside trees and brush become more gnarled the higher you climb. Then you reach the 5,721-foot top. A communications tower commands the rock crest, but a wooden viewing deck awaits your final steps. From here the land falls away in all directions. The Blue Ridge zigzags northeasterly toward Asheville. The Pigeon River flows west into Tennessee, while the verdant French Broad valley flows north to Asheville. Mount Mitchell rises proudly in the distance. To the south stand the rugged mountains of Shining Rock. Look for the Frying Pan Mountain tower, another worthy destination. In the near you can see the Buck Springs parking area and trailhead. After looking out on a clear day, it is easy to draw comparisons with Moses's view from the first Mount Pisgah.

Miles and Directions

0.0 Start from the north end of Buck Springs Overlook Road and join the Mount Pisgah Trail as it leaves north on a wide, level track. After a short distance, the Picnic Area Connector leaves left to Mount Pisgah Campground, Pisgah Inn, a picnic area, and Frying Pan Mountain. Stay straight with the Mount Pisgah Trail as you curve into a cove.

0.1 Pass a broad open rock face rising to your right.

0.4 Cross a spring branch feeding Pisgah Creek.

0.6 Reach a gap dividing Mount Pisgah from Little Pisgah Mountain. Curve left, ascending under craggy, windswept hardwoods.

1.0 The trail makes a sharp switchback to the right. Views open to the Parkway below.

1.2 Arrive atop Mount Pisgah, where a transmission tower rises. A wooden observation deck stands a few feet above the ground, offering incredible panoramas in all directions. Return the way you came.

2.4 Arrive back at the trailhead.

13 Avery Creek Falls and Twin Falls Loop

This circuit hike in Pisgah National Forest near Brevard leads you to three fine water-falls tucked deep in the hollows of the Davidson River valley. Head up scenic Avery Creek and view warm-up Avery Creek Falls, then cross numerous bridges before turning up Henry Branch. Find Twin Falls, a pair of 80-foot cataracts that converge at their base. This hike then winds along the slopes of Clawhammer Mountain before diving into narrow Clawhammer Cove to complete the circuit. Hiker bridges make this water-centric hike a year-round dry-footed affair.

Start: FR 477 on Avery Creek

Distance: 5.8-mile loop

Hiking time: About 3 hours

Difficulty: Moderate

Trail surface: Natural

Best season: Late fall through spring for bolder waterfalls

Other trail users: Mountain bikers on some parts, a few equestrians

Canine compatibility: Leashed dogs allowed

Land status: National forest

Fees and permits: No fees or permits required

Schedule: 24/7/365

Maps: USGS Pisgah Forest, Shining Rock; National Geographic #780: Pisgah Ranger District

Trail contacts: Pisgah National Forest, Pisgah Ranger District, 1001 Pisgah Hwy., Pisgah Forest, NC 28768; (828) 877-3265; fs.usda.gov/nfsnc

Finding the trailhead: From the intersection of NC 280 and US 276 in Brevard, take US 276 North for 2.1 miles. Turn right on FR 477; a sign here directs you toward Pisgah Riding Stables. Follow FR 477 for 2.5 miles; the trailhead will be on your right, 0.8 mile beyond the Pisgah Riding Stables. GPS: N35° 18' 58.0" / W82° 45' 08.2"

The Hike

This rewarding and not too difficult loop hike explores streams flowing off the slopes of Rich Mountain, highlighted by the visit to Twin Falls, a pair of thrilling 80-foot-high cataracts. These cascades make some heady spills, each showing off

Left: Henry Branch forms the left-hand cataract of Twin Falls.
Right: Crossing one of the many hiker bridges on this hike

distinctive characteristics—dropping as narrow charging chutes, delicate curtain falls, splashing cascades, slaloming rapids, and just about everything in between.

Even if there were no waterfalls on this hike, the overall beauty of Avery Creek and its tributaries and the mountainsides that separate them would be worth the visit. Richly vegetated valleys create a temperate near-jungle. The trails are never too far from water. A slew of hiker bridges not only allow dry passage but also provide close-up looks at Henry Branch and Avery Creek and other unnamed streams, including the one cutting the vale known as Clawhammer Cove, an all-time Southern Appalachian name candidate. While looping around back to the trailhead, you do climb, but overall elevation changes are less than 600 feet, easing the strain.

The hike starts where the Buckhorn Gap Trail leaves FR 477. While driving in you will pass a perhaps better trailhead—the Avery Creek Trail starting point—just before reaching the Buckhorn Gap trailhead, but parking at the Avery Creek trailhead is limited to one or two cars beside a precarious slope, making the Buckhorn Gap Trail a superior embarkation point. The Buckhorn Gap Trail soon comes alongside Avery Creek. The song of falling water fills your ears—Avery Creek Falls. In their zeal to reach Twin Falls, many hikers bypass this initial

Left: Henry Branch tumbles 80 feet.
Right: This unnamed stream forms the right-hand spill of Twin Falls.

cataract, as evidenced by less-than-beaten-down spur to the two-tiered spiller, which first descends as a 10-foot sloped cascade then gathers steam in a flat stretch before dropping in a 12-foot-high creek-wide sheet. Don't bypass Avery Creek Falls, especially if you are looking to play around in the creek. Twin Falls lacks plunge pools and big waters into which to wade or swim.

The Buckhorn Gap Trail is open to hikers, bicyclers, and equestrians, although horseback riders are very infrequent. Hikers have to be on guard because the trail often splits at creek crossings—hikers go one way on log footbridges; mountain bikers and equestrians go another, crossing the streams via fords. The diverging paths then reconverge.

Eventually the Buckhorn Gap Trail leaves Avery Creek and heads up Henry Branch, a tributary of Avery Creek along which Twin Falls is found. Paths work up both sides of Henry Branch. Our hike heads up the left (west) side of Henry Branch and passes a wet-weather fall spilling about 20 feet over a rock ledge just before coming to a steep cove where Twin Falls echo off the hillsides.

The first sight of these two tall cataracts is a thriller. You rush up the path ready to snap your best shots. The left-hand fall—Henry Branch—of the Twin Falls comes first. It pours white through rhododendron then widens and rolls in four stages, the last of which is the grandest, descending in a regal curtain over bare rock, then slaloms in shoals over the trail. A spur leads to the base of the curtain.

Then it is on to Twin Falls's right-hand fall—the unnamed tributary of Henry Branch. This multilayer tumbler has a bit less flow and is narrower as it jumps off a ledge then squares itself, down, down, down—dashing over evergreen-shrouded rocks and crossing the trail before meeting Henry Branch. A spur heads up the right-hand side of this fall, where you can see a stage of the cataract lunge from an overhanging ledge.

The Twin Falls can both be seen from the confluence of Henry Branch and the unnamed tributary. Early morning and late afternoon present the best winter shade photography times. After shooting and admiring, take the trail heading down the east side of Henry Branch to meet a horse rack and trail intersection. Here our hike makes its loop, skirting the slopes of Clawhammer Mountain, winding in and out of coves, and joining gated FR 5058 before meeting Clawhammer Cove Trail. This singletrack path wastes no time in making a downgrade into a slender valley. The cove cuts deep, and you follow suit, diving into pines before finding Avery Creek and another hiker bridge. Pass alluring pools and noisy shoals along Avery Creek before climbing back to the trailhead, briefly joining FR 477 on the way.

Miles and Directions

0.0   Start at the FR 477 parking area on the Buckhorn Gap Trail. The signed northbound path, flanked by mountain laurel and rhododendron, soon curves around coves above Avery Creek. Pass under a power line twice.

0.5   Sidle along Avery Creek Falls, accessible by a spur trail leading right and downhill. Come to the lower part of the falls first, as it spills over a 12-foot ledge into a pool. To see the upper part of the spiller, walk upstream past a rock slab to view the angled 10-foot step fall. The rock slab at the top of the lower fall makes for a fine relaxation spot. After resuming the hike, look for a low-flow waterfall tributary coming into the far side of Avery Creek. The Buckhorn Gap Trail then curves along a flat away from Avery Creek.

0.9   Meet the Avery Creek Trail, which has been running roughly parallel to the Buckhorn Gap Trail. Keep straight on the Buckhorn Gap Trail.

Avery Creek Falls and Twin Falls Loop

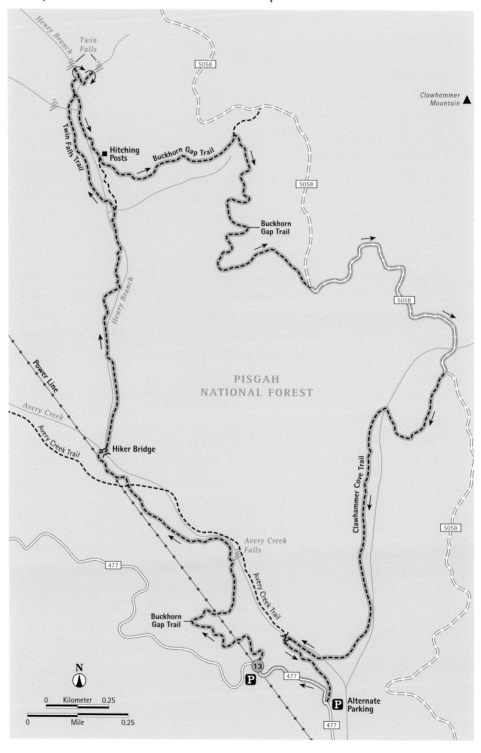

Henry Branch
Twin Falls
5058
Clawhammer Mountain
Hitching Posts
Buckhorn Gap Trail
Twin Falls Trail
Buckhorn Gap Trail
5058
Buckhorn Gap Trail
5058
Henry Branch
Power Line
Avery Creek
Avery Creek Trail
PISGAH NATIONAL FOREST
Clawhammer Cove Trail
5058
Hiker Bridge
Avery Creek Falls
477
Avery Creek Trail
Buckhorn Gap Trail
13
P
477
P Alternate Parking
477

N

0	Kilometer	0.25
0	Mile	0.25

1.0 Cross Avery Creek on a hiker bridge near a power line. Turn into the Henry Branch valley. Encounter several trail splits where hikers cross the stream on bridges and mountain bikers and equestrians use fords. Keep upstream along Henry Branch.

1.6 Reach a signed intersection. Here the Twin Falls Trail crosses Henry Branch on a hiker bridge while the Buckhorn Gap Trail keeps straight up the right bank of Henry Branch. Cross the log bridge on the hiker-only Twin Falls Trail.

1.9 Pass an intermittent cascade on your left just before coming to a campsite and trail intersection. Here the Buckhorn Gap Trail leads down Henry Branch. You will join this path later; for now, head up and explore the Twin Falls. Take the spur trails alongside the cataracts for additional photography opportunities.

2.1 Head down the Buckhorn Gap Trail after backtracking to the campsite below Twin Falls. This path quickly bridges Henry Branch. Hike downstream along the east side of Henry Branch.

2.4 Reach a trail intersection at some horse hitching posts. Head left on the Buckhorn Gap Trail, ascending into a maple-oak-beech cove.

2.7 Hop a small tributary of Henry Branch. Continue up the hardwood-rich cove with scattered grasses.

2.8 Come to a signed intersection. The Buckhorn Gap Trail splits into two arms. Turn right here, curving southeast along coves below Clawhammer Mountain on a doubletrack path toward FR 5058. The left arm also goes to FR 5058.

3.6 Meet gravel FR 5058 in a gap. Turn right here, descending through more coves.

4.2 Leave right from FR 5058 on the signed and blazed Clawhammer Cove Trail. Turn right here, descending a singletrack path.

4.5 Bridge the stream of Clawhammer Cove. Keep downhill.

5.3 Reach a trail intersection after reaching and turning up Avery Creek. Head left, crossing Avery Creek on a hiker bridge on the Avery Creek Trail. Briefly turn downstream on Avery Creek before climbing toward FR 477.

5.7 Emerge at FR 477 and a very limited parking area at the Avery Creek trailhead. Turn right here (northbound) up FR 477.

5.8 Arrive back at the trailhead.

14 Bradley Creek Circuit

Looking for a fun watery hike with minimal elevation change? Look no further. This warm-weather loop circles Buck Mountain, first tracing South Mills River down a wildflower-filled valley, making many fords to then turn up smaller but no less scenic Bradley Creek. Enjoy more streamside backdrops and make more wet-footed crossings. Turn up still smaller Pea Branch, finally leaving the aquatic surroundings to cross a low ridge and then return to South Mills River. The final part of the hike traces an old forest road, adding new trail mileage.

Start: Turkey Pen trailhead

Distance: 7.6-mile double loop

Hiking time: About 4.5 hours

Difficulty: Moderate; does have numerous fords

Trail surface: Natural

Best season: Late spring through early fall

Other trail users: Equestrians, mountain bikers

Canine compatibility: Leashed dogs allowed

Land status: National forest

Fees and permits: No fees or permits required

Schedule: 24/7/365

Maps: USGS Pisgah Forest; National Geographic #780: Pisgah Ranger District

Trail contacts: Pisgah National Forest, Pisgah Ranger District, 1001 Pisgah Hwy., Pisgah Forest, NC 28768; (828) 877-3265; fs.usda.gov/nfsnc

Finding the trailhead: From exit 40 on I-26, south of Asheville, take NC 280 West for 10.2 miles to Turkeypen Road, on your right, just after Boylston Creek Church. (Turkeypen Road is signed on the highway, but the entrance looks like a gravel driveway.) Follow Turkeypen Road for 1.2 miles to dead-end at the trailhead. GPS: N35° 20' 34.6" / W82° 39' 33.9"

The Hike

An excellent, easily accessible trail network emanates from the Turkeypen trailhead, where this hike starts. Don't be surprised if the parking area is crowded, but there's room for everyone in the South Mills River valley, where a wealth of creekside and ridgetop paths form a trail complex that presents multiple loop hike possibilities. I favor this particular circuit, as it stays along mountain

Hikers will become well acquainted with the fords of Bradley Creek.

streams almost the whole hike, allowing you to maximize your aquatic experience. Strictly a warm-season endeavor, multiple fords are required to complete the loop. If you are going to get your feet wet, why not leave 'em wet and soak in the streamside beauty of three waterways: South Fork Mills River, Bradley Creek, and Pea Branch? You'll see a cornucopia of wildflowers in spring, rushing cascades and silent pools, craggy waterside outcrops and repose boulders, lushly wooded flats, and deep mountain scenes that transport you to the Carolina wildlands.

A little planning is in order, however. Since you will be fording repeatedly, wear sturdy-soled shoes you don't mind getting wet. I do not recommend sandals, since I don't favor the prospect of busting my toe on an underwater rock. Low-top hiking shoes covering your entire foot that drain easily are my footwear of choice for this adventure. Additionally, a pair of trekking poles or a good old-fashioned hiking stick will aid your passage across the creeks.

Note: Before coming to the trailhead, check the water level of the South Mills River to determine if the fords are passable for the day of your hike. Check the

Teenage backpackers cross the only bridge on Bradley Creek.

USGS water gauge, "Mills River near Mills River, NC," adding "USGS" to your search. This gauge is downstream of the trailhead but will tell you whether the stream is at, above, or below normal levels for that given day. The gauge will also give you the water temperature for that day!

Water levels will generally be higher in spring, lower through the summer, and at their lowest in autumn. However, heavy rains in spring, thunderstorms in summer, and tropical systems in autumn can cause the watershed to be above normal. In spring the Mills River can be quite chilly. The waters will be tolerable by June, and throughout summer the plentiful pools found along the circuit will become potential swimming holes. By September the fords are downright easy and the water is still mild. The season for this hike is over by the end of October.

Since this is a backcountry area and not a designated wilderness, the trail network is signed and well maintained, making travel and navigation easier. Elevation changes less than 300 feet make the loop more doable. Consider making this an overnight adventure, as there are campsites aplenty.

The first part of the hike navigates through numerous trail intersections then settles down as it descends the South Mills River on the Riverside Trail. The wide, road-like path is shaded by hornbeam, pine, and black birch; the forest floor is carpeted in ferns, dog hobble, and rhododendron. The South Mills runs around 30 to 40 feet wide, alternating in trouty pools and splashy shoals. Make your first ford a little less than 1 mile into the hike. Use this crossing as a rough gauge: If you feel comfortable making this crossing, you can make the following fords. Begin soaking in the everywhere-you-look streamside aura in the form of mossy logs, sun-splashed pools, smooth gravel bars, irregular rock bars, and sparkling waters shooting past mute boulders. The fords continue as you head easterly downriver in first-rate western North Carolina beauty.

The hike then turns up Bradley Creek, where the riparian scenery and fords continue, heading upstream on a gentle grade. At any given point, a streamside flat stretches wide while the other bank of the stream rises hilly. After a final crossing of Bradley Creek, the jaunt on the Riverside Trail ends and you work your way up still smaller Pea Branch. Experience the first meaningful elevation change of the hike while surmounting Pea Gap, then return to South Fork Mills River. After a little backtracking you can take a closed forest road back up to the trailhead, completing the hike.

Miles and Directions

0.0 Start at the Turkeypen trailhead on the South Mills River Trail, one of four trails emanating from the parking area. As you face north at the trail kiosk, you will have a gated trail to your right (your return route) and the singletrack South Mills River Trail to your left. The ridge-running Turkeypen Gap Trail and Vineyard Gap Trail leave behind you. Head left on the heavily trod South Mills River Trail, descending toward the South Mills River, ensconced in rhododendron.

0.4 Reach the South Fork Mills River and a trail intersection. A trail bridge crosses the river here, and South Mills River Trail heads upstream with it. This hike stays right, heading downstream along the South Mills River on the Bradley Creek Trail. Walk a short distance then come to a four-way trail intersection. The road leading right is your return route to the trailhead. A horse ford goes left. Keep straight, still on the Bradley Creek Trail.

0.8 Make the first ford of the hike. If you can successfully execute this stream crossing, you can make the subsequent fords. After crossing the stream, a hiker trail heads left, back toward the trailhead.

Bradley Creek Circuit

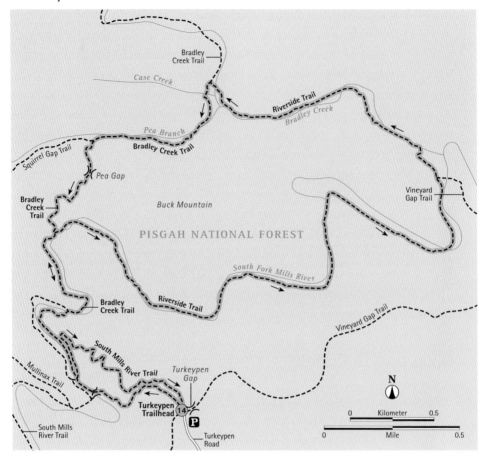

1.1 Bend right, passing under a blasted bluff.

1.3 Come to a trail intersection. Here the Bradley Creek Trail leaves left and is your return route. Our counterclockwise circuit heads right, joining the Riverside Trail.

1.4 Ford South Fork Mills River. Sycamores are prevalent as you trace an old railroad grade. Look for embedded railroad ties.

1.8 Ford the river again.

2.2 Ford the river again. Enjoy a long walk on a level track as you admire the beautiful valley.

2.9 The Riverside Trail curves right, cutting across a long bend in South Fork Mills River. Look for more railroad ties on the elevated bed pushing through a sea of evergreen.

3.4 Ford South Fork Mills River a last time. You are on the left-hand bank. The valley widens. Beard cane prevails in the flats.

3.7 Intersect the Vineyard Gap Trail. It has come from Turkeypen Gap.

3.8 Reach then ford Bradley Creek in a huge flat. The Riverside Trail now turns up the rhododendron-heavy Bradley Creek valley, while an unmaintained path continues down South Fork Mills River. You and the Bradley Creek Trail are now heading upstream instead of downstream.

4.0 Ford Bradley Creek.

4.2 Ford Bradley Creek again. Watch for tall tulip trees.

A mountain laurel blossom settles on a sandbar of Bradley Creek.

4.6 Cut through a meadow. Continue up the Bradley Creek valley.

4.8 Make a final ford of Bradley Creek. Reach a trail junction and the end of the Riverside Trail. At this point, turn left on the Bradley Creek Trail, now following Bradley Creek downstream. Soon rock-hop Case Branch.

5.0 Come alongside Pea Branch. Ascend a slender valley.

5.4 Intersect the Squirrel Gap Trail. Turn left here, hop over Pea Branch, and stay with the Bradley Creek Trail.

5.6 Cut through Pea Gap. Look at the mica in the sandy trailbed. Descend from Pea Gap.

5.9 Return to the South Mills River. Backtrack right, heading upriver.

6.8 Come to a four-way intersection. Head sharply left up the gravel road, making a wide switchback.

7.6 Arrive back at the trailhead.

15 Waterfalls of DuPont Loop

This circuit hike at DuPont State Recreational Forest visits four of the six major waterfalls located at this preserve outside Brevard. Leave the Lake Imaging trailhead and trace mostly doubletrack paths to less-visited Grassy Creek Falls, then nearly circle magnificent and popular High Falls, viewing it from multiple angles. Next, admire roller-coastering Triple Falls. Trace the Little River to wide, rumbling Hooker Falls. Finally, take a quiet path to return to the trailhead, closing the loop. Elevation changes vary just a few hundred feet on the well-marked, well-maintained, but exceedingly popular trail system.

Start: Lake Imaging trailhead
Distance: 6.4-mile loop
Hiking time: About 3.5 hours

Grassy Creek Falls is one of the least-visited cataracts in DuPont State Forest.

Difficulty: Moderate

Trail surface: Natural, gravel

Best season: Year-round; winter for more solitude

Other trail users: Mountain bikers, equestrians

Canine compatibility: Leashed dogs allowed

Land status: State forest

Fees and permits: No fees or permits required

Schedule: Year-round, 5 a.m. to 10 p.m.

Maps: USGS Standingstone Mountain; National Geographic #504: DuPont State Recreational Forest, DuPont State Recreational Forest

Trail contacts: DuPont State Recreational Forest, PO Box 300, Cedar Mountain, NC 28718-0300; (828) 877-6527; dupontstaterecreationalforest.com

Finding the trailhead: From the intersection of NC 280 and US 276 in Pisgah Forest, just north of Brevard, take US 64 East for 3.5 miles to a light at Crab Creek Road. Turn right on Crab Creek Road, follow it 4.2 miles, and turn right on DuPont Road. Follow DuPont Road as it soon becomes Staton Road for a total of 2.5 miles to the Lake Imaging trailhead, on your left. GPS: N35° 12' 32.8" / W82° 36' 55.1"

The Hike

This hike travels through extremely scenic DuPont State Recreational Forest, home to waterfalls, granite outcrops, wildlife aplenty, and an extensive trail system. DuPont came to be after lands ended up under state ownership following a tense time of land bidding, during which key features of this particular hike—including High Falls and Triple Falls—nearly ended up being part of an upscale housing development. Some of the trails you hike on this feature-laden loop were actually roads laid out by the developer. The state forest now contains more than 10,000 acres and is a magnet for hikers, mountain bikers, and equestrians who seek to enjoy nature and get some outdoor exercise on the 90 or so miles of pathways that course throughout the terrain. These trails can range from wide gravel gated roads (open only to forest personnel) to remote singletrack paths winding through the hills and hollows. Almost all the trails here are multiple-use trails, so expect to share the path with mountain bikers as well as equestrians.

The large Lake Imaging trailhead is popular with all three groups, with hikers being the largest assemblage, mountain bikers a close second, followed by

High Falls pours 120 proud feet.

equestrians. Be a defensive hiker and listen for mountain bikers, who will sometimes be traveling excessively fast and not give you time to jump out of the way. However, most of them are courteous to hikers. Both hikers and mountain bikers should yield to horses.

It is just a short distance from the trailhead until you see your first water feature: Lake Imaging. The peculiar name is derived from one of the corporate property owners, Sterling Diagnostic Imaging. Name aside, the small 2-acre impoundment is more of a pond than a lake. A shelter stands astride Lake Imaging and makes for a fine picnic spot. Pathways circle the impoundment. This is one of five lakes in DuPont State Recreational Forest. The largest is Lake Julia, coming in at 99 acres. Anglers vie for bream and largemouth bass on these lakes; trout are found in the Little River, the primary watercourse in the forest, and its tributaries.

Beyond Lake Imaging, the easy, undulating doubletrack takes you to a spur and Grassy Creek Falls—your first moving-water feature. Like many of the cataracts here, 50-foot Grassy Creek Falls sheets over a long, widening, angled stone slab into a plunge pool. Unlike most other waterfalls here, this cataract is decidedly less crowded. Use caution at this and all the other falls here at DuPont. Unfortunately, aquatic accidents are a common occurrence among forest visitors.

Buck Forest Road leads you through the covered bridge above High Falls. Here, enter the busy but beautiful area where the three primary spillers of DuPont are situated together, concentrating the visitation. Do not let this deter you; the three falls—High Falls, Triple Falls, and Hooker Falls—all deserve your attention. You will see 120-foot High Falls from an elevated viewpoint near some picnic shelters as well as viewing it from the base. Here the Little River positively roars in white froth over a solid granite face exuding power and majesty. No wonder it is so popular! Next comes Triple Falls, a three-tiered spellbinder also dropping 120 feet, dancing and dashing over granite in massive stages. Steps lead to the middle of the cataract, but you can also see all three drops at once from a trailside vista.

After crossing Staton Road, trace the Little River past the large Hooker Falls parking area to visit Hooker Falls. This tumbler stands in complete contrast to all the other cascades at DuPont. Here a wide wall of white uniformly spills 12 feet over a ledge into a gargantuan pool that is easily the most popular moving-water swimming spot in the forest.

Beyond Hooker Falls, leave the crowds behind, joining quiet and little-traveled Holly Road. This doubletrack path heads north, winding through hills of pine and oak, eventually leading back to the trailhead, completing the waterfall extravaganza.

Miles and Directions

0.0 Start at the Lake Imaging trailhead and pass around the pole gate. Head northeast on Lake Imaging Road, quickly spanning a stream via culvert.

0.2 Keep straight on Lake Imaging Road as the Ridgeline Trail heads left.

0.3 Come to 2-acre Lake Imaging. Stay left as a trail also goes around the right side of the pond. Just ahead, the Jim Branch Trail leaves left. Span small Hooker Creek via culvert and then ascend.

0.7 Bisect a former clearing, now growing up in pines.

1.2 Stay on Lake Imaging Road as the north end of the Hilltop Loop leaves right. Just ahead, the Locust Trail leaves left. Descend, passing a small quarry on trail left in pine-oak woods.

1.4 Turn right onto the Grassy Creek Falls Trail. Just beyond here, the south end of the Hilltop Trail enters from the right. Descend toward Grassy Creek. Shortly reach an old stone barbecue pit and the top of Grassy Creek Falls. See the cascade sheet downward 50 feet. Backtrack, then resume Lake Imaging Road.

1.8 Turn right onto Buck Forest Road. (As noted, all these roads are open only to forest personnel vehicles.) Immediately bridge Grassy Creek, then ascend a hill with partial wintertime views of the Blue Ridge to the west.

1.9 Chestnut Oak Road leaves left. Stay straight with Buck Forest Road. Grassy Creek Falls spills noisily below.

2.3 Conservation Road leaves left. Stay straight with Buck Forest Road, passing a mountain wetland to your left. Ahead, walk through the covered bridge above High Falls. Do not try to access the top of High Falls from here. After spanning the Little River via the covered bridge, split right on the Covered Bridge Trail.

2.6 Turn right onto the High Falls Trail after crossing a pipeline clearing. Descend, crossing the pipeline clearing a second time.

2.7 Split right toward High Falls as a spur trail goes straight to a pair of picnic shelters. Descend, then come to an astonishing vista of 120-foot High Falls. Continue dropping toward the Little River, passing a second access for the nearby picnic area.

3.0 Turn right onto the dead-end River Bend Trail. Follow the Little River upstream, curving toward the base of High Falls.

Waterfalls of DuPont Loop

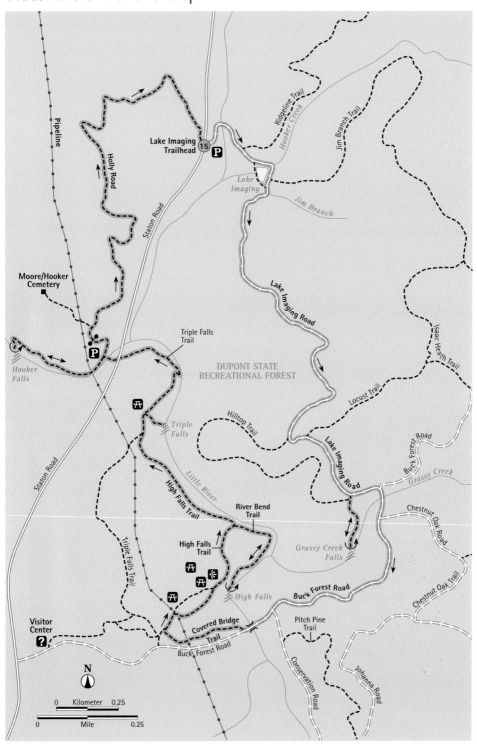

3.3 Reach the base of High Falls. A little rock scrambling is required to get close to the massive, misting roar of white. Backtrack.

3.6 Rejoin the High Falls Trail, paralleling the Little River downstream.

3.8 Stay right on the Triple Falls Trail. Descend.

3.9 Split right, joining a wooden stairwell to the middle of Triple Falls as a trail leads left to a picnic area. Backtrack up the stairs after viewing the falls; rejoin the Triple Falls Trail, descending along the Little River.

4.4 Pass under Staton Road.

4.5 Cross the Little River on a trail bridge. Come to the large upper Hooker Falls parking area. Head left toward Hooker Falls.

4.8 Reach low, wide Hooker Falls and its big pool. Backtrack.

5.1 Return to the Hooker Falls parking area; join Holly Road after passing around a metal pole gate. Quickly pass the spur leading left to Moore/Hooker Cemetery. Ahead, enjoy the interpretive signage about woodland trail and road building along Holly Road.

5.9 Bridge a small creek via a culvert after ascending along a trickling branch.

6.3 The trail devolves to singletrack and drops through pine-oak woods.

6.4 Reach Staton Road. Turn right and arrive back at the Lake Imaging trailhead.

High Falls in summer

16 Mount Mitchell State Park Loop

This circuit hike takes you to the highest point east of the Mississippi River: Mount Mitchell. Start near the park restaurant, traversing rare spruce-fir forest and take the historic Old Mitchell Trail to the summit, where prolific panoramas can be had on clear days. Descend along Lower Creek on the also historic Camp Alice Trail. Finally, join an old logging railroad bed on the Commissary Trail, where still more views open. Make Stepps Gap and the park office, where a final trek on the Old Mitchell Trail returns you to the trailhead.

Start: Mount Mitchell State Park office

Distance: 4.1-mile loop

Hiking time: About 2.4 hours

Difficulty: Moderate

Trail surface: Natural

Best season: Whenever the skies are clear and the Blue Ridge Parkway is open

Other trail users: None

Canine compatibility: Leashed dogs allowed

Land status: State park

Fees and permits: No fees or permits required

Schedule: Nov–Feb, 7 a.m.–6 p.m.; Mar–Apr, 7 a.m.–8 p.m.; May–Aug, 7 a.m.–10 p.m.; Sept–Oct, 7 a.m.–9 p.m.; closed Christmas Day

Maps: USGS Mount Mitchell; Mount Mitchell State Park

Trail contacts: Mount Mitchell State Park, 2388 State Hwy. 128, Burnsville, NC 28714; (828) 675-4611; ncparks.gov/mount-mitchell-state-park

Finding the trailhead: From Asheville take the Blue Ridge Parkway north 34 miles to milepost 355. Turn left on NC 128 into Mount Mitchell State Park. Follow the scenic highway 3 miles to the large restaurant parking area, on your right. GPS: N35° 45' 08.0" / W82° 16' 26.0"

The Hike

Mount Mitchell is the highest point east of the Mississippi River, without a doubt. The mountaintop stands at 6,683 feet along the crest of the Black Mountains. However, there was once considerable controversy as to the true high point in the East. Some thought it was Grandfather Mountain, an impressive crag to the northeast of Mount Mitchell. Others thought it was Clingmans Dome in the

The compass atop Mount Mitchell helps hikers find distant peaks.

Smokies; still others thought it was Mount Washington in New Hampshire. Here in Carolina the debate was primarily between proponents of Grandfather Mountain and what came to be known as Mount Mitchell.

Back in 1835, Dr. Elijah Mitchell, of the esteemed University of North Carolina, made his way to the top of the Black Mountains and determined that they were indeed higher than Grandfather Mountain. However, Thomas Clingman—North Carolina senator, one-time student of Dr. Mitchell, and, later, Confederate general—challenged his former mentor as to the high point. To end the controversy once and for all, in 1857 Elisha Mitchell headed up to the Black Mountains to once again measure the high point. Elisha may have used what is now known as the Old Mitchell Trail—the very path upon which this hike begins—to scale the summit. His climb went well, but on the way back the professor tumbled from a cliff, landing at the base of a 40-foot waterfall, where he drowned.

Mitchell was vindicated posthumously, while Thomas Clingman got nearby Clingmans Peak named for him as well as the Smokies high point of Clingmans Dome. To honor Mitchell's efforts, the high point of the Black Mountains was named for him. Mitchell was later buried at the peak.

Being the high point only added to the attraction for people visiting the Black Mountains. The range is a place where flora and fauna replicate that found in Canada. When the climate was colder, plants such as red spruce and Fraser fir, birds such as juncos, and critters such as red squirrels found a home in the

Southern Appalachians. After the climate warmed, the northern flora and fauna survived on "sky islands" such as the Black Mountains.

Hikers have been coming to scale the Black Mountains since the 1830s, when what became the Old Mitchell Trail was a primary route along the crest. The trail actually started down along the Swannanoa River and worked its way up to the ridgeline, ending at Mount Mitchell. Therefore, when you hike this path you are walking in the footsteps of early Southern Appalachian explorers. What is left of the Old Mitchell Trail starts at the park office. Mount Mitchell State Park was established in 1915 after area citizens cried foul upon seeing the Black Mountains being denuded of vegetation after loggers arrived in the early 1900s equipped with band saws and efficient methods of timber removal via logging railroad lines.

Prior to this, North Carolina did not even have a state park system; the state park system and North Carolina state parks were established simultaneously. The preservation of Mount Mitchell led not only to saving North Carolina's highest peak but also to the protection of all the other parcels in the state park system, from the Atlantic Ocean to the Piedmont to the Appalachian range.

The Black Mountains stretch
out in the distance.

Much of this hike traverses deep evergreen forests.

Of course, early users of the Old Mitchell Trail did not start near a stone building housing an alluring restaurant, as you do on this hike (check ahead for restaurant hours, which are seasonal). Nor did early hikers walk past a developed tent campground. But eventually they made their way to the top of Mount Mitchell, despite the irregular, rooty, and rocky terrain that remains rugged to this day, despite the plethora of stone steps, wooden walkways, and other conveniences employed by modern trail builders.

Mount Mitchell is graced with a low-slung stone observation tower with a 360-degree panorama of the surrounding mountains. To help you get your bearings, signs point out notable places on the horizon. On very clear days—and then is when you should be doing this hike—the views extend impressive distances, from the Black Mountains in the near as well as the immediate state park facilities to far-flung peaks on the horizon and easily identifiable landmarks such as Table Rock and distant points well into Tennessee.

Most visitors to the observation tower will be coming via the short and busy Summit Trail, accessed from a parking area just below the peak of Mount Mitchell. However, once you backtrack on the Old Mitchell Trail, the crowds once again thin out. Join the Camp Alice Trail, a rough path once used by early tourists in the 1930s and 1940s to access the top of Mount Mitchell from Camp Alice, a converted tourist camp that was formerly a logging camp located near Lower Creek. This stream, emerging from springs on the highest mantles of Mount Mitchell, tumbles down in cascades that sing in your ears.

After tackling the Camp Alice Trail, join the Commissary Trail, a wide doubletrack path that most hikers will welcome after the irregular pathways thus far. The gravel track follows an early 1900s logging line that was later converted to haul tourists to Mount Mitchell instead of logs from the mountain. Since the 1930s, tourists have been using the Blue Ridge Parkway to reach the state park, the same as most of us do today.

The hiking is easy on the Commissary Trail, despite the gradual uphill. Nearly continual views open to the east along the path. The first part of the Commissary Trail is the only part of the hike where you are less than 6,000 feet in elevation. Then you reach Stepps Gap and the park office, rejoining the Old Mitchell Trail northbound to cruise the west slope of Mount Hallback before finishing the cloud-top adventure at the park restaurant, where a hot meal awaits in season.

Miles and Directions

0.0 Start from the restaurant parking area and join the Old Mitchell Trail northbound on a singletrack path. Pick up the path near a small building north of the park restaurant, climbing among low balsam trees.

0.2 Top out on a knob, passing a small water tank to your left. Descend. Come near the Mount Mitchell access road.

Mount Mitchell State Park Loop

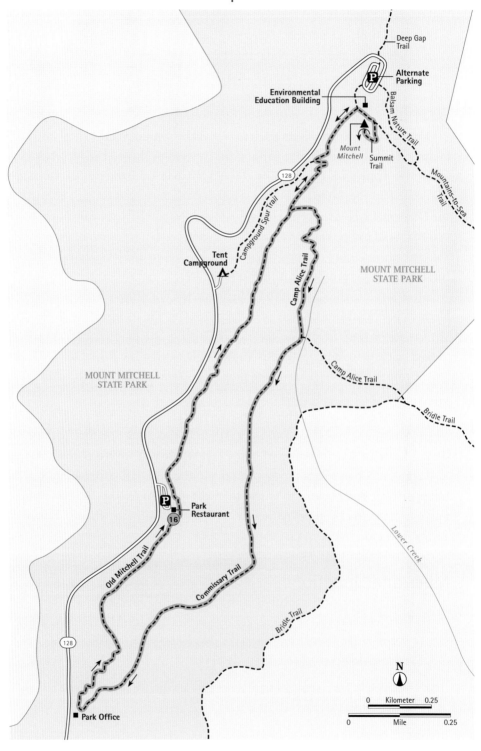

0.4 Turn away from the road and skirt below a rock outcrop. The trail becomes decidedly rougher, working over seeping rock slabs, muddy areas, and irregular rock protrusions. In places, land bridges and steps ease the most-challenging segments.

0.6 Pass under a transmission line. Continue in rough terrain.

0.7 Start the protracted climb to Mount Mitchell's summit amid thick evergreens rising above moss-covered logs and rocks.

0.8 Meet the Camp Alice Trail, your return route. For now stay left on the Old Mitchell Trail, still climbing in lush, perpetually shady woods.

1.0 The Campground Spur Trail comes in after a couple of switchbacks. Stay right with the Old Mitchell Trail.

1.2 Join the Summit Trail, heading right. This wide concrete path is quite a change from the Old Mitchell Trail. Throngs of walkers may also be ascending the Summit Trail. Pass the park environmental education building and also the spur leading left to the Balsam Nature Trail—a signed interpretive walk informing hikers about the boreal forest atop Mount Mitchell.

1.4 Reach the low-slung observation platform atop Mount Mitchell. The four cardinal directions and signage help you identify sights on the horizon, including the Commissary Trail, upon which you are fixing to walk, as well as other destinations included in this guide. Backtrack down Mount Mitchell 0.6 mile to the Camp Alice Trail intersection.

2.0 Descend on the Camp Alice Trail, the path mountain enthusiasts took in the 1930s and 1940s to top out on Mount Mitchell from Camp Alice, the logging camp turned tourist camp. Come alongside Lower Creek, falling in noisy cascades.

2.3 Reach a trail intersection at Lower Creek. To your left, across Lower Creek, the Camp Alice Trail continues east. We turn right, not crossing the creek, and join the Commissary Trail, a wide gravel path. Head south, making a gentle uptick. The footing is good, allowing you to look around. Views extend to your left (easterly) across the South Toe River Valley to points beyond.

3.5 Emerge at a pole gate and the rear of the state park office at Stepps Gap. Walk around to the north side of the office and pick up the Old Mitchell Trail.

4.1 Arrive back at the trailhead after swinging around the west side of 6,320-foot Mount Hallback.

17 Crabtree Falls

This loop hike leads from a popular campground on the Blue Ridge Parkway down to Crabtree Falls—an impressive cataract that plunges 70 feet over a rock face, misting visitors when its flow is up. Spring is a good time to visit the falls, not only for bold flows but also to see the forty-plus species of wildflowers, from lady's slippers to jack-in-the-pulpits to a few relic crabapple trees that gave the area its name. It's a little more than 500 feet of elevation change down to the falls. Your return trip explores the upper Crabtree Creek valley.

Start: Crabtree Falls upper parking area

Distance: 2.7-mile loop

Hiking time: About 1.4 hours

Difficulty: Easy–moderate

Trail surface: Natural

Best season: Winter through early summer and after thunderstorms; late fall

Other trail users: None

Canine compatibility: Leashed dogs allowed

Land status: National park

Fees and permits: No fees or permits required

Schedule: 24/7/365

Maps: USGS Celo; National Geographic #779: Linville Gorge, Mount Mitchell [Pisgah National Forest]

Trail contacts: Blue Ridge Parkway, 199 Hemphill Knob Rd., Asheville, NC 28803; (828) 348-3400; nps.gov/blri

Finding the trailhead: From Asheville take the Blue Ridge Parkway north to milepost 338.9. Turn left into the Crabtree Falls recreation area. Immediately turn left and reach the upper trailhead parking near the former visitor center. Trailhead GPS: N35° 48' 45.2" / W82° 08' 36.1"

The Hike

When developing the Blue Ridge Parkway in the 1930s, the National Park Service knew it wanted to include Crabtree Falls. Except back then it was called Murphy Falls. Just to make things more complicated, official USGS quad maps called Crabtree Falls "Upper Falls." The park service renamed the falls for Crabtree Creek, on which it is located. Others contend the falls were named for an early

Crabtree Falls can be a froth of white during rainy times.

colonial settler named John Crabtree. Name aside, the reality on the ground is a gorgeous 70-foot cataract that spills over a widening ledge; it is one of my favorite sights on the Parkway.

Crabtree Falls makes a worthy hike destination. A loop trail leads to the falls, allowing you to cover new ground the entire route while viewing the cascade. Crabtree Falls is the centerpiece of a recreation area that includes a campground located just off the Parkway. The campground, situated at 3,600 feet, makes a fine hot-weather getaway. It is open during the warm season. Campsites have a picnic table, fire ring, lantern post, and level tent pad. Water spigots and restrooms are spread out among the seventy-one tent and twenty-two RV sites. A designated picnic area is located less than 1 mile south on the Parkway for those who want to dine outside.

The crab (crab-apple) trees that once covered the partly wooded meadows of the recreation area continue to fall to the winds of time and relentless reforestation. However, some of the crab trees still show off their springtime blossoms here atop the Blue Ridge. After leaving the upper trailhead adjacent to the Parkway, you pass through some relic meadows being kept open by the park service with periodic mowing. Beyond the meadows, the hike skirts the campground. Here your descent begins in earnest. The trail falls away through rhododendron then passes an abandoned trail, formerly creating an additional loop. A series of switchbacks on a steep wooded slope moderates the decline. Parts of the trail use well-placed, sturdy but narrow stone steps to lose elevation. Depending on water volume, the roar of Crabtree Falls may already be filling your ears.

Then Crabtree Falls comes into view, a froth of white spreading over rock strata. The 70-foot parade of lather crashes into a pool then splits around a small rock island. A wooden walkway bridge crosses Crabtree Creek, doubling as a first-rate observation/photography platform. On this bridge, waterfall enthusiasts will be snapping pictures using whatever devices they have on hand, from smart phones to big ol' cameras sitting atop tripods, trying to get the perfect shot. And Crabtree Falls is exceptionally photogenic—the stream fearlessly diving over a bare cliff, spilling in sheets, dashing from rock to rock, then regrouping to slalom in shoals and flow under the observation bridge.

Some waterfall visitors go back the way they came, the backtrack being shorter (2.2 miles total out and back). However, you will be going against the flow of hikers, which could be important on those busy, fair Saturdays. Additional viewing opportunities of Crabtree Falls are ahead as you climb stairs away from the creek. More switchbacks lead up past an overhanging rockhouse. Come to a linear outcrop, where you can walk out and look down on the falls as it makes a big drop. This precarious view is better when the leaves are off the trees. You then head up the perched upper valley of Crabtree Creek. The stream drains this elevated vale between Sevenmile Ridge and the Blue Ridge, making a surprisingly large waterway for 3,500 feet elevation. Upper Crabtree Creek speeds along in shoals and pools. The loop crosses Crabtree Creek on a hiker bridge before finally turning away from Crabtree Creek to cut through the campground. Beware of old, closed connector trails. Soon you will hear the cars on the Blue Ridge Parkway, marking your return to the trailhead.

Spring and late fall are the best times to visit Crabtree Falls. In spring you will be rewarded with wildflowers rising from the refreshed soil and a normally fast-flowing Crabtree Creek that will put extra pepper into the falls. In late autumn, the leaves are off the trees and the crowds have thinned, allowing you to view Crabtree Falls through the woods from afar and up close without having to jostle for elbow room on those ideal warm-weather days. You also can better see the geology of the land, the rock strata that make waterfalls happen. Early morning is a good time during the warm season, as you will also beat the crowds. Plus, since Crabtree Falls is on the west side of the Blue Ridge, it takes a while for the morning sun to hit the falls, making for better waterfall photography conditions. No matter the weather, season, or time of day, be sure to carve out a few hours to visit this jewel of the Blue Ridge Parkway.

Miles and Directions

0.0 Start at the upper trailhead near the former visitor center and take the asphalt Crabtree Falls Trail downhill. Lights to access the area amphitheater line the path.

0.1 Pass the amphitheater on your left; the asphalt ends. Keep straight and enter a field-woods mix. A trail comes in on your left; this is your return route. For now, continue through the woods and fields. Look for relic crab trees.

0.2 A spur trail leads left toward the B Loop of Crabtree Falls Campground. Stay right toward Crabtree Falls. Pass some campsites on your left.

0.3 Cross the campground entrance road and reach the now-closed alternative parking for Crabtree Falls. Rejoin the hiking trail, leaving from the back left corner of the parking area. You are now descending to the falls beneath a cloak of rhododendron and black birch.

Crabtree Falls

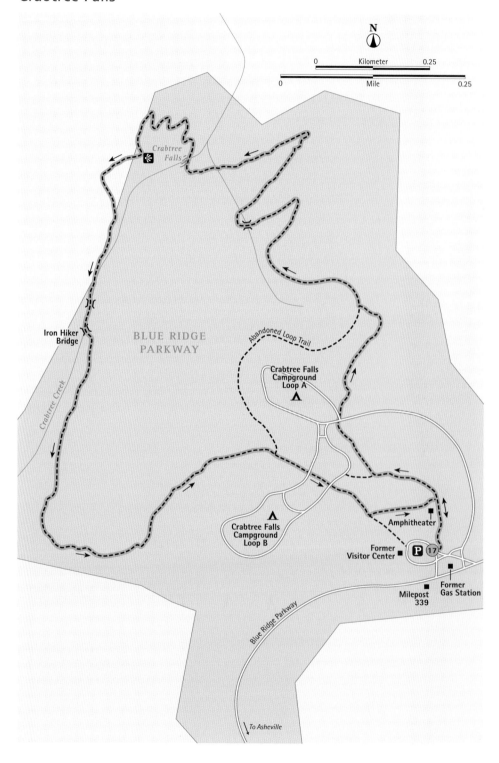

0.5 Stay right as a closed alternative loop trail leaves left. The closed loop grows fainter with time. Continue descending off the west side of the Blue Ridge.

0.7 Stone steps aid your descent on this steep, rocky, and rooty mountainside.

0.8 A hiker bridge takes you over a steep streamlet. More stone steps lead down in a switchback to the right. The stream you just bridged flows over the trail. Depending on water levels, you may need some fancy footwork to keep your feet above water.

0.9 Make a big switchback to the left. Continue descending.

1.1 Come to Crabtree Falls. The setting is gorgeous as the 70-foot cataract plunges over the side of a precipice and widens on its splashy fall. If the water and wind are up, you will soon be tickled with mist. Continue across the combination bridge–waterfall observation platform, admiring the plunger from multiple angles. Climb away from the falls on stone steps and short switchbacks. Alternative views of the falls open when the leaves are off the trees.

1.3 Come along an overhanging rockhouse. Just ahead, reach a rock outcrop that extends left to a potentially dicey precipice with a top-down leaves-off view of Crabtree Falls. Ahead, come alongside Crabtree Creek, viewing lesser cascades.

1.6 A boardwalk leads over a tributary of Crabtree Creek. Next, cross Crabtree Creek on an iron hiker bridge. Keep upstream on the left bank. Walk past more alluring waters.

2.0 Top a hill then curve left, ascending along a tributary of Crabtree Creek.

2.4 Pass the other end of the closed loop trail then shortly enter B Loop of the campground. Keep straight here, bisecting the campground; look for the trail between sites #82 and #84 on the far side of the campground. Open onto mixed fields and woods. Ahead, the trail splits; head left toward the amphitheater. (A right will lead you back toward the visitor center building.) Pass the amphitheater then backtrack.

2.7 Arrive back at the trailhead.

18 Trails of Linville Falls

Explore more than 4 miles of trails centered on renowned 150-foot Linville Falls, off the Blue Ridge Parkway. Leaving the seasonal visitor center, you first view Upper Falls then soak in elevated looks at Linville Falls backed by a panorama of Carolina mountains. Return to the trailhead and take the more-challenging track to Linville Falls and its big, stone-rimmed plunge basin, then grab an additional elevated perspective. Pay a visit to 12-foot Duggers Creek Falls to complete the aquatic tour.

Start: Linville Falls Visitor Center

Distance: 4.2 miles round-trip

Hiking time: About 2.5 hours

Difficulty: Moderate

Trail surface: Natural, some gravel

Best season: Spring through fall for visitor center access

Other trail users: None

Canine compatibility: Leashed dogs allowed

Land status: National park

Fees and permits: No fees or permits required

Schedule: 24/7/365

Maps: USGS Linville Falls; National Geographic #779: Linville Gorge, Mount Mitchell [Pisgah National Forest]

Trail contacts: Blue Ridge Parkway, 199 Hemphill Knob Rd., Asheville, NC 28803; (828) 348-3400; nps.gov/blri

Finding the trailhead: From Asheville take I-40 East to exit 72 (Old Fort). Join US 70 East for 11 miles; turn left on US 221 North near Marion and follow it 22 miles to meet the Blue Ridge Parkway (BRP). Turn northbound on the BRP and follow it for 1.1 miles; turn right onto the access road for Linville Falls Visitor Center and follow it 1.5 miles to dead-end at the trailhead parking. GPS: N35° 57' 16.1" / W81° 55' 40.6"

The Hike

Linville Falls is arguably the signature cataract of the Blue Ridge Parkway in North Carolina. After all, it has its own visitor center and campground and a fine set of nature trails of varying difficulties that add up to more than 4 miles of hiking if you do them all. These paths are not just aimless walks in the woods.

Outdoor adventurers gather along the Linville River below Linville Falls.

The trails lead to multiple vantages of 150-foot Linville Falls from near and far, up and down, below and beside. Photographers can have a heyday shooting the white froth that first spills as Upper Falls then flattens out in a pool before entering a slender, swirling drain-like defile to emerge as an explosive force of white, making a final 45-foot dive off bare rock into an enormous plunge pool.

Superlative scenery comes along with each waterfall view—a melding of rock, water, and forest looking deep into the Linville Gorge and the mountains framing the Linville River. Add old-growth hemlock and white pine trees to the mix. Given to the National Park Service by benefactor John D. Rockefeller Jr., the cataract and more than 1,000 adjacent acres became part of the Blue Ridge Parkway. The access, trail system, and campground were subsequently developed. This access is often closed during winter, but you can still reach the trail system via a Pisgah National Forest trailhead off Wisemans View Road, which is off NC 183 near the falls.

The trail system is composed of two primary paths, each on its respective side of the Linville River. Each route offers views, but one is decidedly more difficult than the other. The Erwins View Trail is easier, more popular, and designed to handle large numbers of lesser-able hikers. However, do not blow it off just because it is easy and popular. Absorbing the views along the Erwins View Trail helps you create a mosaic of perspectives of Linville Falls. You leave directly from the visitor center on a wide and easy path, shortly bridging the surprisingly large

Left: Linville Falls charges into its plunge pool.
Right: Duggers Creek Falls provides contrast to the roaring cataracts of the Linville River.

and wide Linville River. The waterway's size is remarkable considering that the watershed upstream of Linville Falls is above 3,000 feet in elevation.

A spur takes you to Upper Falls, a view attainable by almost everybody. Here a large rock slab and promontory allow hikers to view Upper Falls and its wide pool. Visitors can also peer down into the main body of Linville Falls as the waters funnel together into a swirling, tunnel-like rock chute where whitewater boils down and out of sight. Linville Falls handles the most volume of any waterfall spilling off the Blue Ridge!

The next three vistas on the Erwins View Trail are elevated panoramas. On the way you pass through a grove of preserved old-growth hemlocks. Chimney View affords a look at the primary drop of Linville Falls and the rock basin plunge pool, where continual washing from the falls limits vegetation growth. Next comes the Gorge View. This outcrop gives you a non-waterfall downstream perspective of the upper Linville Gorge and the river below, the wooded gorge walls falling off the Blue Ridge.

Erwins View, actually two separate but adjacent viewpoints, offers truly magnificent mountain prospects. Here Linville Falls forms a centerpiece of water and rock, framed by thick forests, contained in an outer frame of distant mountain ridges extending to the horizon. Wow!

You have to return to the visitor center to begin the less-used, more-challenging Plunge Basin Trail. It explores the other side of the Linville River, making an initial steady climb and leaving most waterfall visitors behind. First visit the base of Linville Falls. The trail here is primitive as it squeezes past bluffs then descends a cliffline using stairs. From there an irregular, extremely rocky trail leads to the river's edge, where some final rock scrambling brings hikers face to face with the falls, a true reflection of nature's power and majesty, spilling from an opening in a rock cleft, widening and diving in white chaos as the spilling cataract echoes off the stone walls, forming continual waves in the plunge pool.

The final look at Linville Falls is from a rock outcrop just above the plunge basin. Work your way from the river to this stone outlook. Here you are close to the falls but above the final plunge, lending a final perspective to your tour of Linville Falls.

But wait—there is more. Though puny by comparison, Duggers Creek Falls and the trail to it put an exclamation point on your Linville Falls adventure. The short path passes near the parking area then turns up Duggers Creek, where faucet-like Duggers Creek Falls makes its tapered dive into a slot canyon through which you view the spiller. From there the hike leads amid outcrops before returning to the trailhead.

Miles and Directions

0.0   Start from the visitor center and walk under the breezeway on the wide Erwins View Trail. Ahead, cross the Linville River on a pedestrian bridge.

0.3   Bridge a small tributary of the Linville River.

0.4   Keep straight as a spur trail goes right to Wisemans View Road. Just ahead, turn left toward Upper Falls. The trail narrows.

0.5   Open onto a large, wide outcrop with a view of Upper Falls to your left and the top of the main falls to your right. Backtrack then continue toward Chimney View. Pass beneath preserved old-growth hemlocks.

0.8   Split left to Chimney View. Descend to two overlooks on an outcrop with a raised view of Linville Falls as well as good looks up- and downriver. Backtrack.

1.0   Rejoin the main trail near a rain shelter and continue toward Erwins View and Gorge View.

1.1   Come to the Gorge View. This non-waterfall look affords a downstream view of upper Linville Gorge. Resume toward Erwins View, ascending steps.

Trails of Linville Falls

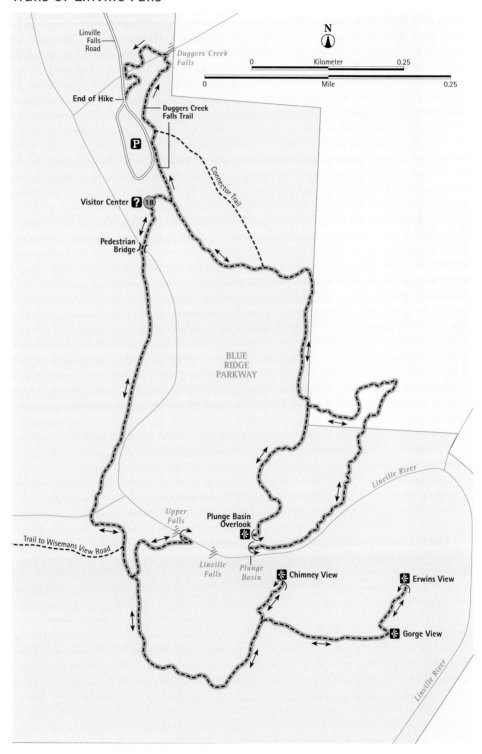

N

| 0 | Kilometer | 0.25 |
| 0 | Mile | 0.25 |

Linville Falls Road

Duggers Creek Falls

End of Hike

Duggers Creek Falls Trail

P

Visitor Center 18

Connector Trail

Pedestrian Bridge

BLUE RIDGE PARKWAY

Linville River

Upper Falls

Plunge Basin Overlook

Trail to Wisemans View Road

Linville Falls

Plunge Basin

Chimney View

Erwins View

Gorge View

Linville River

Your reward is this distant view of Linville Falls and the Blue Ridge.

1.2 Reach Erwins View and one of the finest vistas on the Blue Ridge. Backtrack all the way to the visitor center.

2.1 Join the Plunge Basin Trail after leaving the trailhead. Walk a narrower, steeper path, immediately passing the Duggers Creek Falls Trail.

2.2 Keep straight at a connector heading left to intersect the Duggers Creek Falls Trail.

2.4 Head left at the next intersection toward the plunge basin. This path traverses a wooded hillside then narrows at some outcrops, through which you squeeze. Descend steps. The trail becomes rocky and rough.

2.8 Reach the base of the falls after scrambling along the Linville River. At high water levels, rock scrambling may prove difficult. Boulders aplenty provide ample seating. Note the shaded defile to your right, an almost cave. Backtrack.

3.2 Head left toward the Plunge Basin Overlook. Walk under arbors of mountain laurel.

3.4 Reach the Plunge Basin Overlook, with an elevated, close-up view of the falls. Backtrack toward the visitor center.

3.9 Veer right onto the Duggers Creek Falls Trail just before reaching the visitor center. Cruise alongside the parking lot.

4.0 Leave left on the Duggers Creek Falls Trail after meeting the Connector Trail. Ascend.

4.1 Bridge Duggers Creek. Look upstream from the bridge at faucet-like Duggers Creek Falls. Climb from the bridge, circling an outcrop. Descend to the park access road. Cross Duggers Creek on the road then head left, rejoining the foot trail.

4.2 Arrive back at the visitor center, at the opposite end of the parking lot.

19 Linville Gorge Wilderness Hike

Take a hike in legendary Linville Gorge to the Tower of Babel, where fantastic views await from a stony perch deep in the Linville Gorge Wilderness. Travel along the gorge slope on a rugged path that makes for slow going. Pass a river access and panoramas of the gorge, as well as a waterfall and big pool. Your ultimate destination is worth the challenging trail. The Tower of Babel is a notable stone knob nearly encircled by the Linville River. Soak in views of the wild canyon and mountains in the distance.

Start: Pine Gap trailhead
Distance: 5.8 miles out and back
Hiking time: About 4.5 hours
Difficulty: Difficult due to rugged trail

Soak in this classic panorama from atop the Tower of Babel.

Trail surface: Natural

Best season: Whenever the skies are clear

Other trail users: None

Canine compatibility: Leashed dogs allowed

Land status: National forest

Fees and permits: No fees or permits required

Schedule: 24/7/365

Maps: USGS Linville Falls; National Geographic #779: Linville Gorge, Mount Mitchell [Pisgah National Forest]

Trail contacts: Pisgah National Forest, Grandfather Ranger District, 109 Lawing Dr., Nebo, NC 28761; (828) 652-2144; fs.usda.gov/nfsnc

Finding the trailhead: From Asheville take I-40 East to exit 85, near Marion. Join US 221 North and continue approximately 24 miles to the town of Linville Falls and NC 183. Turn right on NC 183 East and follow it for 0.7 mile to gravel Kistler Memorial Highway. You will see a sign indicating Linville Falls and Linville Gorge Wilderness. Veer right here and follow the gravel road for 0.9 mile to the Pine Gap trailhead, on your left. *Note:* Along Kistler Memorial Highway you will pass the Pisgah National Forest access for the trails of Linville Falls and the Linville Gorge Wilderness information cabin before reaching the Pine Gap trailhead. GPS: N35° 56' 27.7" / W81° 55' 55.1"

The Hike

Linville Gorge is a "must" hiking destination for residents of greater Asheville. The deeply carved valley is a federally designated wilderness and certainly exudes the qualities expected in such an untamed place. The terrain is rugged and rocky, and wildfires regularly sweep through the gorge. The Linville River slices its way through a brawling chaos of rocks, boulders, and cliffs, occasionally slowing in inviting pools then hurtling through unruly rapids. The trail system reflects the wild and rugged nature of the gorge. Because this is a designated wilderness, the Pisgah National Forest maintains the trail system at a primitive standard. When you combine the unforgiving pathways with the rocky terrain and inevitable fallen trees, the result is slow travel for the wilderness hiker. Allow ample time to make this hike, and include time to relax and enjoy the hard-earned scenery.

Linville Gorge Wilderness is popular not only with day hikers but also with backpackers. However, permits are required to backpack the wilderness during summer and holiday weekends. Backpacking permits can be obtained at the information station on your right, 0.4 mile before reaching the Pine Gap trailhead. Your starting point—the Pine Gap Trail—is also utilized by kayakers. These intrepid paddlers actually carry their boats down to the Linville River via this trail. Improvements were made to the Pine Gap Trail in 2016, making it easier for kayakers to tote their boats the 0.5 mile to the river. Brush was cleared in a wider swath from the path and footing improved—rocks were removed and the trailbed smoothed out. This has made the first part of the hike a little more user-friendly than in days gone by. The upstream access off the Blue Ridge Parkway requires boaters to either paddle through or around Linville Falls, both dangerous propositions that all but a few maniacs avoid. The National Park Service, which manages the Linville Falls area, officially prohibits boating on its part of the Linville River, making the Pine Gap Trail the uppermost legal entry point.

The trails at Linville Gorge are also used by anglers fishing for trout, smallmouth bass, and bream in challenging waters, as well as rock climbers who dare the stony cliff faces so abundant in this jewel of the Blue Ridge. Being hikers, we will enter the gorge on foot. The improved Pine Gap Trail leads past an overlook, revealing the depth and magnitude of the gorge, and keeps angling downhill using switchbacks to reach the Linville River after 0.5 mile. This is where the paddlers jump in the water and descend nearly 2,000 feet before exiting near Lake James at the NC 126 bridge. You can check out the river here too.

The Pine Gap Trail continues following the Linville River then turns away to cut across a bend, coming to a signed trail intersection in aptly named Pine Gap, where aromatic evergreens rise in tall ranks. Here hikers join the rugged Linville Gorge Trail, tracing the winding course of the Linville River among pine, mountain laurel, and oaks. The trail then comes to the edge of a cliff, where excellent upstream panoramas open.

Ahead, a few switchbacks lead to the river itself. Enjoy trailside looks into the mix of stone and water. Next on the highlight list is an unnamed 15-foot waterfall just around the bend. A spur leads to an elevated rock ledge where you can peer down on the combination tier and slide cascade with a huge recovery pool ideal for dipping.

The hiking is still slow and challenging as you work alongside rock walls, over outcrops, and over fallen trees. The river is now making tortuous bends. Then you reach the signed trail intersection next to the Tower of Babel. Here a rockhouse is downhill to your left. Visit the rockhouse. The network of user-created trails

Table Rock stands out in the distance of Linville Gorge.

can be confusing. However, a little persistence will take you to the top of the outcrop, where the maw of Linville Gorge opens wide; Hawksbill Mountain and Table Rock rise in the yon. Below, the Linville River nearly encircles the tower. Allow plenty of time for the slow backtrack to the trailhead.

Miles and Directions

0.0 Start on the Pine Gap Trail, a singletrack path leaving the southeast corner of the parking area. The narrow way descends over an improved surface, but still with plenty of roots, rocks, and imperfect footing.

0.1 A rock outcrop to the left of the trail provides your initial vista into the Linville Gorge. Hike along the base of sheer stone bluffs.

0.5 Reach a spur trail going left to the Linville River after a few switchbacks. Visit the river if you please. Boulders overlook slow pools and beckon hikers to the moving aqua amid still stone.

0.8 Come to a four-way trail junction in Pine Gap. Here a spur trail leads left 0.2 mile down to the inside of a bend in the Linville River, where a rocky bar faces a vertical bluff. The Bynum Bluff Trail leads acutely right up the nose of a rocky ridge to Kistler Memorial Highway. Join the Linville Gorge Trail. It curves slightly right here, turning southwest with the bend of the river.

1.1 The trail takes you next to a rockhouse.

1.1 Bridge a tributary, continuing uphill.

1.2 Reach a rocky precipice. Hikers can peer upstream into the river gorge, with Brushy Ridge and Long Arm Mountain rising in the background. Note the rapids and pools below.

1.3 Come to the Linville River at a big rock slab after passing a dripping cliffline. Gain a close-up look at the wild waterway.

1.4 Pass an unnamed 15-foot waterfall as the trail and river curve left. A spur leads to the cataract with a big plunge pool. Continue cruising beneath bluffs.

1.7 A spur descends left to the river. Stay with the Linville Gorge Trail.

1.9 Pass a spur trail leading left to a view along a narrow outcrop just before coming to the Cabin Trail. It makes a nearly 1,000-foot climb in 1.0 mile before reaching Kistler Memorial Highway. Stay with the Linville Gorge Trail as it curves around a hollow.

2.2 Come alongside a rock promontory with a down-gorge view of the Tower of Babel rising from the heart of the gorge.

2.3 Step over a clear, perennial stream then turn downstream along it. Ahead, look for a user-created spur here leading left to the river. Stay right with the Linville Gorge Trail.

Linville Gorge Wilderness Hike

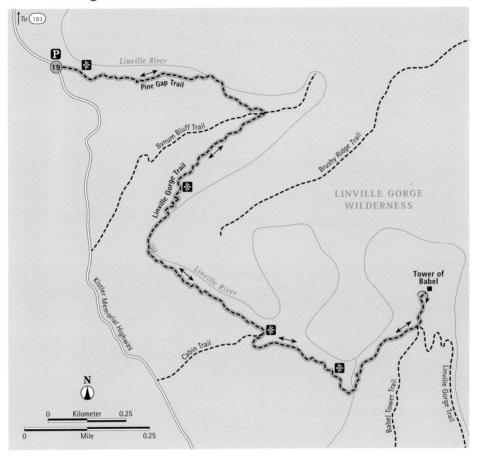

2.7 Come to a four-way intersection just after passing a rockhouse to your left. The Babel Tower Trail leaves right; the Linville Gorge Trail keeps straight. A wide rock flat stands to your left, above the rockhouse. Take yet another trail leading left and downhill, then climb into the rock flats. Circle around the left side of the pinnacle, cloaked in scraggly pines, and find a very steep primitive path leading to the top.

2.8 Reach the top of the Tower of Babel. Widespread panoramas open down Linville Gorge, with Table Rock and Hawksbill Mountain rising dramatically into the sky. Look upstream for additional vistas. Backtrack.

5.8 Arrive back at the trailhead.

20 Lake James State Park Hike

This state park trek gives western Carolina hikers a chance to explore a different environment—the piedmont-like lands bordering Lake James. This hike takes trail walkers along rolling shores, where views open across the clear water with piney peninsulas in the near and the rising Blue Ridge in the distance. Elevation changes are minimal, and the state park offers additional trails and activities that are sure to make your trip here worthwhile.

Start: Near the East Shelter of the Paddy's Creek Area
Distance: 3.4–mile loop
Hiking time: About 2 hours
Difficulty: Easy–moderate
Trail surface: Mostly natural

Autumn leaves color the shoreline of Lake James.

Best season: Early fall through late spring

Other trail users: None

Canine compatibility: Leashed dogs allowed

Land status: State park

Fees and permits: No fees or permits required for entrance or hiking

Schedule: Dec–Feb, 7 a.m.–6 p.m.; Mar, Apr, and Oct, 7 a.m.–8 p.m.; May–Sept, 7 a.m.–9 p.m.; Nov, 7 a.m.–7 p.m.

Maps: USGS Oak Hill, Ashford; Lake James State Park Trails

Trail contacts: Lake James State Park, 6883 NC 126, Nebo, NC 28761; (828) 584-7728; ncparks.gov/lake-james-state-park

Finding the trailhead: From Asheville take I-40 East to exit 90 (Nebo/Lake James). Turn right and join Harmony Grove Road; pass over the interstate. After 0.6 mile reach an intersection and stay right on Harmony Grove Road, following it for 2.2 more miles to reach the intersection with US 70 in Nebo. Turn left and follow US 70 West just a short distance then turn right on NC 126. Follow NC 126 for 5 miles, passing the Catawba River section of Lake James State Park; turn right into the Paddy's Creek area. Follow the main park road for 2.2 miles to dead-end at the large swimming beach area with its large parking lot. Drive along the lowermost parking area past the concession/ranger station/swim beach entrance to the signed East Shelter. Park near the shelter. GPS: N35° 45' 04.5" / W81° 52' 28.7"

The Hike

If you look at a map of Lake James, the lake looks rather strange. Rather than your typical reservoir, where a river is dammed and flooded, Lake James was created by damming both the Catawba and Linville Rivers then linking them by canal, giving it that unusual look. The canal linking the two dammed waters created a 6,812-acre impoundment. Duke power built these dams in the 1920s to generate electricity, as they do to this day. Its location at the base of the Blue Ridge Mountains makes Lake James one of the most scenic impoundments in North Carolina. From many locales, you can see Lake James in the foreground with the Southern Appalachians rising in the distance. The best views are arguably from the lake into the heart of Linville Gorge—a superlative vista that should grace North Carolina newcomer and tourist brochures from Kitty Hawk to Murphy.

Back in the 1920s, people weren't thinking of vacationing here and purchasing lakefront and mountain land on which to build houses with scenery in mind.

However, as all western North Carolinians know, that situation has changed. Land prices have gone through the roof. A century later, locals and transplants alike are seeking to build homes with panoramas of undulating mountains and placid waters on now-expensive properties.

That is precisely what makes Lake James State Park so valuable. Set along the shores of Lake James in two parcels, the preserve offers visitors the type of scenery desired by homebuilders. Today we can come here to engage in outdoor recreation, soaking in this marvelous landscape without even having to pay an entrance fee!

Luckily, local legislators saw the value of creating a shoreline state park, and Lake James State Park came to be in 1987. After the land was acquired, the park was developed with both aquatic and land recreation in mind. Trails were laid out for hikers like us and a separate set of pathways constructed for mountain bikers. This creates a good situation for both parties. More than 10 miles of hiking trails

The swim beach and fishing pier stand quiet this early spring morn.

and about 15 miles of mountain biking trails were constructed. These pathways traverse low hills bordering peninsulas extending into the lake. The rolling lands are low by western North Carolina standards and exhibit physical characteristics as well as flora and fauna of both the Piedmont and Appalachians. For example, you will see the red clay associated with the Piedmont as well as trees that find a home in the Piedmont, such as shortleaf pine, sweetgum, and winged elm, offering a different experience than hiking in the mountains to the west.

Hiking here is an excellent winter proposition and enjoyable spring and fall as well. Hiking at Lake James State Park in the summer can be very hot, and boat traffic can make the lake noisy on weekends. Nevertheless, I suggest coming here for an extended visit, as the park has an excellent walk-in tent camping area in the park's Catawba River Area as well as drive-up tent camping in the Paddy's Creek Area. The camps have hot showers and flush toilets. Trails emanate directly from the campgrounds, adding to the hiking possibilities.

Multiple picnic areas make dining here a breeze. There is even a picnic shelter at the trailhead as well as multiple shaded lakeshore picnic tables. Anglers will enjoy vying for largemouth and smallmouth bass as well as walleye. Kids will have a ball fishing for bluegill and sunfish from a fishing pier located near the trailhead. If you don't have a motorboat to ply the water, the park rents canoes and kayaks, allowing boat-less visitors to paddle and fish the alluring shoreline. You can rent a boat here near the trailhead as well. The large swim beach is located here too. There is a fee in effect when lifeguards are on duty; if lifeguards are not on duty, there is no fee.

This hike uses the Mill Creek Trail, the park's longest hiker-only path. The adventure will take you directly through the swim beach when making your loop. However, the trek starts by heading away from the swim beach and facilities, making a counterclockwise loop. It then skirts the first of many quiet coves as the Mill Creek Trail roughly parallels the shoreline. You have opportunities for multiple views of the lake, especially when curving along the Mill Creek arm of the impoundment, including vistas of the Blue Ridge rising in the distance. The Mill Creek Trail then turns away from the water and works over a low peninsula and returns to the water at the Paddy's Creek arm of the lake, where more panoramas await. The final part of the trek leads through the main facilities of this area, including the swim beach, concession area, boat rental, ranger office, picnic areas, and shelters. This area will get crowded on warm summer weekends. Plan accordingly, but do come here. It will add a new perspective to hiking in the greater Asheville area.

Lake James State Park Hike

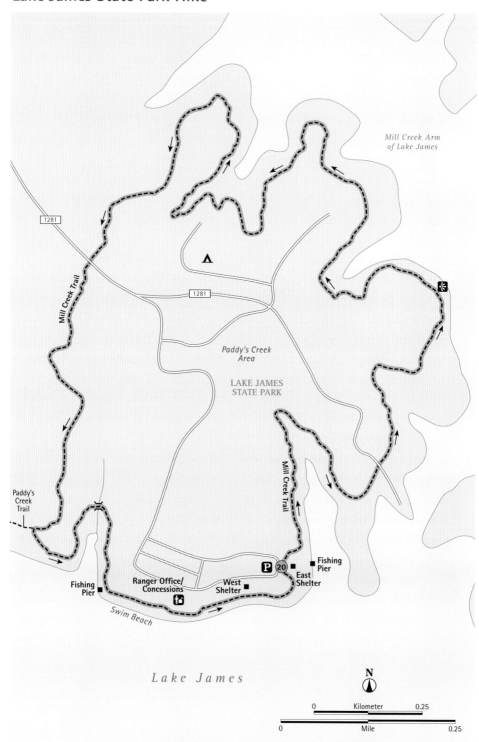

Miles and Directions

0.0 As you face the signed East Shelter at the greater swim beach/ranger office and concession area, head right on the gravel Mill Creek Trail, immediately crossing the asphalt track leading down to a fishing pier. The path quickly becomes natural surface, bordered by tightly grown young pines. Shortly come along an embayment of Lake James.

0.1 Leave the embayment and head up a wooded intermittent drainage. Notice the red clay, shortleaf pines, and sweetgum trees characteristic of the Carolina Piedmont. Curve around the embayment.

0.5 Briefly return to the shoreline then split left, bisecting a peninsula stretching into the lake. Mountain laurel, American holly, and clubmoss are common along the path.

0.8 Reach a bench and lake overlook. View a cove in the near and mountains in the distance. Continue to follow the lake's curves along the sloping shoreline.

1.5 Turn around the head of a rhododendron-choked spring. Head back toward the lake then curve away yet again.

1.7 Come very near the Paddy's Creek Area campground.

1.8 Lake James is back in view. Walk among young, spindly trees, regenerating in former farmland.

2.0 Cross the paved main park road of the Paddy's Creek Area. Quickly reenter woods. Start a gentle downhill.

2.7 Reach a trail intersection. Here the Paddy's Creek Trail leads right, up the Paddy's Creek arm of Lake James. Our hike turns left, toward the developed facilities of the swim beach area.

2.9 Curve around a small cove then cross a little creek on a pedestrian bridge.

3.0 Come to the end of the natural surface trail and find another fishing pier. A spur trail goes left up to the parking area. Keep straight on an asphalt track then reach the swim beach. Hike along the swim beach, enjoying distant views. Come near the large concession building/ranger office.

3.2 Leave the beach area. Keep easterly, walking amid picnic tables with the lake to your right and the parking area uphill to your left.

3.4 Arrive back at the East Shelter.

BICYCLING ADVENTURES

B icyclers of all stripes have a treasure trove of pedal-ing opportunities in and around Asheville. The mountain biking community here is strong, dedicated, and involved. You will find every level of mountain biking difficulty among the many fat-tire trails systems in the area—and in this guide—though most of the treks here are in the beginner–intermediate range. Take a spin at the mountain biking mecca that is Bent Creek, or tackle the superlative pathways at DuPont State Forest. Beginners can try the loops at Lake James State Park. Other bicycling opportunities exist beyond the natural-surface trails. Two-wheelers can also ply hard-surface greenways such as the in-town French Broad River Greenway and Hendersonville's Ocklawaha Greenway as well as the historic Point Lookout Trail. The Estatoe Greenway ride includes both natural-surface woodland trailway and asphalt trails in a scenic setting in and near Brevard. Whether you are looking for a technical singletrack challenge, a flat family pedal, or an in-city ride, there's a bicycling adventure here for you.

The Wimba Loops at Lake James State Park are exclusively for mountain bikers.

21 French Broad River Greenway

This ride takes you on an existing part of Asheville's fast-expanding greenway system. Starting at French Broad River Park, cruise an asphalt path along the scenic French Broad River, linking to several other parks. Pass a bicycler's velodrome you can use along the way. End at Hominy Creek Riverfront Park. Multiple facilities at existing parks as well as links to future greenways make this segment of the French Broad River Greenway a hub for in-town bicyclists.

Start: French Broad River Park

Distance: 5.8 miles out and back with small loop

Riding time: 1–1.5 hours

Difficulty: Easy

Terrain and surface type: Asphalt on flat river bottom

Highlights: River views, multiple parks; optional velodrome

Hazards: None

Other considerations: Hominy Creek Riverfront Park offers alternative parking.

Maps: French Broad River Greenway West

Trail contacts: The City of Asheville, 70 Court Plaza, PO Box 7148, Asheville, NC 28802; (828) 259–5805; ashevillenc.gov/service/enjoy-greenways/

Finding the trailhead: From exit 2 (US 19 Business/US 23 Business) on I-240/I-26 in Asheville, take Haywood Road east. Turn right (south) on Hanover Street and follow it 0.4 mile. Turn left on State Street and continue 0.7 mile. Turn left on Amboy Road and follow it 0.5 mile. Make a quick left turn onto Riverview Drive then a quick right turn into French Broad River Park. GPS: N35° 34' 11.5" / W82° 33' 53.1"

The Ride

Greenways continue to grow in popularity throughout our country, and Asheville is no exception. The city lies along the French Broad River, and river corridors are favored areas for greenways. In addition to greenways, Asheville also has recognized the value of greenspace along the French Broad River by establishing riverfront parks throughout town. These riverfront parks provide river accesses and bike and walking trails—places for people to get a quick nature fix.

Momentum for building greenways in Asheville is in full swing now, but it took a while. A connected network of greenways, of which the French Broad

Pedaling by the velodrome

River Greenway will be a central part, will ring downtown and the River Arts District. The network will also link the French Broad River to the surrounding Blue Ridge Mountains. This plan makes sense, as the French Broad River is very much the lifeblood of outdoor adventures in the greater Asheville area, whether you are bicycling, hiking, or paddling.

For now we have this segment of greenway. And it is a good one. The ride starts at French Broad River Park, one of Asheville's larger riverfront parks. It offers a loop trail, riverfront decks, a very popular dog park, picnic areas, and restrooms. It is also where the greenway system will extend north along the west bank of the river.

Locals flock to the shaded greenspace on nice days. After making a loop through French Broad River Park, the greenway heads under Amboy Road and upriver, with the French Broad to your left. You then cruise through narrow

Amboy Riverfront Park before jumping on the sidewalk along Amboy Road to then enter Carrier Park. This preserve has lots of side trails to explore as well as the velodrome, a circular banked track that is open to bicyclers. Often, bicyclers pedaling the French Broad River Greenway will see the velodrome and take a few spins around. Just as often, you will find hotshot bicyclists charging around the track at impressive speeds. Beyond Carrier Park, the greenway curves south with the river and you enjoy cruising alongside the waterway under tree cover. This is a pleasant section. All too soon you are at Hominy Creek Riverfront Park, where Hominy Creek flows into the French Broad. This is also a popular paddling access site. For now, turn around and enjoy your second cruise on the greenway. In the very near future, you will be able to use French Broad River Park to access much more trail. Remember the rules: Traffic along the greenway is both ways, and stay to the right except when passing others. Make sure to call out when you pass.

The French Broad River Greenway is an excellent urban ride.

French Broad River Greenway

Meadow Road

Swannanoa River

40

N

Kilometer

Mile

0

0.5

0.5

0

Future
Greenway

Riverview Drive

French Broad
River Park

21

Bradley Street

State Street

Amboy Riverfront
Park

Amboy Road

Carrier Park

French Broad River

Short Michigan Avenue

State Street

40

26

240

French Broad River Greenway

Hominy Creek Road

Hominy Creek
Riverfront Park

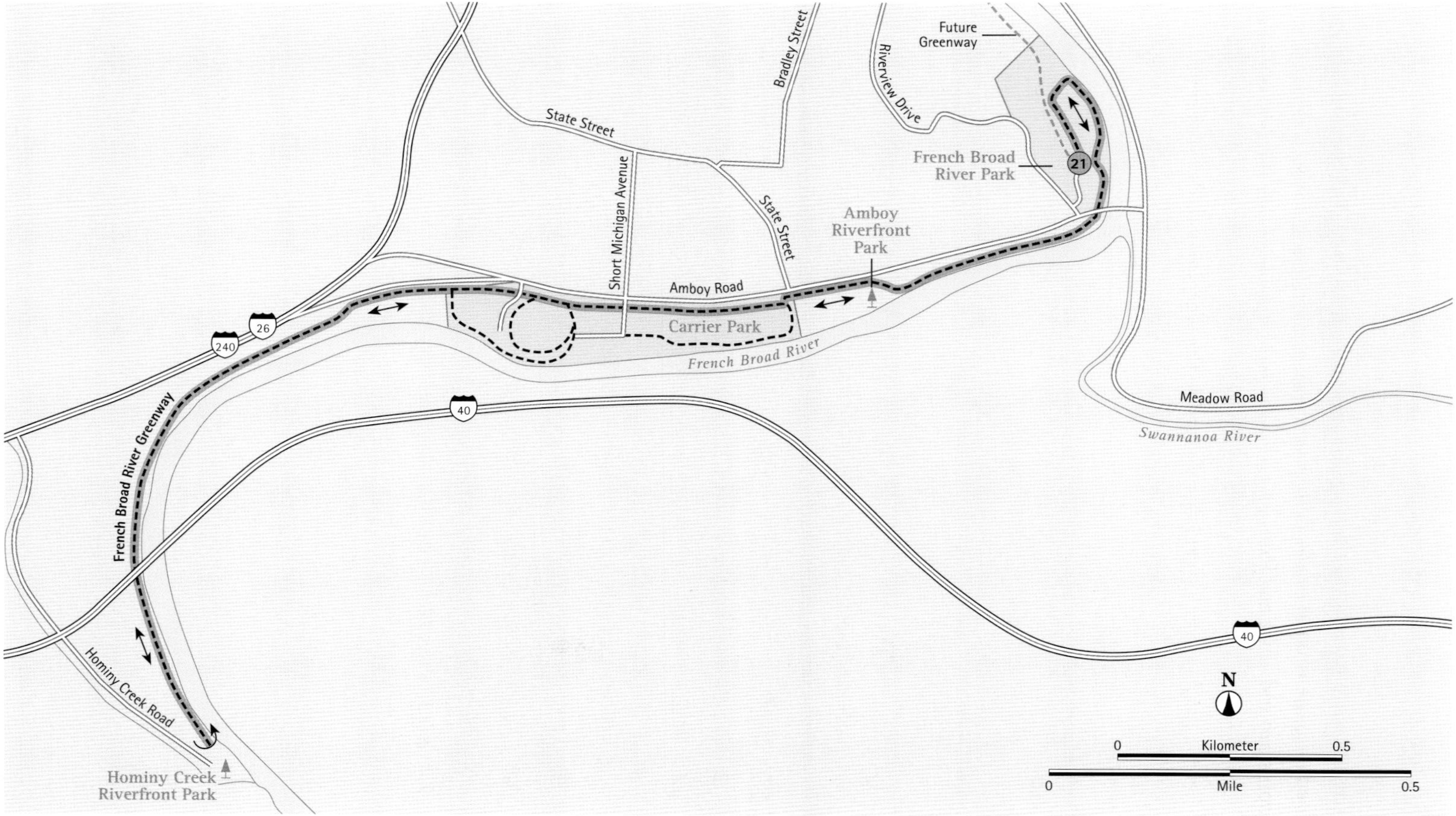

Miles and Directions

0.0 Start at the signboard at the circular auto turnaround inside French Broad River Park. Head left (north) on the paved path, making a circle around this preserve. To your left, the future extension of the French Broad River Greenway also will head north. After curving south, the French Broad River will be to your left. Pass a wooden pier overlooking the water before completing the mini loop.

0.5 Pedal under Amboy Road, curving west with the river. You are under a screen of trees, including many tall sycamores.

0.7 Enter Amboy Riverfront Park. This is a narrow greenspace hemmed in by Amboy Road on the right and the river on the left.

1.0 Leave Amboy Riverfront Park and join the concrete sidewalk running alongside Amboy Road, continuing west.

1.2 Leave the sidewalk and Amboy Road, turning left into Carrier Park. This preserve has additional asphalt and natural-surface trails for exploring. The park also has a bicycle repair station and restrooms. Stay with the asphalt greenway in a mix of sun and shade.

1.6 Pass the velodrome on your left. It is open for public access if you want to take a few spins around the banked circular track. You will likely want to stop and check out the hard-core speed riders as well as more casual pedalers trying it out. A pedestrian bridge allows access to the center of the velodrome.

1.8 Leave the west end of Carrier Park. The trail follows a sidewalk in front of a business.

1.9 The trail passes through the center of a small private RV park, following a marked right-of-way.

2.1 Reenter woods. A steep hill rises to your right. You are cruising bottomland, soaking in views of the French Broad as you ride. Sycamore and maple ash rise overhead. Contemplation benches are scattered along the asphalt trail.

2.6 Ride under I-40.

2.9 Reach Hominy Creek Riverfront Park, set on a peninsula between the French Broad River and the mouth of Hominy Creek. Here you will find alternative parking as well as a river access for canoes and kayaks. Backtrack.

5.8 Arrive back at French Broad River Park, completing the bicycle adventure after looping through the preserve one more time. *Note:* In the future you will be able to continue north on the greenway.

ALL ABOUT GREENWAYS

Greenways are linear paths that can be asphalt, gravel, or mulch, often following creeks, rivers, or lakes. Greenways can utilize former railroad and utility rights-of-way or already established parklands linking two parks together, such as here along the French Broad River. New land is sometimes purchased; other times easements are granted across private land, such as on this ride, where the trail crosses an RV park. Greenways are most often linear but can be a loop confined to one city park, such as part of this ride at French Broad River Park. Greenways are primarily used for recreational travel but can also be used by commuters and other citizens simply trying to get from point A to point B.

Greenways have broad appeal. You will see mothers with strollers pushing their newborns, runners huffing and puffing, couples strolling hand in hand, dogs walking their masters, or birders with binoculars pushed against their eyeballs. Bicyclists use greenways for exercise and travel. Any reason and venue for exercise helps cut down on America's sky-high obesity rate. Greenways are more than family recreation venues. Urban wildlife inhabits these oases of nature amid the city. The corridor along the French Broad River is rich in birdlife. Critters use greenways to travel from one greenspace to another, wildlife corridors if you will. These corridors help create overall larger territories for wildlife to exist, improving animal health since gene pools are not isolated.

Greenways have practical benefits too. Wooded streamsheds cut down on urban flooding, reducing erosion for property owners. Wooded streams also absorb water and filter pollutants from urban runoff. Greenway forests help keep cities cooler, reducing the urban heat island effect and cutting down on summertime electric bills. Trees also filter air, improving air quality in the French Broad River valley.

Greenways also improve property values of adjacent lands. Most residents realize that greenways are more likely to carry alert citizens on the lookout for criminals rather than criminals themselves. Integrating greenways into developments addresses many questions. For example, when a greenway cuts down on stormwater runoff, it reduces flooding, which addresses public safety. A greenway helps protect an area's natural resources. Developing a greenway enhances overall aesthetics, improving "quality of place." The whole process is known as integration. That is government-speak for putting it all together. Greater Asheville is growing fast. Let us continue to add greenways as we develop new areas of the region.

22 Explorers Loop at Bent Creek

Bent Creek Experimental Forest is *the* destination for Asheville mountain bikers. With a wealth of trails of all types and difficulties, Bent Creek is a place to literally expand your universe as a two-wheeled trail treader. This circuit ride discovers the forest using the Explorers Loop as well as other paths, taking you low, high, and in between, with plenty of challenging terrain along the way. After a trip or two to Bent Creek, you will be creating additional loops of your own, never tiring of the extensive trail system.

Start: Hard Times trailhead

Distance: 8.0-mile balloon loop

Riding time: 2–3.5 hours

Difficulty: Moderate–difficult (Novices, prepare for a challenge.)

Terrain and surface type: Natural-surface singletrack and doubletrack in mountains

Highlights: Varied forest scenes, Lake Powhatan, meeting other mountain bikers

Hazards: All trails are two-way for bicyclers and pedestrians.

Other considerations: Trails can be busy; be watchful for others.

Maps: National Geographic #780: Pisgah National Forest—Pisgah Ranger District

Trail contacts: Pisgah Ranger District, 1001 Pisgah Hwy., Pisgah Forest, NC 28768; (828) 877-3265; fs.usda.gov/nfsnc

Finding the trailhead: From exit 33 on I-26 South in Asheville, take NC 191 South for 2 miles to the signed right turn at a traffic light. Keep straight on Wesley Branch Road for 2.3 miles then turn left into the Hard Times trailhead. GPS: N35° 29' 15.5" / W82° 37' 27.4"

The Ride

Bring up mountain biking with anyone in the greater Asheville area and within 5 minutes the name "Bent Creek" will be mentioned. I guarantee it. That is the standard moniker for a huge interconnected set of trails within the Bent Creek Experimental Forest, itself a part of Pisgah National Forest. Lake Powhatan Recreation Area also lies within the experimental forest and is a destination in itself. Lake Powhatan lies in the heart of the Bent Creek trail system. The recreation area features fishing and swimming at the impoundment as well as a campground popular with both RV and tent campers. If you've never overnighted at Lake Powhatan, I highly recommend the experience.

Trailside view of Lake Powhatan

The trail system is mostly used by area residents, both hikers and mountain bikers. The dual-use and dual-direction trails see mostly mountain bikers, while foot sloggers dominate the hiker-only trails. The Hard Times trailhead is a good place to break into the Bent Creek trail network. A little less technical and steep than trails on the other side of Wesley Branch Road, specifically the Rice Pinnacle trailhead, the Hard Times area—especially the trails south and southwest of Lake Powhatan—offer miles and miles of pathways, allowing you to build your skills and graduate to the more difficult paths. Trails are a mix of singletrack and doubletrack. The trail intersections are well signed as a whole.

In addition to being good for mountain biking, Lake Powhatan has a fine campground. This camp is not only well located for immediate recreation but is also within easy striking distance of downtown Asheville and other attractions for which this area is known, such as the Biltmore. Take advantage of this gorgeous parcel convenient for both outdoor and urban adventures in greater Asheville.

Mountain bikers flock to Bent Creek.

Miles and Directions

0.0 Start at the busy Hard Times trailhead; pass around a pole gate and descend on a doubletrack, Hard Times Road. (All the roads within the trail system are gated and open only to forest personnel.)

0.2 The signed Hard Times Connector leaves left. Stay straight on doubletrack, descending.

0.3 Reach a T intersection. Old Bent Creek Road leaves left toward the North Carolina Arboretum. Our ride heads right a short distance along Bent Creek to a concrete bridge over Bent Creek. Cross the bridge. Look at the stream and see how it is channeled with native rock and concrete here. Once across the bridge, you can go left on Hard Times Road or right on singletrack Homestead Trail. Go right and follow the Homestead Trail as it heads upstream on an irregular track along Bent Creek amid rhododendron tunnels and rocks. Soon you can hear the outflow of Lake Powhatan; views open of the impoundment.

0.7 Head left on the Small Creeks Trail as the Homestead Trail goes straight and becomes foot only, passing the Lake Powhatan swim beach. Bridge small creeks along a heavily wooded slope.

Explorers Loop at Bent Creek

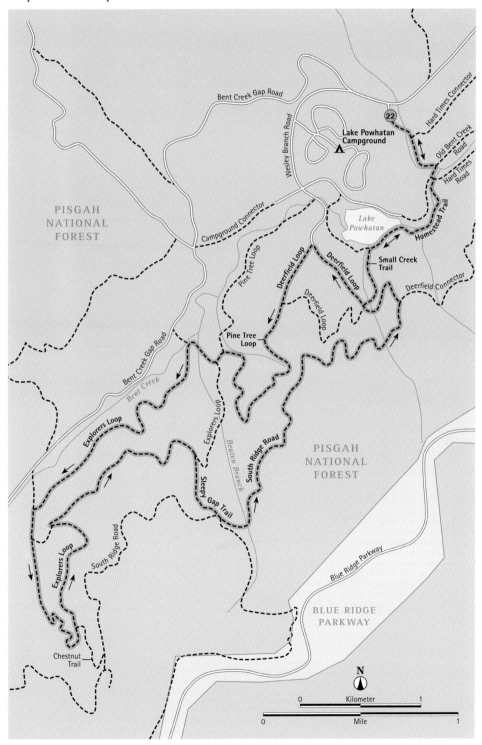

1.0 Reach a complicated intersection with old foot trails and signed trails. The signed Deerfield Connector goes left, as does one leg of the Deerfield Loop. For now, join the leg of the Deerfield Loop heading right.

1.2 Come to Wesley Branch Road and a parking area. Follow paved Wesley Branch Road.

1.3 Turn left on natural-surface Deerfield Loop. Begin a solid climb in woods.

1.5 Come to another intersection in a gap. Keep straight on the Pine Tree Loop. Climb then make a fast descent.

2.3 Reach an intersection. Head left toward the Explorers Loop.

2.5 Meet the Explorers Loop and turn right; splash your way across Beaten Creek. (There's a hiker-only bridge here too.) Come to yet another intersection; stay left with the Explorers Loop. Climb away from the stream in rhododendron then level off.

3.3 Come to another intersection. Head left on the wide 479H Trail. Ahead, pass the Explorers Loop Alternate.

3.6 Climb steadily into Chestnut Cove, using switchbacks as the path transitions from doubletrack to singletrack.

4.0 Reach an intersection. Here the Chestnut Cove Trail climbs right; our ride keeps straight, again on the Explorers Loop. Enjoy level riding and some fun downhill.

4.5 Stay right after meeting the other end of the Explorers Loop Alternate. Enjoy fun and easy riding in woods.

5.2 Leave right on the Sleepy Gap Trail. Climb 170 feet in 0.3 mile.

5.5 Head left on the South Ridge Road, a wide gravel track heading downhill. Roll into coves and on ridges, another fun part of the ride.

6.8 Turn left on the Deerfield Connector. Look for a sign indicating "Lake Powhatan 0.4 mile." Descend sharply.

7.0 Come to another intersection, completing the loop portion of the ride. You have been here before. Head right here on the Small Creeks Trail, backtracking to the trailhead after crossing Bent Creek.

8.0 Arrive back at the Hard Times trailhead.

23 North Carolina Arboretum Ride

This ride starts at Bent Creek Experimental Forest then makes its way into the North Carolina Arboretum, a special place for plants in the Asheville area, using Old Bent Creek Road, a gated gravel doubletrack. Enjoy stream scenes and access to other arboretum trails and facilities such as the Education Center. Bottom out and take the Old Mill Trail to reach Hard Times Road, another gated track. From here you have a 1.5-mile climb through attractive woods, nearing the iconic Blue Ridge Parkway. After reaching a high point, roll downhill all the way back to Bent Creek before making a short backtrack to the trailhead.

Start: Hard Times trailhead

Distance: 6.3-mile balloon loop

Riding time: 1.5–2 hours

Difficulty: Moderate

Terrain and surface type: Doubletrack gravel in mountains

Highlights: Bent Creek, North Carolina Arboretum

Hazards: None

Other considerations: Route can be busy; be watchful for hikers and runners.

Maps: National Geographic #780: Pisgah National Forest—Pisgah Ranger District; The North Carolina Arboretum map for trails and gardens

Trail contacts: Pisgah Ranger District, 1001 Pisgah Hwy., Pisgah Forest, NC 28768; (828) 877-3265; fs.usda.gov/nfsnc. The North Carolina Arboretum, 100 Frederick Law Olmsted Way, Asheville, NC 28806; (828) 665-2492; ncarboretum.org.

Finding the trailhead: From exit 33 on I-26 South in Asheville, take NC 191 South for 2 miles to the signed right turn at a traffic light. After the turn, keep straight on Wesley Branch Road for 2.3 miles and turn left into the Hard Times trailhead. GPS: N35° 29' 15.5" / W82° 37' 27.4"

The Ride

This fun bicycle adventure starts at the mountain biking heaven known as Bent Creek. However, this ride is unusual in the respect that it comprises a long, gentle downhill followed by a long, continuous but easily doable climb followed by a second long descent, this one steeper. Don't fear the climb. It rises a little more than 400 feet in 1.5 miles. The uptick is made easier since it is on a gravel road. And you can always stop and take a break, pretending you are admiring some

This bridge crosses Bent Creek near ride's end.

flora inside the arboretum or the Pisgah National Forest, through which this circuit ride also travels.

The arboretum is community supported, with more than 17,000 members. In addition to nature-made forest, the arboretum contains 65 acres of formal landscaped gardens, including a special bonsai collection. A total of 10 miles of trails are located within the bounds of the arboretum. A little more than half the trail mileage is for foot traffic only. Our ride uses the gravel road trails open to bicycles. However, on this ride you will see and be able to connect to many of these foot trails.

Kids come to the arboretum with their parents and on field trips, engaging in geocaching and interpretive learning or checking out the cool model train, which runs on weekends during the warm season. Kids can also visit the Nature Discovery Room to see wild animals in realistic habitats. For older kids, also known as adults, classes are held on subjects from natural history to horticulture and landscape design as well as arts and crafts. The arboretum even has an on-site restaurant, open for lunch. Special events are held throughout the year at the North Carolina Arboretum.

So there's a lot going on here, and the preserve is worth a visit, whether you pedal through the arboretum or return for a longer stay. It is one more worthy outdoor destination in greater Asheville.

Miles and Directions

0.0 Start the arboretum adventure from the Hard Times trailhead in Pisgah National Forest. Pass around a pole gate and descend on a doubletrack, Hard Times Road. (All the roads within the trail system are gated and open only to forest personnel.)

0.2 The signed Hard Times Connector leaves left. Stay straight on doubletrack, descending.

0.3 Reach a T intersection. Head left with doubletrack Old Bent Creek Road. Continue your easy downgrade with Bent Creek to your right. This part of the ride passes through a stand of kudzu, a nonnative plant from Asia that has covered thousands of acres of formerly viable forest and cropland in the South. Kudzu was widely planted after the Dust Bowl of the 1930s to cover barren lands—and hasn't stopped growing since. It is truly a threat to forests such as here in the Pisgah, growing all the way down to Bent Creek in places.

0.9 Come to the gated entrance to the North Carolina Arboretum. The gates are locked after hours but open during the daytime. No more kudzu. Old Bent Creek Road is more open and well maintained inside the arboretum. Look for Wolf Branch Road leaving left just beyond the gate. It connects to the main greenhouse. Hiker-only trails (not shown on the map) run through the grounds.

Looking upstream on Bent Creek

1.3 Bridge Bent Creek as it makes a sharp bend, then meet Rocky Cove Road. (**Option:** You can shortcut the loop using Rocky Cove Road.) Keep straight, tracing Bent Creek downstream. The waterway is shrouded in rhododendron and heavy vegetation, but can be accessed via short hiker-only paths.

1.5 Running Cedar Road heads left (uphill) to the Education Center, formal gardens, and other exhibits. If you are going to explore the arboretum, this would be a good place to visit first.

2.0 Come to an intersection. Ahead you can see where Old Bent Creek Road is gated. Split right onto the Old Mill Trail, which continues to follow Bent Creek in lush forest. You will twice pass under an elevated roadway while cruising the creek bottom.

2.4 Meet the other end of Hard Times Road. Head right here under mountain laurel and pine-oak-hickory woods. Begin the gradual 420-foot climb, angling up the west side of Shut-in Ridge.

3.1 Reach an intersection. Here, Owl Ridge Road leaves right, connecting to Rocky Cove Road down below. Stay straight, still climbing along Hard Times Road.

3.2 Reach a gate. Here you leave arboretum property and reenter Pisgah National Forest. The gate is unlocked during daylight hours. Continue the uptick in forest below now-wooded Glen Bald.

3.8 Level off and come alongside the Blue Ridge Parkway to your left. Bicyclers and hikers use this informal access from the Parkway to get on the trails of Bent Creek and the arboretum. Enjoy the non-hilly track before beginning your long downhill, turning away from Shut-in Ridge.

4.2 Watch left for a stone wall and steps that lead up to a little rocked-in spring. This sight is worth checking out and maybe getting a cool drink.

4.3 Meet Rocky Cove Road, as it has climbed from Bent Creek. You are in a truly rocky cove below Lance Mountain. Continue with Hard Times Road, winding in and out of more coves where small tributaries of Bent Creek flow in season.

5.0 Meet South Ridge Road as it climbs, away from a gap. We stay right with Hard Times Road. The descent sharpens as you speed along unless you grab your brakes.

5.4 Curve into the immediate valley of Bent Creek. You can hear the creek down below. Watch for pedestrians in this area.

6.0 Return to Bent Creek and an intersection. Here, the Homestead Trail leaves left. Stay straight, bridging Bent Creek where it flows in a rocked-in channel. After the bridge,

North Carolina Arboretum Ride

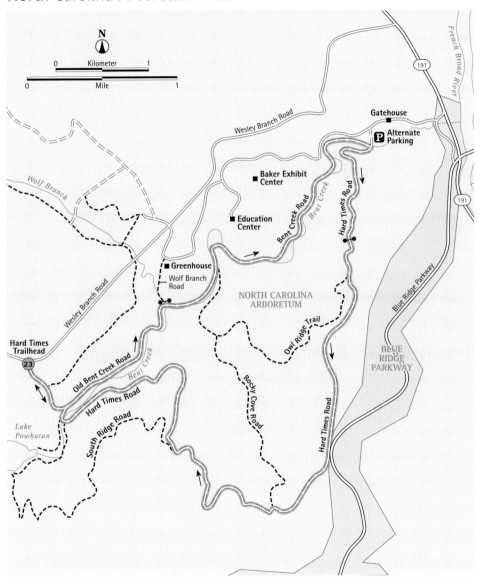

turn right (a left takes you to Lake Powhatan) and go just a short distance to complete the loop portion of the ride. Turn left and backtrack on Hard Times Road.

6.3 Arrive back at the trailhead.

24 Point Lookout Trail

This gem of a ride traces a long-closed highway through the mountains above Old Fort and Black Mountain. The asphalt track ascends the valley of Swannanoa Creek through attractive woods, winding amid coves before rising to a shoulder of Bernard Mountain, where you will find Point Lookout, a fantastic and long-appreciated vista. From there the Point Lookout Trail continues, going over a railroad line to end near Swannanoa Gap. Your return trip is one long and fun coast back to the trailhead.

Start: Parking area near Piney Grove Baptist Church

Distance: 7.4 miles out and back

Riding time: 1–1.5 hours

Difficulty: Moderate; does climb 900 feet

Terrain and surface type: Asphalt along mountain slope

Highlights: Trailside scenery, views from Point Lookout

Hazards: Speed going downhill

Other considerations: Trail is closed to auto traffic.

Maps: National Geographic #779: Linville Gorge, Mount Mitchell [Pisgah National Forest]

Trail contacts: Pisgah National Forest, Appalachian Ranger District, 632 Manor Rd., Mars Hill, NC 28754; (828) 689-9694; fs.usda.gov/nfsnc

Finding the trailhead: From Asheville take I-40 East to exit 72 (Old Fort/Mountain Gateway Museum) and head left on US 70/Main Street for 0.4 mile. Turn left onto NC 1400/Old US 70 and follow it for 2.8 miles to end at the trailhead parking area, on your left, near Piney Grove Baptist Church. Do not park in the gravel lot on Sunday morning during church services. GPS: N35° 38' 06.3" / W82° 13' 27.7"

The Ride

These days, when executing our bicycling, hiking, and paddling adventures in and around Asheville, we often use the interstates that (most of the time) zip us through town and onward to enjoy some precious time in the great outdoors. There was a time when Asheville and the rest of the country had to use winding two-lane roads to get from point A to point B. In North Carolina, US 70 was (and still is) a primary east–west route, stretching from the Atlantic Ocean to the Tennessee state line. The part of US 70 east of Asheville, near the hamlet of Old Fort, wound its way up the Swannanoa Creek valley en route to the town of Black

Pedaling near Point Lookout

Mountain. The road passed Point Lookout, with its spectacular view to the east, and stopping there became a rite of passage for travelers. Hotels even sprang up around Point Lookout (people weren't in such a hurry back then). Later, the interstates came and a portion of I-40's route used the old US 70 route, closing part of US 70. An adjacent part of US 70 passing through the Pisgah National Forest was closed down, gated on both ends, and left to grow over, surrendering back to the woods on the slopes of Bernard Mountain and the valley of Swannanoa Creek.

Locals began using the old concrete highway for walking and bicycling, tracing the former highway that once had seen parades of automobiles chugging their way into the mountains from the Piedmont and vice versa. The highway had lived through untold numbers of cars breaking down on the climb—radiators steaming, gas tanks on empty, smoke bellowing from the tailpipe until the engine ran no more. And then it became a quiet woodland access for those who knew its secrets.

But word about the "secret" trail to Point Lookout got out. Subsequently, a plan developed to open Old US 70 as an official trail managed by the USDA Forest Service, through whose property much of the trail ran. The road was stabilized, landslides cleaned up, and culverts scoured. Finally, the old concrete highway was topped with a layer of asphalt, making for a smoother track. In 2008 the newly christened Point Lookout Trail was opened.

Old US 70 had a second chance. Instead of cars and trucks, hikers and bicyclers wound its curves and traveled under its leafy roof. Occasional breakdowns these days might be a turned ankle or a sprung chain instead of a blown engine or steaming radiator. Why don't you give the Point Lookout Trail a chance? I enjoy its sense of history, the woodland scenery, and the challenge. The ride is uphill the whole way—not steep, just steady—starting at 1,680 feet and ending at 2,590 feet. Worry not; resting benches are located throughout the trek should you desire a breather—or just want a place to soak in the mountainside splendor.

And about the return trip . . . you truly can coast the entire way back. I like to go slow, riding the brakes a little, savoring the ride. And I stop at Point Lookout on the way up and on the way back down. So gather up the crew and make your own adventure on the Point Lookout Trail.

Miles and Directions

0.0 Start from the gravel parking area open to the public but used by Piney Grove Church on Sunday mornings and pedal west on Old US 70 just a short distance to a gate. (There's a house on the left at the gate.) Pedal around the gate and begin ascending the Point Lookout Trail, recycled US 70. Immediately enter attractive hardwood forest with Swannanoa Creek down in the hollow to your left and Bernard Mountain rising to your right.

0.2 Gated FR 4026 goes left. Stay with the asphalt Point Lookout Trail, westbound. The atmosphere is serene here, nestled between Youngs Mountain to your left and Bernard Mountain to your right.

0.5 Pass a bluff, blasted to allow US 70 to ascend the mountain. Curve into wooded coves where streams flow under the trail via culvert. You might call this a mountain greenway, with elevation change included.

1.0 Make a sharp left curve, crossing a major unnamed tributary of Swannanoa Creek in thick rhododendron. Begin angling up a shoulder ridge of Bernard Mountain. Enjoy a view east as you pass a fenced area along the trail with a steep slope.

1.2 Turn back west, gaining the crest of the shoulder ridge. Swannanoa Creek splashes below. More views open ahead. Walnut trees are common. The variety of trees makes this a great autumn-color destination. Kudzu covers still other areas.

2.2 Come below Norfolk Southern Railway.

Point Lookout Trail

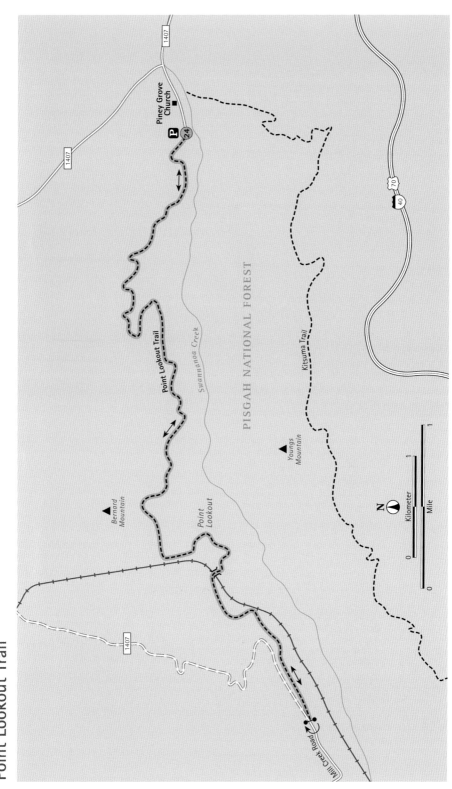

This trail used to be US 70.

2.5 A gravel track leads acutely right and is used by railroad personnel for track management.

2.6 Come to Point Lookout. Here a spectacular view stretches into the horizon, over the Swannanoa River valley east through the mountains toward the Piedmont. A signboard details interpretive information, and a pair of flagpoles flies North Carolina and American flags. Soak in a view from observation benches. Beyond, turn back into the Swannanoa Creek valley.

2.9 Pedal above the rail line where it emerges from a tunnel.

3.4 Begin a long straightaway.

3.7 Reach the west terminus of the Point Lookout Trail at Mill Creek Road. A gate divides the trail from the road. There is shoulder parking along Mill Creek Road, but it is not recommended. Backtrack and see if you can coast the entire way back. Or take a slower pace, soaking in the trailside scenery

7.4 Arrive back at the trailhead.

25 Wimba Loops at Lake James State Park

Explore the hills above and the shores of Lake James at this first-rate, quality-made pair of mountain bike loop trails. Wind through hollows and along ridges, undulating on fun rollers—an ideal pedaling adventure to help you up your mountain biking game.

Start: Lake James State Park mountain bike trailhead

Distance: 10.0-mile double loop

Riding time: 2–3.5 hours

Difficulty: Moderate

Terrain and surface type: Natural surface on hilly terrain

Highlights: Mountain bike designated trails, state park–level scenery

Hazards: None

Other considerations: Trails are one way.

Maps: Lake James State Park Mountain Bike Trail System

Trail contacts: Lake James State Park, 321 NC 126, Nebo, NC 28761; (828) 584-7728; www.ncparks.gov

Finding the trailhead: From Asheville take I-40 East to exit 90 (Nebo/Lake James). Turn right and join Harmony Grove Road; pass over the interstate. After 0.6 mile reach an intersection; stay right on Harmony Grove Road, following it for 2.2 more miles to reach the intersection with US 70 in Nebo. Turn left and follow US 70 West just a short distance; turn right on NC 126. Follow NC 126 for 5 miles, passing the Catawba River Area of Lake James State Park to turn right into the Paddy's Creek Area. Follow the main park road for 0.9 mile to the mountain biking trailhead, on your left. GPS: N35° 45' 34.3" / W81° 53' 16.8"

The Ride

Lake James State Park is one of North Carolina's better planned and laid out preserves, not only maximizing the attractive parcels along the shores of Lake James but also creating a smart infrastructure where outdoor adventurers can mountain bike, hike, paddle, camp, swim, and fish—all in a special setting.

The park wanted to create a mountain bike trail system usable by everybody from beginners to experts and thus fashioned a series of loops varying in difficulty. The Tindo Loops are the easiest. The circuits on this adventure—West Wimba and East Wimba Loops—are moderate in difficulty, with the East Wimba

Loop being the more difficult. The superlative layout and condition of the trails will make you appreciate this network of mountain bike paths as they wander through the park's pine-clad hills and hollows. The scenery is excellent throughout, whether you are in deep woods, crossing bridges over creeks, or glancing through the trees toward Lake James. The thick woods make this a viable choice on a hot summer day. Fall is fine for viewing colorful hardwoods. In winter you will gain more extensive views of Lake James. Spring brings wildflowers in the many stream drainages you will explore.

The East Wimba and West Wimba Loops are on the easier side, with climbs and drops generally less than 100 feet. In fact, the entirety of the two loops entails only 1,200 feet of elevation change over 10 miles—the full adventure if you do both loops. If you are looking for a shorter bike ride, simply ride only the West Wimba Loop, making the ride about 6 miles. To access the East Wimba

Rolling through a section of the Wimba Loops

Loop, you must utilize part of the West Wimba Loop, making it a ride of almost 10 miles. Therefore, the best course of action if you want to do the East Wimba Loop is to go ahead and do the full West Wimba Loop too. If you are looking for the shortest ride of all, pedal the Tindo Loops, also detailed in this guide.

Miles and Directions

0.0 Start from the north side of the parking area, which has a restroom, changing area, picnic table, and signboard. Enter woods, going downhill on a singletrack path marked with circular blazes. This first part is two-way traffic.

0.1 Reach an intersection. Here the Tindo Loops go left; go right, toward the Wimba Loops. Pedal a rolling track of red dirt, roots, and pine needles under pines, holly, and sweetgum trees. Go just a short distance and reach the West Wimba Loop. Head right here. Roll on singletrack through woods with banked turns on a flowy track with not much rock.

0.6 Bridge a creek and turn east toward Lake James. The trail often crosses old roads but doesn't stay on them for long, instead tackling wilder terrain. The woodland floor can be a sea of ferns during the warm season. Cross intermittent stream drainages, with only minor ups and downs.

1.4 Circle the head of a hollow.

2.0 Gain views of Lake James through the trees. This is about as close as you will get to the shoreline without getting off your bike.

2.4 Come to the intersection of the East Wimba and West Wimba Loops after pulling away from Lake James. For the full experience, stay right here on two-way track toward the East Wimba Loop.

2.5 Bridge the biggest creek along the mountain bike trail system on a sturdy wooden span. The normally clear unnamed waterway flows into wetlands linking the creek to Lake James. Continue on the two-way connector.

2.7 Reach the East Wimba Loop. Head right here, turning back toward Lake James on a climb. Back on one-way track, resume undulations, twisting, turning, and rolling as designed for mountain bikes. Watch for a few rocky sections ahead. Tree roots are also encountered along the track.

3.4 Bridge another stream, continuing the counterclockwise circuit. Come within sight of the lake again before pulling away from the impoundment.

Wimba Loops at Lake James State Park

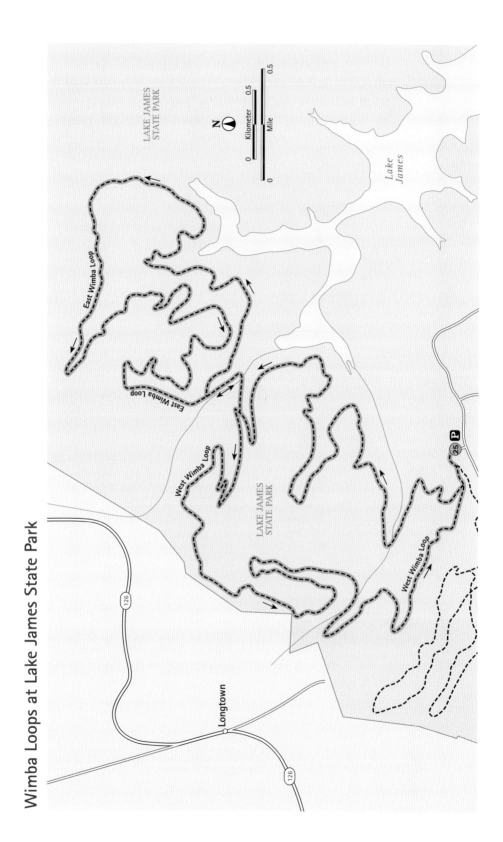

4.6 Turn left at the head of a hollow centered with a small stream. Ahead, bound through a series of rollers in pine woods. Fun!

6.1 The trail continues to take advantage of all available lands, curving into the head of another hollow. There is no bridge here. Beyond here, cruise down the hollow on more fun rollers into a widening hollow with springs at the bottom. You can pick up speed here and appreciate not having to worry about someone coming at you.

6.4 Complete the East Wimba Loop. Head right on the two-way connector, once again bridging the biggest stream of the mountain biking area.

6.7 Come to the intersection you were at earlier. This time head right, bridging a little stream, counterclockwise on new one-way trail on the West Wimba Loop. Make a solid ascent up a thickly wooded hollow. Rise for 0.5 mile before leveling off, part of it on a banked S-turn.

7.8 Reach the highest elevation of the ride, a little over 1,400 feet, atop a ridge. The trail is rooty here in places as you cruise a flat.

8.5 Return to 1,400 feet after rolling along the side of a steep slope and returning to the aforementioned ridge. Now enjoy a prolonged descent of 0.5 mile, dropping about 100 feet.

8.9 The trail briefly splits, with a technical feature you can ride on the left.

9.1 Bridge a stream in a hollow. Climb and turn east.

9.4 Cross an intermittent streambed.

9.9 Complete the West Wimba Loop. Backtrack toward the trailhead.

10.0 Arrive back at the trailhead.

26 Tindo Loops at Lake James State Park

This pair of short loops at Lake James State Park presents trails constructed specifically for mountain bikers. Designated one-way trails take you through deep pine and hardwood forests. The Tindo Loops have been laid out with entry-level mountain bikers in mind, with fewer elevation changes, level sections, and a mere modicum of technical ridings, to help you break into the exciting adventure that is mountain biking.

Start: Lake James State Park mountain bike trailhead

Distance: 3.6-mile figure-eight loop

Riding time: About 1 hour

Difficulty: Easy

Terrain and surface type: Natural surface on slightly hilly terrain

Highlights: Mountain bike designated trails, state park–level scenery

Hazards: None

Other considerations: Trails are one way.

Maps: Lake James State Park Mountain Bike Trail System

Trail contacts: Lake James State Park, 321 NC 126, Nebo, NC 28761; (828) 584-7728; ncparks.gov

Finding the trailhead: From Asheville take I-40 East to exit 90 (Nebo/Lake James). Turn right and join Harmony Grove Road; pass over the interstate. After 0.6 mile reach an intersection; stay right on Harmony Grove Road, following it for 2.2 more miles to the intersection with US 70 in Nebo. Turn left and follow US 70 West just a short distance. Turn right on NC 126 and continue for 5 miles, passing the Catawba River Area of Lake James State Park to turn right into the Paddy's Creek Area. Follow the main park road for 0.9 mile to the mountain biking trailhead, on your left. GPS: N35° 45' 34.3" / W81° 53' 16.8"

The Ride

Lake James State Park is a treasure of the greater Asheville region. A place where multiple adventures can be undertaken, the park was established in 1987 but took a while to flower into the full development we see today. Adventures here run the full gamut. Here you can not only mountain bike but also tread a well-established hiking trail system running along the shores and lands of the preserve. Being astride a lake means water activities as well. The park boasts a full-scale swim beach and lake recreation area, where you can rent canoes and kayaks as well as launch your own craft to paddle the shores of Lake James. Two paddling adventures in this guide utilize Lake James State Park and the surrounding waters of Lake James. Boat ramps afford opportunities for motorized watercraft as well. A fishing pier allows you to cast a line if you are boatless. Before or after your adventure, you can enjoy a picnic at multiple areas, including shaded shelters.

The park's two areas—Catawba River and Paddy's Creek—offer camping possibilities. True to its signature multiple options, at Lake James State Park you can boat to a primitive campground, drive to a more-developed camp, or venture to walk-in campsites on foot. This preserve is nothing if not a place for adventurous outdoor enthusiasts!

This ride is ideal for beginner mountain bikers.

The park is easily accessible from Asheville via I-40; consider staying for an extended period to enjoy the multiple offerings. Everything here is built first rate and is in fine condition, and the mountain bike trail system is a perfect example. Constructed for mountain bikers, the trails are laid out with the two-wheeled set in mind. The trails have good flow and plenty of rollers to keep the excitement going. The trail system is all one way except for a few small connectors, allowing you to concentrate on riding your mountain bike rather than watching for oncoming trail users. The direction of the one-way trails is occasionally changed to keep the pathways in the best possible shape. Unlike other mountain biking destinations, you don't have a nest of confusing unmarked trails. The trail system is clear, simple, and signed, keeping you from having to constantly stop to figure out which way to go.

The Tindo Loops are two shortish circuits that are laid out for newbie mountain bikers to get their feet wet, a place where experienced riders can take an apprentice. Elevation changes for the entire loop are a little less than 300 feet. The paths aren't too steep or too technical or too long, or too confusing. Even Goldilocks could mountain bike here. They're just right! When you enter the loops, just follow the directional arrows and you too can have an adventure that is just right.

Miles and Directions

0.0 Start from the north side of the parking area, which has a restroom, changing area, picnic table, and signboard. Enter woods, going downhill on a singletrack path marked with circular blazes. This first part is two-way traffic.

0.1 Reach an intersection. Here the Tindo Loops go left and the Wimba Loops go right. Stay left with the Tindo Loops. Cruise state park–level scenery on a mostly level track in rich woods of pine, sweetgum, and holly. The trees are somewhat close to the trail, so be watchful.

0.2 Cross a gravel road open only to state park personnel. Quickly reenter shady woods, with pine needles scattered on the forest floor.

0.4 Dip into and out of an old eroded roadbed.

0.5 Reach an intersection; go left toward the loops. The trail to the right is the return of one of the loops. Descend in woods on a two-way trail segment.

Tindo Loops at Lake James State Park

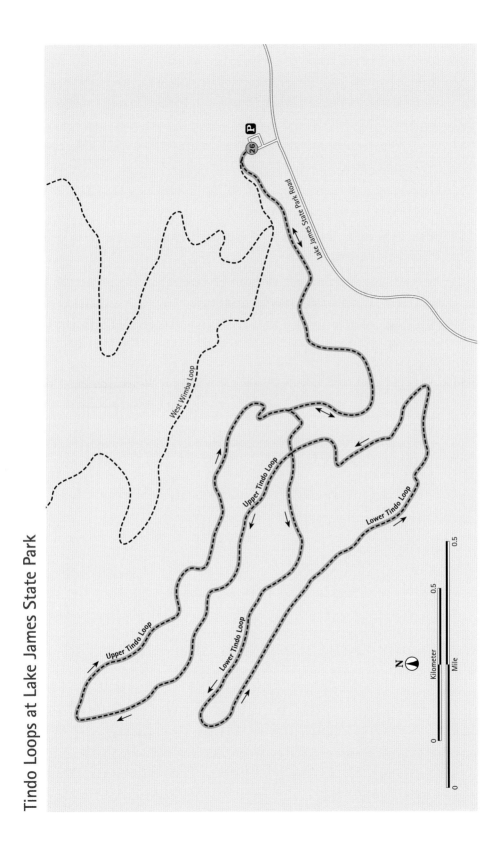

0.6 Come to a three-way intersection, where you can go straight, right, or left. Go right on the Upper Tindo Loop. Here the trail is mostly level, but it does have some bouncy, rooty segments. Your speed is largely determined by how hard you want to pedal. A few sections feature ups and downs.

1.1 Curve back on the Upper Loop near the state park boundary. The singletrack does have some undulations, rollers, and banked turns.

1.7 Return to the earlier intersection at 0.5 mile. Go straight on the two-way section, descending toward the Lower Tindo Loop.

1.8 Return to the earlier intersection at 0.6 mile. Go straight on the Lower Tindo Loop. This circuit is also mostly level.

2.1 The Lower Tindo Loop makes a U turn to the left. Descend and pick up speed. Watch out for young trees growing directly beside the trail.

2.6 Cross a rocky drainage and bang your way past exposed roots, the biggest technical test of the Lower Tindo Loop, and your low point. Climb from here, soon making a sharp left turn.

3.0 Complete the Lower Tindo Loop. Backtrack toward the trailhead.

3.5 Meet the Wimba Loops. Stay right, toward the trailhead.

3.6 Arrive back at the trailhead. If you are still itching to go, do the Tindo Loops over again, or tackle the West Wimba Loop.

27 Oklawaha Greenway

This Hendersonville greenway takes you along a stream and through trailside parks. The fun paved ride just east of downtown starts at Berkeley Mills Park and heads to and alongside Mud Creek. You then cruise an attractively landscaped floodplain. Take the spur to Patton Park then return to the main trail, exploring long King Memorial Park. Make another detour to Sullivan Park before continuing south to end at big Jackson Park. Though the trail is mostly level, it does have some hills to keep things lively.

Start: Berkeley Mills Park

Distance: 7.3 miles out and back with side trips

Riding time: 1.5–2.5 hours

Difficulty: Easy

Terrain and surface type: Asphalt mostly along stream

Highlights: Quality trail, pollinator-friendly landscaping, interpretive information

Hazards: Flooded areas of trail after heavy rains

Other considerations: Jackson Park has nearly unlimited parking.

Maps: Oklawaha Greenway

Trail contacts: City of Hendersonville, North Carolina, 145 Fifth Ave. East, Hendersonville, NC 28792; (828) 697-3000; hendersonvillenc.gov/parks-recreation

Finding the trailhead: From Asheville take I-26 East to exit 44 (US 25 North/US 25 South Business). Head south on Asheville Highway and follow it for 4.6 miles. Turn left onto Berkeley Road and continue 0.1 mile; turn left again onto Balfour Road. Follow Balfour Road for 0.2 mile; you will see Berkeley Park on your left (not to be confused with the greater Berkeley Mills plant, which you are near.) Continue just a short distance past the left-hand-turn entrance into Berkeley Park and turn right into the parking area for the Oklawaha Greenway. If this lot is full, park at the main part of Berkeley Park. GPS: N35° 20' 54.3" / W82° 28' 05.3"

The Ride

In some respects, in relation to Asheville, Hendersonville is treated like an afterthought—the lesser of the two metropolitan areas, although they are only 20 miles apart. Asheville is set along the French Broad River, from which rises the majestic Blue Ridge, whereas the land in Henderson County is more rolling; the mountains a little lower, a little tamer. But Henderson County has plenty going

Pedaler's-eye view of the Ocklawaha Greenway

for it. It is home to DuPont State Forest, an adventurer's paradise, whether you like hiking, mountain biking, or waterfalling. Celebrated for its agricultural heritage, Henderson County is also known as "Apple Country." More than 150 orchards can be found in the vicinity, producing many of the apples that make North Carolina one of the top-ten apple producing states in the country.

So what does all this have to do with the Oklawaha Greenway? I am making the case to look southward from Asheville into Henderson County, Hendersonville specifically, to find new outdoor adventures. And the Oklawaha Greenway is a great starting point. The linear trail along the banks of Mud Creek was a long time coming. Starting as just an idea in 1999, the greenway was constructed in phases from 2004 to 2015. Plans call for the greenway to be expanded north to Fletcher and south to Flat Rock.

The greenway has become very popular. Most any day you will see bicyclers, runners, walkers, and nature enthusiasts. The Audubon Society has declared the Oklawaha Greenway to be a birding hotspot, so don't be surprised if you see groups wearing pith helmets and knee socks walking around with binoculars pasted against their eyes and bird-identification apps open on their phones, looking toward the sky with excitement. Butterfly- and bee-attracting greenery has been planted along the trail, enticing those pollinators.

The Oklawaha Trail starts at Berkeley Mills Park, a multiuse facility with ballfields, picnic areas, and a lake. At one time hereabouts, a huge granite quarry extracted nearly all the granite used at the famed Biltmore Estate. In 1924 a textile mill was established in the locale and has been in operation ever since. The 60 acres of Berkeley Mills Park and part of the right-of-way for the Oklawaha Greenway were donated by current mill owner Kimberly-Clark. The route works along the edge of the plant, descending to Mud Creek. "Oklawaha" is Cherokee for "slow-moving waters." The trail heads south, passing under Berkeley Road and North Main Street before reaching long King Memorial Park. Here a spur trail goes west to Patton Park. The Oklawaha Trail makes its way through King Memorial Park, with another side trail heading to a neighborhood and Sullivan Park. After that the trail uses the Seventh Avenue bridge to span Mud Creek, joining the east bank where it passes under MLK Jr. Boulevard. From there it enters big Jackson Park, a large preserve with a mountain bike skills park, ballfields, disc golf course, nature trail, and picnic areas. After wandering through Jackson Park, the trail ends on a hill beside a large parking area and the park office, set in a building from pre-park landowners.

The path is a 10-foot-wide asphalt strip with a yellow line in the middle in most places, keeping two-way traffic safe. Benches are located at intervals, and trail distances are marked every 0.25 mile, keeping you apprised of your whereabouts. You will find three bicycle repair stations along the way. Blue safety phones are also spaced along the trail.

Thus are the details, but isn't an outdoor adventure all about the experience? I think yours will be a good one. The views are pleasing to the eye; the trailside vegetation enhances the urban setting. Mud Creek is much more scenic than the name implies. Much of the greenway travels through already existing parks. The ride is mostly flat, with a few hills to offer a little challenge. I find it a winner of an adventure, and no slouch compared to Asheville's greenway system. So give good ol' Hendersonville a chance, and expand your universe of bicycling adventure possibilities.

Miles and Directions

0.0 Start at the trail's beginning at its intersection with Balfour Road. Head east then south, passing the recommended parking area. Follow the asphalt track as it skirts the edge of the Kimberly-Clark plant, descending and rolling through woods.

This is a fun greenway; try it out.

Oklawaha Greenway

0.4 Come alongside Mud Creek, an often clear stream following drier spells. A heavy screen of trees shades the waterway. You have descended 60 feet from the trailhead. Grassy areas and planted trees landscape the winding path.

0.8 Pedal under Berkeley Road. A short spur trail leads right to alternative parking. Keep south, passing pollinator-friendly vegetation.

1.1 Bridge a tributary of Mud Creek.

1.4 Pedal under North Main Street. Be watchful under road bridges after rains; silt can wash onto the trail. If Mud Creek floods, crews are quick to remove silt from the trail. Soon enter King Memorial Park.

1.5 Reach an intersection and signboard. Head right toward Patton Park, passing a wetland on your left. Soon climb a small hill to cross North Main Street and a railroad track; turn right toward Patton Park.

2.0 Reach Patton Park—19 acres of ballfields, tennis courts, walking trails, a pool, picnic tables, and a pavilion. Backtrack to the main branch of the Oklawaha Trail.

2.5 Continue south on the main branch of the Oklawaha Trail through King Memorial Park, a long 6-acre preserve with a wetland. Enjoy trailside interpretive information.

2.8 Split right with the heavily wooded connector toward Sullivan Park, a 5-acre neighborhood park with a playground, picnic tables, and basketball courts.

3.0 Reach Sullivan Park; backtrack.

3.2 Return to the Oklawaha Trail, still southbound. Quickly bridge a stream entering from your right.

3.5 Cross Mud Creek on the Seventh Avenue bridge and come to Pets Own Place Dog Park on your left. Here, carefully cross Seventh Avenue, still southbound, now on the east side of Mud Creek.

3.7 Pass under MLK Jr. Boulevard. The trail winds south.

4.1 Cross Fourth Avenue, a small two-lane road, then enter big Jackson Park and shortly bridge a small stream. Cruise through the park, passing near a paved nature trail.

4.3 Reach the trail terminus after climbing a hill. Shaded picnic tables are nearby the large parking area. From here it is a 3.0-mile backtrack without taking the side paths.

7.3 Arrive back at the parking area for Berkeley Mills Park.

28 DuPont State Forest Ride

Enjoy fast, well-marked and -maintained trails in a first-rate scenic setting at DuPont State Forest. This loop explores the northern part of the forest. It passes Lake Imaging then climbs above Little River and nears Grassy Creek Falls. From there you continue on a mix of singletrack and doubletrack trail, winding through gorgeous forestlands before returning via the renown Ridgeline Trail, where some fast riding takes you back to the trailhead.

Start: Lake Imaging trailhead

Distance: 7.4-mile loop

Riding time: 1.7–2.5 hours

Difficulty: Moderate

Terrain and surface type: Natural-surface singletrack and doubletrack in mountains

Highlights: Beautiful woods, waterfalls nearby, great trail conditions

Hazards: All trails are two way for pedestrians and equestrians.

Other considerations: Trails can be busy; be watchful for others.

Maps: National Geographic #504: DuPont State Recreational Forest, DuPont State Recreational Forest

Trail contacts: DuPont State Recreational Forest, PO Box 300, Cedar Mountain, NC 28718; (828) 877-6527; dupontstaterecreationalforest.com

Finding the trailhead: From the intersection of NC 280 and US 276 in Pisgah Forest, just north of Brevard, take US 64 East for 3.5 miles to a light at Crab Creek Road. Turn right on Crab Creek Road and follow it for 4.2 miles. Turn right on DuPont Road and continue as it soon becomes Staton Road, for a total of 2.5 miles to the large Lake Imaging trailhead parking area, on your left. GPS: N35° 12' 33.3" / W82° 36' 55.5"

The Ride

When I think of my favorite place to mountain bike around Asheville, it is undoubtedly DuPont State Forest. I prefer a well-organized, well-taken-care-of trail system as opposed to spiderwebs of user-created trails where you don't know whether you are coming or going. And the scenery: The forested hills and hollows of DuPont are alluring enough to distract you from your ride.

Trail intersections here are marked with signs.

All trail intersections are signed, allowing you to focus on the ride itself rather than navigating. And the trails are in such great shape you can become a human extension of your two-wheeled machine, rolling down winding single-track, climbing banked turns, slashing past trees close to the trail, making the most of a downhill before pushing the pedals at just the right moment to maximize momentum while beginning an uphill. The doubletrack sections will leave you to cruise through the charming landscape, eyes on the woods, pedaling along without watching your every move. This combination of trail types adds up to a winning ride. By the way, the trip gains and loses a little over 1,000 feet in its 7.4-mile distance.

The adventure starts at the large Lake Imaging trailhead, with a restroom and large signboard displaying the entire trail system on a map. You join double-track Lake Imaging Road and get your heart pumping to quickly reach small Lake Imaging, with its covered picnic shelter and fishing possibilities. From there you experience the first climb of the trip, on the Jim Branch Trail. The beginning of the Jim Branch Trail features erosion-preventing cobblestone track, adding challenge to the short but quick ascent as it climbs above upper Hooker Creek. Next, pedal along the valley edge on the Isaac Heath Trail to roll over knobs and pick up the Locust Trail before coming near Triple Falls and High Falls on the Little River using the Hilltop Trail. You won't be able to see the cataracts from the trail but should be able to hear their roar. Ahead, the Hilltop Trail dumps you

Rolling through a curve

The last part of this ride can be a downhill blur.

out within easy walking distance of Grassy Creek Falls. Take the time to jump off your bike and walk the short spur to the top of the spiller as it flows white over an open granite slide.

After the falls, the trail utilizes doubletrack Lake Imaging and Buck Forest Roads. Gear down to climb again on a gentle but steady grade, nearing a place known as The Flatwoods. It is an easy ride on the White Pine Trail, then you turn onto the Hooker Creek Trail, which goes nowhere near Hooker Creek. Reach the Ridgeline Trail and enjoy a raucous downhill end to your ride. Be mindful of your speed here, and keep an eye on the trail ahead.

This is just one of many rides you can undertake at DuPont State Forest. The 10,000-acre preserve features 90 miles of trails and doubletrack roads open only to forest personnel. The trails to and around the falls are generally the most crowded, and most of them are hiker-only. All trails are open to hikers, whereas specific ones are also open to mountain bikers and equestrians. As always, mountain bikers yield to hikers and equestrians. Mountain bikers are encouraged to keep their speed under control, especially around blind curves.

The state forest came to be after various tracts of land were acquired between 1995 and 2000. The final tract, containing many of the waterfalls for which the forest is now known, was acquired through a controversial use of eminent domain and cost much more than the rest of the forest combined. Once DuPont State Recreational Forest was established, a trail system was quickly developed; over the past two decades, the locale has deservedly become one of the most loved and appreciated outdoor adventure destinations in the greater Asheville sphere.

Note: Around 1,800 acres of DuPont is protected under the North Carolina Natural Heritage Program for its special ecological characteristics. In my opinion, the forest as a whole is one of the most scenic properties in the entire North Carolina state forest and state park system. Take some time in places to soak in the landscape through which you ride.

Miles and Directions

0.0   Start at the Lake Imaging trailhead by passing around the pole gate near the trailhead kiosk on Lake Imaging Road, a doubletrack trail.

0.2   Intersect the Ridgeline Trail, coming in on your left. This will be your return route. For now stay straight with Lake Imaging Road, soon coming alongside small Lake Imaging.

0.3   Head left on the Jim Branch Trail, climbing a rock trailbed. The singletrack trail soon levels off in pine-oak–mountain laurel woods. Ahead, however, you are going up more than not, including using switchbacks.

DuPont State Forest Ride

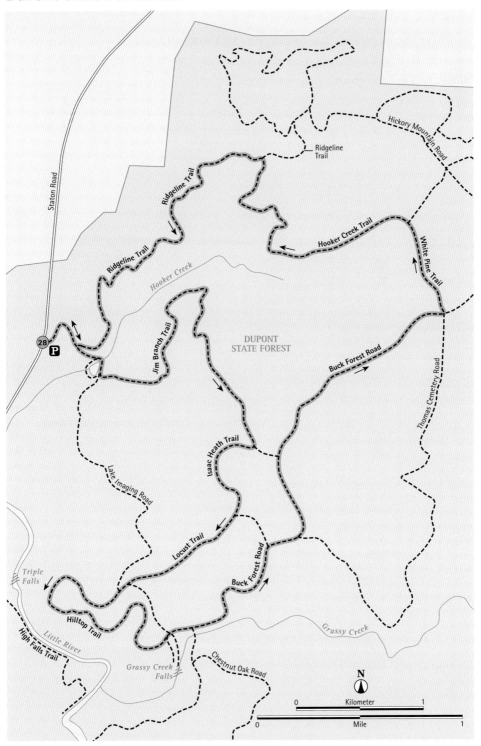

1.5 Reach a trail intersection in a gap. Head right on the Isaac Heath Trail. Circle around a knob on a smooth, fast track.

1.8 Stay straight with the Locust Trail as the Isaac Heath Trail splits left. Climb away from the intersection then make a longer downhill, with part of the trail traveling over rock slabs.

2.2 Meet Lake Imaging Road again. Follow it right just a short distance then stay left, joining the Hilltop Trail, a singletrack path. Cruise smooth track along a hilltop high above Triple Falls and High Falls. In places the trees are tight on the trail.

3.2 Reach a horse hitching post and intersection. You can take the hiker trail right to view Grassy Creek Falls, just a short distance away. Otherwise, keep left then meet Lake Imaging Road yet again; turn right (downhill) on the doubletrack.

3.3 Head left on Buck Forest Road, another doubletrack. To your right, Lake Imaging Road bridges Grassy Creek. Begin a prolonged but moderate ascent in rich woods.

3.7 Pass the other end of the Isaac Heath Trail while on a right-hand turn, still climbing.

3.8 Stay with Buck Forest Road as Thomas Cemetery Road goes right. The track levels out for a bit.

4.1 Stay with Buck Forest Road as the other end of the Jim Branch Trail enters on your left. Continue more up than not.

4.9 Reach a four-way intersection near The Flatwoods; head left on the White Pine Trail among mountain laurel and pines. Climb more. Note the trailside interpretive signage explaining best management practices in the state forest. Pass through a wildlife meadow.

5.1 Reach the high point of the ride and a trail junction. Head left here with the Hooker Creek Trail, making an extended descent on a somewhat rocky track.

5.6 Watch for a sharp right turn at the bottom of a downhill. Climb, then wind along the upper drainages of Hooker Creek.

6.0 Intersect the legendary Ridgeline Trail, a favorite for downhill riding. However, at this juncture you first climb a doubletrack, then drop left onto singletrack, and finally start rolling on a 1-mile downhill. Balance your speed with awareness. High-banked turns and switchbacks add to the fun.

7.2 Meet Lake Imaging Road a final time and head right.

7.4 Arrive back at the trailhead.

29 Estatoe Trail and Greenway

This exciting, fun, and scenic trail ride starts at the Pisgah National Forest ranger station outside Brevard and follows the Estatoe Trail along the Davidson River through attractive riverside woods to enter the town of Brevard, joining the Estatoe Greenway. From there you wind through town, enjoying town scenes as well as distant mountain views. End the adventure near Brevard College and downtown Brevard, completing a transition from forest to city.

Start: Pisgah National Forest ranger station/visitor center

Distance: 10.4 miles out and back

Riding time: 2–3 hours

Difficulty: Moderate

Terrain and surface type: Gravel along river, asphalt through town

Highlights: Davidson River scenes, mountain views, downtown access

Hazards: Crossing a few busy roads

Other considerations: None

Maps: Estatoe Trail

Trail contacts: Pisgah National Forest, 1600 Pisgah Hwy., Pisgah Forest, NC 28768; (828) 877-3265; fs.usda.gov/nfsnc. City of Brevard, 95 West Main St., Brevard, NC 28712; (828) 885-5600; cityofbrevard.com.

Finding the trailhead: From Asheville take I-26 East to exit 40 (NC 280/Asheville Regional Airport) and follow NC 280 West for 16 miles. Turn right onto US 276 North in Pisgah Forest and continue for 1.5 miles. Turn right into the large parking area at the Pisgah National Forest ranger station/visitor center. GPS: N35° 17' 05.3" / W82° 43' 34.7"

The Ride

Talk about transitioning! On this ride you will enjoy a lot of what western North Carolina bicycling is all about. Start in Pisgah National Forest at the busy and informative ranger station/visitor center then make your way through the forests along the clear, highland-draining waters of the Davidson River. Pass pools and shoals under a thick mantle of hardwoods and evergreens, bridging the Davidson River. The route continues along the mountain waterway, passing near Davidson River Campground, then pops out along US 64, crossing that road to join Brevard's Estatoe Greenway. Here the ride morphs into a city greenway

This boardwalk is bordered by woods and the Davidson River.

experience as the dedicated asphalt path works along roads and through parkland, where views open of the adjacent mountains. It finally picks up an old railroad right-of-way before ending near Brevard College and downtown Brevard at McLean Street, where it is ultimately slated to continue through downtown into the Railroad Arts District and onward to Tannery Park.

It all begins in the historic Pisgah National Forest. The very first tract of national forest east of the Mississippi River was purchased in North Carolina in 1912, shortly after the passage of the Weeks Act, the federal law establishing national forests in the East. Before Pisgah National Forest came to be, fertile bottoms in the mountains were subsistence farmed by backwoods settlers. Later, lands were bought out by Vanderbilt himself when acquiring vast tracts for his estate. The magnate had regard for his wooded properties and hired the first professional foresters to operate in the United States. This led to a school of forestry being opened just a few miles up US 276 from the beginning of this ride. The buildings of the school as well as adjacent acreage have been declared a Natural National Historic Site. Before or after your ride, you can learn more about this history at the Forest Discovery Center.

The Blue Ridge rises above this greenway in Brevard.

Stop at the national forest ranger station at the ride's beginning.

On the way to the trailhead, when first getting on US 276, you can still see a constructed pillar denoting Pisgah National Forest. The ranger station/visitor center where this ride starts is also chock-full of historical and practical information about Pisgah National Forest. The visitor center also offers water, restrooms, and shaded picnic tables. If you prefer a riverside picnic, you will pass Sycamore Flats Picnic Area en route to the trailhead.

Consider combining a camping excursion at Davidson River Campground with your ride. It couldn't be more convenient. The large wooded camp with 144 sites is spread out onto eight loops just across from the trailhead. Open April through November, hot showers and water spigots are available at Davidson River Campground. Located within Pisgah National Forest, it is close to many attractions there yet is within 2 miles of Brevard. Speaking of Brevard and its sister town of Pisgah Forest, they both offer all manner of shopping and dining, with Brevard leading the way in live music. Using this ride you could easily visit Brevard and pedal back to your campsite on the Davidson River or just make a day trip of it.

Miles and Directions

0.0 Start at the Pisgah National Forest ranger station/visitor center. Pedal the entrance road east to two-lane US 276. Carefully cross the road and join a gravel doubletrack running alongside the Davidson River to your right.

0.4 Reach the Davidson River Campground access bridge over the Davidson River. The large camp is to your right. Keep straight here, passing through a parking area for the Art Loeb Trail, also popular with tubers and anglers. Continue down the left bank of the Davidson River in attractive woods (a trail also runs down the right bank here). In summer, all manner of water activities will be taking place in the cool, clear mountain stream.

0.7 Cross an iron pedestrian/bicycle bridge over the Davidson River. Look upstream and downstream to appreciate the well-loved waterway. Cruise on a smooth gravel path through a flat, curving right with a bend in the river. Look around for some huge sycamore trees shading the path. User-created side trails extend to the Davidson River.

1.2 Come directly alongside the Davidson River at a bend. Sycamore Flats Picnic Area stands across the moving water. A gravel bar inside this bend is a popular water play area. On our side of the river, a stream comes in on the right and is spanned by a

Estatoe Trail and Greenway

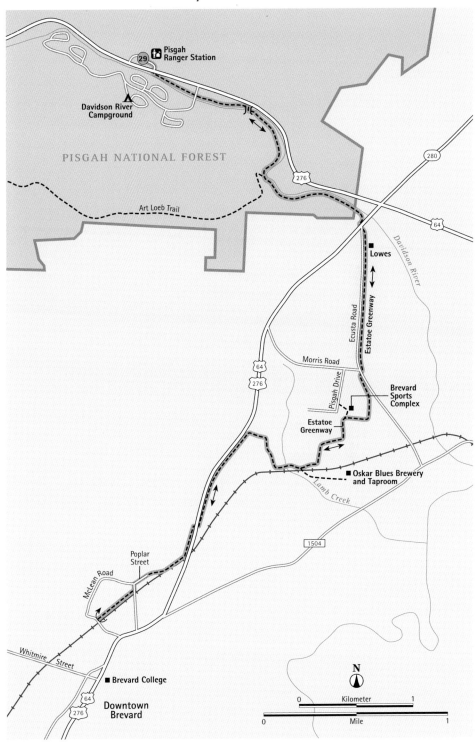

bridge. Just beyond the bridges the Art Loeb Trail leaves right for the high country. The Estatoe Trail continues down the right bank of the Davidson River, banked against a wet bluff with many spring seeps over which boardwalks have been lain.

1.5 Pedal beside an old quarry, now partly grown over and looking almost natural. Keep downriver.

1.8 Leave the national forest, passing a USGS water gauge, then emerge at US 64. Cross US 64 at a traffic light, picking up the Estatoe Greenway, Brevard's primary dedicated bike path. You are running parallel to Ecusta Road and pedaling in front of Lowes. Pass a roundabout and keep along Ecusta Road.

2.6 Cross Ecusta Road. Here the greenway enters the greater Brevard Sports Complex, with ballfields aplenty. Roll through parkland, gaining good mountain views to the north as the highlands of Pisgah National Forest rise to mile-high heights and the Blue Ridge Parkway.

3.0 Reach a T intersection. Head left here as a spur going right heads to a neighborhood. Continue winding through fields and woods.

3.4 A spur leads left to Oskar Blues Brewery and Taproom and a neighborhood.

3.5 Bridge Lamb Creek, draining Pisgah National Forest then flowing through Brevard. The trail turns north.

3.8 Briefly come along Hospital Road then turn south, running along US 64, still on dedicated greenway.

4.4 Cross US 64 at a traffic light with Osborne Road. Keep south along a busy section of US 64, passing businesses.

4.6 Head away from US 64, now following a long boardwalk overlain on the former Southern Railroad right-of-way. Head southwest. Ahead, turn away from the rail line and bridge a small stream.

4.8 Emerge onto quiet Poplar Street at a dead end. Follow the road to then cross Fisher Road. Here the greenway turns south then heads right, back on the old railroad right-of-way.

5.2 Reach McLean Road and current trail terminus. Brevard College and downtown are very close. Backtrack.

10.4 Arrive back at the ranger station/visitor center.

30 Blue Ridge Parkway Ride

This Blue Ridge Parkway sampler road ride starts high and stays high. But despite the elevation, the hills on this road riding adventure aren't bad. In fact, it is one of the more level stretches of the Parkway in the greater Asheville area. You will start at Devil's Courthouse Overlook then head southbound on the scenic road, passing numerous views, overlooks, and hiking trails along the way. The first part of the ride is the most level, with a final climb to end at Cowee Mountains Overlook. From there, return to the point of origin.

Start: Devil's Courthouse Overlook

Distance: 16.8 miles out and back

Riding time: 2–3 hours

Difficulty: Moderate

Terrain and surface type: Asphalt track on crest of the Blue Ridge

Highlights: Extensive views, high-elevation forest

Hazards: Vehicles on Blue Ridge Parkway

Other considerations: Avoid this high-elevation ride in winter.

Maps: Blue Ridge Parkway

Trail contacts: Blue Ridge Parkway, 199 Hemphill Knob Rd., Asheville, NC 28803; (828) 348-3400; nps.gov/blri

Finding the trailhead: From Asheville take I-26 East to exit 33 (NC 191/Blue Ridge Parkway). Join NC 191 South and continue for 2.4 miles to the Blue Ridge Parkway. Turn right and follow the Parkway southbound for 29 miles. Turn left into the Devil's Courthouse Overlook parking area, on the left at Blue Ridge Parkway milepost 422.4. GPS: N35° 18' 18.9" / W82° 53' 58.2"

The Ride

Don't we wish we could ride the entire 469 miles of the Blue Ridge Parkway? The scenic road starts at Virginia's Shenandoah National Park and runs along the crest of the Blue Ridge into North Carolina to end at Great Smoky Mountains National Park. For most of us this Parkway ride will remain a dream—we're hampered by either time or ability. It is very important to be an accurate judge of your pedaling prowess before tackling long stretches of this asphalt ribbon winding over mountains, down to gaps, and over creeks and rivers. Be a defensive bicycler—and be alert for motorists. Parkway drivers travel slower than on

Start your Parkway ride at the Devil's Courthouse.

other roadways, but auto tourists are enjoying the sights too. Take your time and savor the overlooks, allowing for rest. *Note:* Bicycles are not allowed on Parkway trails but are allowed on many of the trails in Pisgah National Forest, which abuts Parkway property on both sides in this area.

Although it serves as a bridge between two worthy parks, the Blue Ridge Parkway is rich with destinations of its own. In addition to road bicycling, an abundance of outdoor adventures awaits you, whether exhilarating drives to inspiring overlooks, walks to waterfalls, hikes to historic sites, or camping where you can reconnect with nature.

Whether it is a few days or a few hours, adventures on the Blue Ridge Parkway will scratch your mountain itch yet leave you desiring to see more of what lies around the next curve. Here are the Parkway basics: The Blue Ridge Parkway is a linear, two-lane scenic road designed for auto touring, with leisure and sightseeing in mind. Concrete posts—numbered every mile—keep you apprised of your whereabouts. The Parkway has limited entrances and exits and also has a lower than average vehicle speed limit—maximum 45 miles per hour.

Plenty of wildlife can and will be seen. Watch for alluring sights and picturesque pullovers—and for deer crossing the road. Keep an eye peeled for motorcyclists as well. The motorized two-wheeled set loves the Parkway too.

The Parkway is not only a scenic motorway but also a conduit for exploring trails along the Blue Ridge. Hiking is a time-honored favorite of visitors, who engage in treks ranging from little leg stretchers to all-day adventures, even overnight backpacks for those so inclined. Road riders can pull over and take a little walk themselves.

Closures for snow and inclement weather are not uncommon. Luckily, the Parkway's website (nps.gov/blri) offers real-time road closure information for specific stretches of road, sparing you the time and hassle of finding the Parkway closed.

Even if we aren't ready to take on the whole thing, we can pedal a part of the Parkway, especially considering that it runs directly through the Asheville area. If driving the Blue Ridge Parkway during the warm season, you will almost always see bicyclers tackling the mountains over which the scenic road rolls. And some of the climbs are staggering for your average bicycler. Making the ascent from Asheville to the Mount Pisgah area—more than 3,000 net feet in 14 miles, not counting downhills as the Blue Ridge rolls—requires training before undertaking it. However, you can start your ride in the high country and make the long downhill run from Mount Pisgah to Asheville. You can pick up some serious speeds on that ride—be very careful.

The stretch of Parkway on our recommended ride is a microcosm of the greater, longer endeavor along America's favorite scenic road. For almost the entire ride, you are over a mile high, making it a great place to pedal during the summer season. Additionally, you can enjoy the spruce-dotted high-country forests found only along the higher mantles of western North Carolina. The net climb is 1,300 feet and net descent 900 feet. (Of course when you turn around, you will descend 1,300 feet and climb 900 feet.) By the way, if you want to pedal through a tunnel, start your ride 0.7 mile toward Asheville at Fetterbush Overlook, milepost 421.7. Then you can ride through the 665-foot-long Devil's Courthouse Tunnel, adding the tunnel experience, for better or worse.

The Devil's Courthouse is your starting point. The massive rock outcrop looms on the horizon; because it is a peregrine falcon nesting place, the trail to its summit is periodically closed. Head southbound (more than 5,400 feet high), where northern hardwoods of birch mingle with red spruce and Fraser fir. Elevation changes are less than 200 feet for the first 4 miles, then you reach Haywood Gap and the ride's low point at 5,225 feet. Along the way you will pass

Views like this will lure your eyes
toward distant horizons.

Blue Ridge Parkway Ride

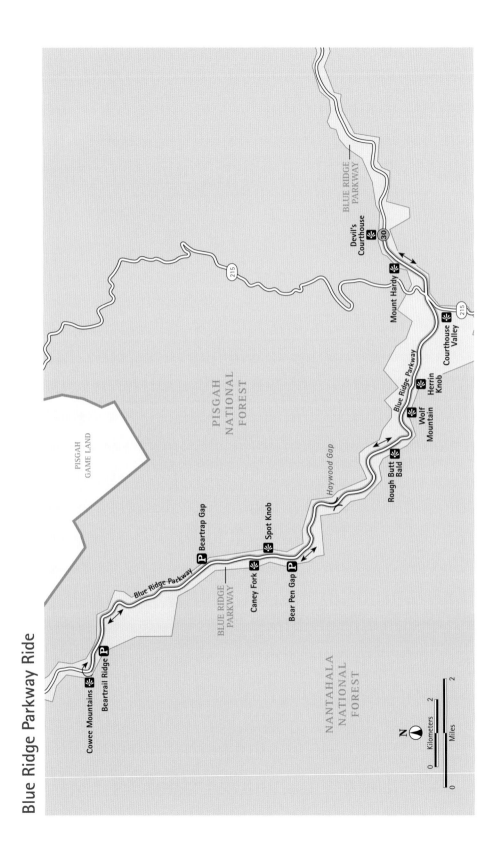

the intersection with NC 215 as it crosses the Blue Ridge. From there you have more up than down, rising to Spot Knob; then comes a respite. The last 1.7 miles are up, but you near 6,000 feet before reaching Cowee Mountains Overlook, an inspiring long and open view, and a just reward for your efforts. The backtrack is easier. Hopefully this ride will be a good primer for you to try other road rides on the Parkway.

Miles and Directions

0.0   Start at Devil's Courthouse Overlook, with a scenic view, hiking trail, and picnic table. Head southbound on the Parkway. The road dips to Beech Gap then toward the base of prominent Mount Hardy.

0.4   Pass the Mount Hardy Overlook. Ahead, roll beyond the intersection with NC 215.

1.1   Pass the Courthouse Valley Overlook.

1.6   Pass the Herrin Knob Overlook.

2.0   Pass the Wolf Mountain Overlook, with a good view to the west.

2.6   Reach the Rough Butt Bald Overlook. A short connector foot trail links to the Mountains-to-Sea Trail. Keep rolling southbound.

3.7   Come to the ride's low point at Haywood Gap; no parking or overlook here, just a hiking trail crossing.

5.3   Pass the Bear Pen Gap parking area.

6.0   Enjoy the spruce-fir forest around the Spot Knob Overlook.

6.2   Pass the views from Caney Fork Overlook.

6.7   Reach Beartrap Gap Overlook, labeled "Reinhart Gap" on official USGS quadrangle maps. Begin the final climb, ascending around the east side of Reinhart Knob.

8.0   Pass the Beartrail Ridge parking area, on your left. Keep climbing.

8.4   Come to Cowee Mountains Overlook. You are just short of 6,000 feet elevation. Immense panoramas open to the west. This is a good place to turn around. Backtrack.

16.8   Arrive back at Devil's Courthouse Overlook.

PADDLING ADVENTURES

Paddling is a fun way to complement hiking and bicycling adventures. The paddling possibilities in and around Asheville run the gamut from whitewater to stillwater and waters between the two. Should we expect anything less? Here you can paddle the mighty French Broad River straight into downtown Asheville—seeing nearby city sights and green mountains rising in the yon. Other segments of the French Broad present rapids and scenery in a more-remote setting. Flatwater enthusiasts will find paddles on nearby Lake Julian and the large impoundment of Lake James. Perhaps you will seek a smaller mountain impoundment such as Bear Creek Lake, with its wild waterfalls. You can grab a first-rate view at Lake Oolenoy while paddling its clear, clear waters, or visit the quiet coves of Lake Adger. Do you hear them? The paddling waters of greater Asheville are calling you.

Lake James is a great place to paddle in summertime (adventure 34).

31 French Broad River: Redmon Dam to Barnard

Have a fun, action-packed paddle amid easy but often-rocky rapids.

Start: Redmon Dam River Access

End: Barnard River Access

Length: 5.5 miles

Float time: About 2.4 hours

Difficulty rating: Moderate

Rapids: Class I–II

River/Lake type: Big mountain river

Current: Moderate

River gradient: 11.2 feet per mile

Water gauge: French Broad River at Marshall (Check frenchbroadpaddle.com/gauges/ for runnability.)

Season: Apr through Oct

Land status: Private

Fees or permits: No fees or permits required

Nearest city/town: Marshall

Maps: USGS Spring Creek NC; French Broad Paddling Trail

Boats used: Kayaks, canoes, a few johnboats, a few rafts

Organizations: French Broad River Paddling Trail; frenchbroadpaddle.com

Contacts/Outfitters: Nantahala Outdoor Center—French Broad River Outpost, 9825 Hwy. 25/70, Marshall, NC 28753; (828) 649-9480; noc.com

Put-in/Takeout Information

To the takeout: From Asheville take I–26 West to exit 19 (Marshall), and join US 70 West for 15 miles. Turn left on Sharp Hollow Road and follow it for 1.1 miles; turn left on Barnard Road. Stay with Barnard Road for 1.2 miles to the bridge over the French Broad River, turning left just before the bridge to the Barnard river access. GPS: N35° 50' 18" / W82° 45' 16"

To the put-in from the takeout: Backtrack from Barnard to US 70. Turn right on US 70 East and follow it for 2.6 miles. Turn right onto Little Pine Road and continue for 1 mile. Turn left onto Sweet Water Road and continue 0.4 mile. Turn

A paddler scans downstream for rapids.

right onto Redmon Road and follow it for 0.6 mile, passing under a one-lane railroad bridge just before reaching the put-in, on your left. GPS: N35° 47' 39" / W82° 42' 43"

Paddle Summary

This is an excellent training paddle for those who want to break into a little whitewater action without getting in too deep. The river run is generally Class I rapids but does have a single Class II spiller that is not difficult. What makes this section of the French Broad both fun and a great training section are the nearly continuous rapids and shoals among which you will navigate. Sometimes you will work around rocks and at other times through shallows, twisting and turning and scanning downriver for a line. It keeps the action going. And the scenery is wonderful too—wooded mountains rise from this section of the river just as it is beginning to cut through the chain of the Appalachians. Just make sure the water levels are not too high, where you may get swamped, or too low, where you will be constantly dragging through the rocks.

River/Lake Overview

Purportedly the third-oldest river in the world (only the New River of the United States and the Egypt's Nile River are older; these claims are not settled), the French Broad River is born in the high mountains of western North Carolina near the town of Rosman, where the forks of the French Broad come together. From there the waterway flows 116 miles in a wide arc through Asheville and the Tar Heel State to push through the crest of the Appalachians into Tennessee. An already big waterway by the time it crosses the Tennessee state line, the French Broad continues dropping in shoals and pools before slowing as it enters Douglas Lake. It once again begins flowing below Douglas Dam and travels a little less than 40 miles to its end near Knoxville, for a total of 102 miles in the Volunteer State. Here the Holston and French Broad Rivers meet to form the Tennessee River, all part of the greater Mississippi River watershed.

The Paddling

Despite having a gradient of more than 10 feet per mile, this section of the French Broad is paddleable by recreational kayakers and canoeists. And it offers the gorge-like mountain scenery for which the next downriver segment—flowing through the Appalachian chain—is known. At the Barnard takeout you will see whitewater rafters and helmeted kayakers preparing to paddle. But don't be alarmed; they are all heading downstream. It is at Barnard where the rapids of the French Broad get hairy. Our section from Redmon Dam to Barnard is ideal for recreational paddlers who want to dip their toes in a little fast-moving water—no helmets required.

At the put-in below Redmon Dam, you will see anglers casting a line from shore as well as recreational paddlers like us. Just upstream, the river roars from 80-foot-high, river-wide Redmon Dam, making for a noisy put-in. At this point the French Broad stretches more than 200 feet across and is already showing its dark tan, partly submerged rocks. The waterway shows no mercy, instantly requiring heads-up navigation amid the stones and shallows that pose no real hazard yet do necessitate continual attention. Ridges rise 1,000 feet or more above the river, giving the gorge a montane touch. A rail line runs along the right bank throughout the paddle yet does not deter from the scenery.

Sunscreen is always a good idea, even if you look goofy putting it on.

At 0.5 mile float under the Little Pine Road bridge then curve left, coming to the confluence with Caney Creek at 1.1 miles. This is a major tributary in this section and also marks where no roads pass completely through the gorge for some miles, giving you an idea of the ruggedness of the vale the French Broad is cutting. The river narrows here and shows off some straightforward Class I shoals.

Continuing downstream, a partly wooded bluff with rhododendron, maple, and other thick vegetation crowds the bank. Heading north, you will run downstream in a segment typical of the French Broad here. The waterway is wide and at normal flows offers multiple routes downstream—no single clear, simple route—meaning that if you went down this segment five times, I bet you would take five different lines working down the river. So just keep on your toes and try to look downstream, planning your next move, while you are making the moves right in front of you. Depending on the water level, you may have to ferry across the river side to side while working your way down. Tipping over is less of a hazard than is simply bumping into rocks or picking the wrong channel and having that channel become too shallow for your boat. If this happens, simply push yourself from the shallows and carry on. Most important, just take your time and enjoy the ride, not fretting over taking the perfect route—there isn't one.

Willows and ash line the banks. At 1.8 miles, as you are bending right, come to the Class II rapid. You have some initial shoals and then drop off a little ledge with multiple routes. A nice little beach on river right just after this rapid makes

French Broad River: Redmon Dam to Barnard

Dancing among the rocks on this segment of the French Broad

for a good stopping spot. At 2.0 miles pass some islands on river right. At 2.6 miles the river bends left and becomes a continuous Class I shoal, fun to navigate. While you are in the middle of this long rapid, Pawpaw Creek enters on river left and Walnut Creek enters on river right. Gravel bars are normally formed at these creek mouths. Beyond the water, wooded ridges rise overhead, lending a wild aspect to the adventure.

The river is narrower here than it was at Redmon Dam. At 3.9 miles the French Broad curves left (northwesterly). At 4.1 miles you enter a long section of Class I rapids that include a plethora of exposed rocks. Here the paddle can resemble a fun paddler's slalom event. This is another spot to gain valuable experience, making your way downstream without significant hazard at normal flows. At 4.6 miles Anderson Branch enters on river left and you begin to see a few riverside dwellings in the riverside flats. Continue working down the river; when you see the Barnard Road bridge, start getting over to river right. Before the bridge on your right, reach the Barnard river access at 5.5 miles, completing this fun, action-packed paddle. Now you can hold your head high among the intrepid whitewater kayakers and rafters heading downstream from Barnard.

32 French Broad River: Westfeldt to Bent Creek

This classic urban float leads you through relaxing waters and easy shoals, ending at Bent Creek near the Blue Ridge Parkway.

Start: Westfeldt River Park

End: Bent Creek River Access

Length: 8.6 miles

Float time: About 4 hours

Difficulty rating: Moderate

Rapids: Class I

River/Lake type: Large river

Current: Moderate

River gradient: 4.1 feet per mile

Water gauge: French Broad River at Blantyre (Check frenchbroadpaddle.com/ gauges/ for runnability.)

Season: Year-round

Land status: Private

Starting out at the Westveldt boat ramp

Fees or permits: No fees or permits required

Nearest city/town: Asheville

Maps: USGS Skyland NC; French Broad Paddling Trail

Boats used: Kayaks, canoes, tubes, johnboats, rafts, dories

Organizations: French Broad River Paddling Trail; frenchbroadpaddle.com

Contacts/outfitters: Lazy Otter Outfitters, 10 Banner Farm Rd., Mills River, NC 28759; (828) 756-1386; lazyotteroutfitters.com

Put-in/Takeout Information

To the takeout: From Asheville take I-26 East to exit 37 and then US 191 South for 2.4 miles to the Bent Creek river access, on your left. GPS: N35° 30' 05.9" / W82° 35' 35.3"

To the put-in from the takeout: Leave the Bent Creek river access and continue on US 191 South for 5.8 miles. Turn left on Old Fanning Bridge Road and follow it for 1.9 miles; keep right at the traffic circle, joining Ferncliff Park Road. Stay with Ferncliff Park Road for 0.6 mile. Turn right into Westfeldt River Park; follow the park road to end at the parking area and boat ramp. GPS: N35° 25' 19.5" / W82° 32' 30.9"

Paddle Summary

This urban paddle run with a simple shuttle is convenient for Asheville and Hendersonville residents. Start at Westfeldt River Park then make an easy float north, with Blue Ridge views from a wide stretch of the French Broad River. Occasional simple shoals speed you up along the way. A popular run in summer, you will share the river with river floaters of all stripes, from anglers to tubers. This being an urban float, you will paddle by the Asheville airport as well as along I-26 for a distance, but the pluses far outweigh the minuses.

River/Lake Overview

Purportedly the third-oldest river in the world (only the New River of the United States and Egypt's Nile River are older; these claims are not settled), the French Broad River is born in the high mountains of western North Carolina near the town of Rosman, where the forks of the French Broad come together. From there

Summer is a great time to be on the river.

the waterway flows 116 miles in a wide arc through Asheville and the Tar Heel State to push through the crest of the Appalachians into Tennessee. An already big waterway by the time it crosses the Tennessee state line, the French Broad continues dropping in shoals and pools before being slowed as it enters Douglas Lake. It once again begins flowing below Douglas Dam and travels a little less than 40 miles to its end near Knoxville, for a total of 102 miles in the Volunteer State. Here the Holston and French Broad Rivers meet to form the Tennessee River, all part of the greater Mississippi River watershed.

The Paddling

This section of the French Broad is squeezed between more-popular runs for kayakers and canoers. However, all sections of the French Broad in the urban area are well loved. This keeps the accesses hopping, so consider executing these urban trips early in the morning or during off-times, such as during the week or in cooler weather. A mild day during the cold season would be an excellent time to enjoy this paddle.

Westfeldt River Park offers a large parking area, a single ramp and a dock—and a walking trail if you are so inclined. The NC 280 bridge (Boylston Highway) is just upstream of the put-in. Leave the ramp on the French Broad, at this point a relatively narrow waterway about 100 feet in width. It will get much wider downstream, especially where the rocky shoals are found.

French Broad River: Westfeldt to Bent Creek

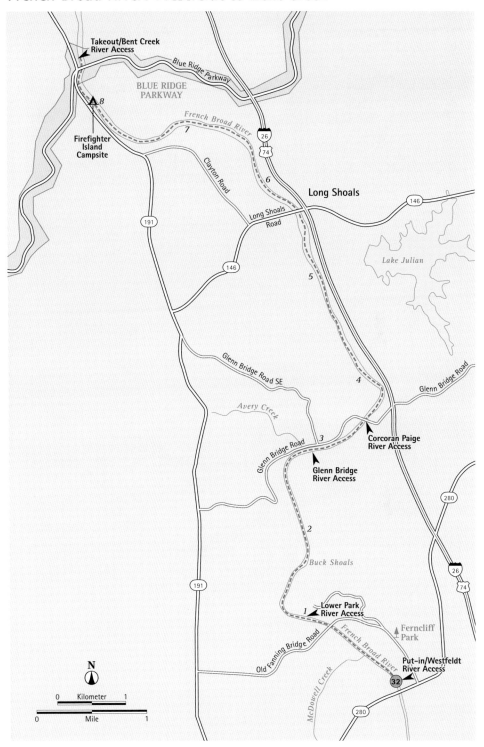

The launch at Bent Creek is a great place
to interact with other paddlers.

The first part of the paddle presents a steady current and smooth surface, allowing you to get organized and in paddling mode. River birch, maple ash, and sycamore rise from soil banks. Fallen trees are common in the waters beside the banks. At 0.4 mile McDowell Creek enters on your left. Continue paddling north, floating under the Old Fanning Bridge Road bridge at 0.7 mile. Just ahead, on your right at 1.0 mile, is the Lower Park river access. Lower Park is on Sierra Nevada Brewing Company property. They open Lower Park seasonally on weekends during the warm season, April through October. I don't recommend it as an access; other nearby accesses are more reliably open year-round.

The paddling remains easy on a gentle river run. You may hear planes from the airport nearby. The river bends right and you reach named Buck Shoals at 1.7 miles. Note the V-shaped lower end of the shoals. This may have been a Native American fish trap at one time. The shoals are mild. The French Broad widens here, and rocks become exposed. At 2.9 miles the river bends right. Here, Avery Creek enters on your left and the signed Glenn Bridge access is on the right. Keeping downstream, paddle by Corcoran Paige River Park, on your right at the Glenn Bridge Road crossing at 3.5 miles.

Beyond Glenn Bridge, the French Broad widens and runs roughly parallel to I-26. Ahead, views open of the Blue Ridge rising to your left. Light rapids and shoals speed you along. Watch out for submerged rocks here. The water speeds. In this section you will also pass a tubing outfit that sends floaters on the water in the summertime. It makes for an entertaining people-watching experience. This long section culminates at 5.3 miles in Long Shoals, light but extended rapids that are fun to run. The Long Shoals Road bridge is in sight below; you float under it at 5.6 miles. From here the river pulls away from I-26 and the banks are forested.

The French Broad makes an easy curve left; the Blue Ridge Parkway stands on a forested ridge above. Come to Firefighter Island at 7.2 miles. This is one of the designated riverside campsites you can reserve through the French Broad River Paddling Trail organization. Stay right around the island, passing the main camp on the isle's sandy lower end. Ahead, curve into light shoals and edge toward the left side of the river, passing the tube operation takeout at a flat known as Sandy Bottom. The French Broad narrows at the Blue Ridge Parkway bridge that you float under at 8.5 miles. Just ahead on your left is the Bent Creek river access and your takeout at 8.6 miles. I recommend paddling to the lower end of the access then paddling up Bent Creek itself to take out.

33 Lake Julian

This paddle at Lake Julian—a Buncombe County park—is close, local, and fun.

Start/End: Lake Julian Park boat ramp

Length: 3.7 miles

Float time: About 2 hours

Difficulty rating: Easy

Rapids: None

River/Lake type: Power plant cooling lake

Current: None

River gradient: None

Water gauge: None

Season: Year-round

Land status: Mostly public

Fees or permits: Daily boat launch fee required

Nearest city/town: Asheville

Maps: USGS Skyland NC

Boats used: Kayaks, canoes, standup paddleboards, sailboats, johnboats, paddleboats

A confidant paddleboarder on Lake Julian

Organizations: North Carolina Wildlife Resources Commission, 1701 Mail Service Center, Raleigh, NC 27699; ncwildlife.org

Contacts/Outfitters: Lake Julian Park, 406 Overlook Extension, Arden, NC 28704; (828) 684-0376; buncombecounty.org

Put-in/Takeout Information

To the put-in/takeout: From I-26 south of Asheville, take exit 37 (Skyland/Long Shoals Road). Join NC 146 East for 1.1 miles then turn right at a traffic light on Overlook Road Extended. Immediately enter Lake Julian Park; follow the park loop road right then descend toward the lake, reaching the boat ramp on your right. Remember to get a launch permit, available at the small office just south of the boat ramp. GPS: N35° 28' 50" / W82° 32' 22"

Mountains frame a paddleboarder on Lake Julian.

Paddle Summary

Paddle this clear, no-motors lake conveniently close to Asheville. Launch from a facility-rich Buncombe County park, replete with mountain views. From there begin circling the impoundment, first cruising along the park shores, where you will see picnicking and relaxation possibilities. Curve past the park marina and boat rental area before cruising along Buck Shoals Road. Continue along wooded shores, entering an arm of the lake, also part of Lake Julian Park. From here paddle by the Asheville steam plant—the reason for the lake's existence—to circle the lake near its dam. Enjoy more wooded scenery before completing the paddle circuit. Although a steam plant sits beside the lake, the park facilities and the no-gas-motors lake more than make up for the plant's presence. The convenience of Lake Julian is an added bonus.

River/Lake Overview

Lake Julian came to be in 1964 as part of a Duke Energy coal-fired plant delivering electricity to the greater Asheville area. The lake provided water for the plant and was used as a cooling agent. The dam here backs up approximately 300 acres of lake fed by streams flowing off nearby Brown Mountain and Crescent Hill, uplands rising approximately 800 feet above Lake Julian. Below the dam, an unnamed stream pushes the waters of Lake Julian a short distance to the French Broad River at Long Shoals.

The Paddling

This paddle is on a lake created as part of a power plant facility, and you can't escape that fact. However, the lake itself is very attractive, and much of the time the power plant is not in view. I believe the convenience of the paddling location and the existence of the county park here more than outweigh the negatives. A trip around the lake can make for a great morning or evening outing. On a nice day the impoundment will be alive with area residents on their favorite watercraft—as long as it doesn't use a gas motor. Kayakers and canoers will be out in force, and families will be renting paddleboats. Lake Julian is also a standup paddleboard hotbed. Others will be on the water in their own boats—the park offers a private boat storage facility. Even the Asheville Sailing Club is located here!

Formerly a coal-fired steam plant originally built by Carolina Power & Light in 1964, the Duke Energy facility has been replaced by a much cleaner natural gas plant on its 700 acres south of Lake Julian. The price tag for replacing the coal-fired plant was nearly 1 billion dollars, but sulfur dioxide emissions have been reduced by 99 percent and mercury emissions completely eliminated. While paddling, appreciate the delivery of power in a cleaner fashion.

Make sure to get your boat launch permit before embarking onto Lake Julian. The permit office is within sight of the launch. A single ramp and small dock are located on a quiet cove of Lake Julian Park. Leave the dock and paddle the extraordinarily clear lake with a greenish tint. Head southeast from the cove, making a clockwise circuit of the impoundment. The Duke Energy complex is across the lake. First paddle by the park office and paddleboat rental dock area while circling a peninsula containing most of the park facilities, including picnic areas, benches, and fishing piers.

On a nice day you will see parkgoers relaxing in the shade, feeding the ducks, and just kicking back. At 0.4 mile float past a park fishing pier and then come to the park's boat storage facility. Here you will see watercraft of all descriptions, including small sailboats, johnboats, kayaks, and canoes, which local residents leave here for a fee then conveniently launch here at Lake Julian. Continue working into a cove near Long Shoals Road, paddling by a second fishing pier. Here, tucked into a corner of the lake at 0.6 mile and standing above an alluring little beach, is a restaurant. If they are open, you can land your watercraft on the beach and grab a cold beverage and a meal. Otherwise continue circling the cove, coming directly alongside Long Shoals Road, which brings a little traffic noise to the otherwise scenic atmosphere.

Explore wooded shoreline, leaving the cove; turn into a second cove at 1.2 miles, heading easterly. Mountain views open in the distance. Here you circle a designated bank fishing area, where churning water enters the lake from below—part of the power plant. This is no danger to the paddler, but the moving water may surprise. Your paddling circuit now comes to its most easterly point near some railroad tracks. An upper part of the lake is on the far side of the tracks but is closed to paddlers. Enjoy more natural shoreline with westerly views of the Blue Ridge before coming to the plant facility at 2.3 miles.

This is not the best part of the paddle, but bear with it. You will skim over shallows beside the facility (note the abundance of shells) and come to the lake dam at 2.9 miles. More mountain views open beyond the low dam. Open lake views will reveal paddlers and anglers aplenty on the lake.

Lake Julian

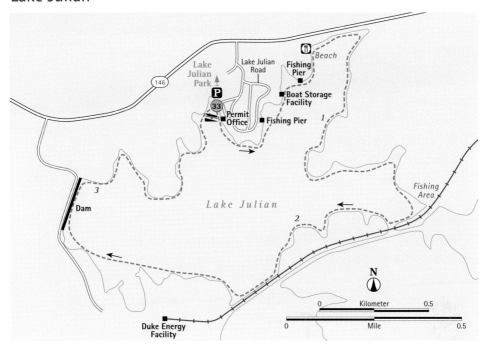

Standup paddleboarders love Lake Julian and are often seen here. Water lovers have been transporting themselves on some form of "paddleboard" on the water for thousands of years, and of course surfboarding is a popular activity along the coasts, but today's standup paddleboarding took off around the world after 2000, reaching the US mainland in force a decade later. Today the paddlers of standup boards ply both flat and moving water, and the market continues to expand. Designs and materials used continue to evolve. Enthusiasts also fish, take overnight trips, and even do yoga while atop a standup paddleboard. Give it a try here at Lake Julian.

You soon find yourself on the wooded north shore of Lake Julian, reaching the mouth of a cove at 3.1 miles. Curve around a point and pass a few houses above the water before returning to the park boat ramp, completing the paddling adventure at 3.7 miles.

34 Lake James: Catawba River Arm

Explore scenic, mountain-rimmed Lake James along the shoreline of Lake James State Park.

Start/End: Canal Bridge boat ramp

Length: 4.5 miles

Float time: About 2.8 hours

Difficulty rating: Easy

Rapids: None

River/Lake type: Mountain impoundment

Current: None

River gradient: None

Water gauge: duke-energy.com/community/lakes (Lake levels are reported with normal full pond elevation of 100 feet.)

Season: Year-round; best May through Oct

Land status: Public—Lake James State Park; some private, Duke Energy property

Fees or permits: No fees or permits required

Nearest city/town: Marion

Maps: USGS Ashford NC; Lake James State Park

Lake James is a great place to paddle in summertime.

Boats used: Kayaks, canoes, motorboats, houseboats

Organizations: Duke Energy

Contacts/outfitters: Lake James State Park, 321 NC 126, Nebo, NC 28761; (828) 584-7728; ncparks.gov

Put-in/Takeout Information

To the put-in/takeout: From exit 94 on I-40 east of Marion, take Dysartsville Road north for 0.7 mile. Turn left on US 70 West and follow it for 1.7 miles. Turn right on Bridgewater Road and continue 1.3 miles. Turn left on Benfields Landing Road and follow it for 2.2 miles; turn left on NC 126 West. Follow NC 126 West for just a short distance; turn right and follow the access road into the Canal Bridge boat ramp, 0.2 mile from NC 126. GPS: N35° 44' 22.0" / W81° 51' 194"

Paddle Summary

This paddle explores the shoreline of Lake James near the main lake dam and along the shores of the Catawba River Area of Lake James State Park. Leave the Canal Bridge boat ramp and paddle south, passing the main dam and spillway of Lake James. Come along the wooded and protected shoreline of Lake James State Park. Here you curve in and out of attractive forest-bordered coves, passing trail overlooks and park facilities, including a camper-only dock. Return to the main part of the impoundment, crossing the old Catawba River channel before returning to the Canal Bridge boat ramp. Along the way you can enjoy shoreline views in the near and mountain views in the distance.

River/Lake Overview

Lake James is a historic, large impoundment where the Catawba River, Paddy's Creek, and Linville River were dammed a century back. These three waterways drain a significant part of western North Carolina's high country east of the Blue Ridge, including fabled Linville Gorge. Lake James sits at the base of the Blue Ridge, where expansive mountain panoramas open from its waters. When Lake James was established in 1923 after seven years of work on its dams, not many people cared about living near mountains for the views or paddling the open waters under their mantle. James B. Duke, founder of Duke Power Company, was establishing hydropower for use in a growing Carolina market. The upper-most lake on the Catawba River, Lake James, named for Duke, stands at 1,200 feet elevation. More than 10 square miles of water surface—6,812 acres to be exact—stretch out beneath the hills and highlands. Around 150 miles of curving shoreline rise along the impoundment. The majority of shoreline is private, but there are public lands, such as the park shore of Lake James State Park, where this paddle takes place.

Unleashed below Lake James, the Catawba River takes an easterly tack through the foothills before turning southeasterly, making its way through the Charlotte–Gastonia metro complex, and is dammed numerous times. The Catawba River enters South Carolina then reaches Lake Wateree, where it becomes the Wateree River, is dammed a final time, then flows 80 miles to meet the Congaree River southeast of Columbia, where the two waters merge to create the Santee River.

The Paddling

The Canal Bridge area is where the two major segments of what became Lake James—the dammed waters of the Catawba and Linville Rivers—were linked by canal, explaining the unusual aerial map view of Lake James. The impoundment is essentially two lakes connected by this canal. The canal and the bridge over the canal are less than 0.5 mile from the put-in/takeout and are clearly visible during much of the paddle. Also visible is the long, angled, grass-topped dam by which you will soon paddle. This dam slowed the Catawba River, stopping its old channel.

Canal Bridge boat ramp has three lanes and can be busy on warm weekends. However, a self-propelled craft can easily launch on either side of the ramps. The launch area also offers a dock and a restroom. Do not park in the trailer-only spots.

Leave south from Canal Bridge, immediately cruising along the edge of the dam, where rock riprap rises to a grassy top. It isn't long before vistas open; the Blue Ridge rises to the northwest, and it is those majestic highlands that drain to form Lake James. At 0.5 mile pass the open spillway of the dam. In the distance to the south rise the South Mountains, much of which are protected as South Mountains State Park. Buoys line the spillway, rising above the clear green waters of Lake James. You will share the waters with fishing boats, pontoons, and personal watercraft during the warm season. However, boat traffic is less-ened once you are past the dam and paddling along the shoreline of Lake James

Billowing clouds rise above Lake James.

State Park, reached at 0.7 mile. Now you begin curving westerly with the shore. White oak, dogwood, pine, and cedar stand on the hillsides rising from the lake. Carolina red clay is exposed where wave action has eroded the shoreline. Look for ospreys watching you from the treetops.

The state park shore creates a natural environment along which to paddle; though, as a whole, Lake James is not heavily populated with homes compared to most other North Carolina lakes. These coves also cut down winds that can be troublesome to lake paddlers. Fallen trees form water obstacles and improve fish habitat. At 0.9 mile reach the Hidden Cove boat ramp, complete with a ramp dock and restroom. The name's origin is easy to figure out. The small cove bends in such a way that the head of the short cove cannot be seen from the main body of Lake James. Turn out of Hidden Cove, back into the main lake. Linville Mountain rises in the yon as you paddle beneath a tall soil bluff before turning into the next cove, much bigger than Hidden Cove, at 1.3 miles. Trace the windings of this multipronged backwater, ideal for a paddler to explore. Note the frequent but small sand beaches that make convenient stopping spots for kayakers and canoers. Exposed rock protrudes from other areas.

When you paddle into the head of the small coves where streams enter, the air can feel decidedly cooler on a hot summer day. On land look for blackened tree trunks where the state park has used prescribed burnings to manage the terrain. Part of the state park's mission is to restore parcels of natural Carolina to its pre-Columbian state. Emerge from this second cove at 2.4 miles. You can clearly see the Canal Bridge, the Canal boat ramp, and the dam. Overhead, a large bluff

Lake James: Catawba River Arm

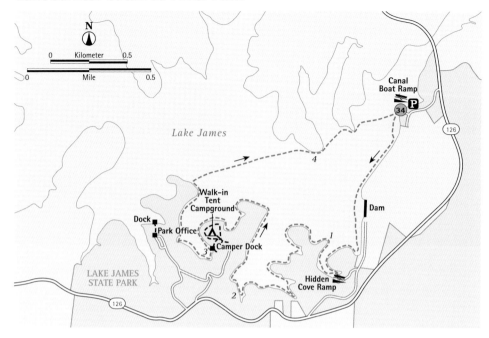

rises. Turn into the next cove at 2.6 miles. Here you will be coming along the twenty-site walk-in tent campground, favored by the active set. Campers must carry their gear 150 yards or more to their designated campsites, many of which overlook Lake James. Still others paddle their gear to the walk-in tent campground dock, reached at 3.0 miles, then carry their gear to their chosen campsite. This campground can be an ideal base camp for paddling this part of Lake James. The state park also presents a drive-up campground with thirty-three sites as well as a paddle-in camping area with thirty sites spread over three spots on the Long Arm Peninsula, in the Paddy's Creek area of the park.

The paddling continues beyond the walk-in campground. Continue along the thickly vegetated shoreline. At 3.3 miles enjoy a welcome beach in a small cove, delivering afternoon shade. This makes a good stopping spot before you cross Lake James. Leave the cove at 3.5 miles, where another tall bluff rises. If you are looking for more mileage, follow the park shoreline another 1.0 mile, passing the park office and its dock along the way. Otherwise, aim east-northeast, crossing the lake channel to reach the far side of the impoundment at 4.0 miles. Enjoy the montane panoramas while crossing the lake. Scattered houses with docks stand over here but are not obtrusive. The Canal Bridge boat ramp is within sight. Aim for the ramps, watching for boat traffic, and complete the loop paddle at 4.5 miles.

35 Lake James: Paddy's Creek Area

Enjoy shoreline paddling along the Paddy's Creek Area of Lake James State Park.

Start/End: Lake James State Park Swim Beach

Length: 6.1 miles

Float time: About 3.2 hours

Difficulty rating: Moderate

Rapids: None

River/Lake type: Mountain impoundment

Current: None

River gradient: None

Water gauge: duke-energy.com/community/lakes (Lake levels are reported with normal full pond elevation of 100 feet.)

Season: Year-round; best May through Oct

Land status: Public—Lake James State Park; a little Duke Energy property

Fees or permits: No fees or permits required

Nearest city/town: Marion

Maps: USGS Ashford NC; Lake James State Park

Boats used: Kayaks, canoes, motorboats, houseboats

Organizations: Duke Energy

Contacts/Outfitters: Lake James State Park, 321 NC 126, Nebo, NC 28761; (828) 584-7728; ncparks.gov

Put-in/Takeout Information

To the put-in/takeout: From Asheville take I-40 East to exit 90 (Nebo/Lake James). Turn right and join Harmony Grove Road then pass over the interstate. After 0.6 mile reach an intersection and stay right on Harmony Grove Road, following it for 2.2 more miles to the intersection with US 70 in Nebo; turn left. Follow US 70 West just a short distance then turn right on NC 126. Continue for 5 miles, passing the Catawba River section of Lake James State Park; turn right into the Paddy's Creek Area. Follow the main park road for 2.2 miles to dead-end at the large swimming beach area with its large parking lot. After parking, find the asphalt trail leading from the right side of the parking area as you face the lake. Follow it down to the right-hand side of the beach and launch from there. GPS: N35° 45' 02.0" / W81° 52' 45"

Paddle Summary

This fun paddling adventure explores intimate coves and waters of Lake James where nearly all the surrounding land is part of Lake James State Park. Being on less wide-open waters, you are less subject to wind and motorboats; though most likely you will experience some of both. The paddle starts with a boat carry from the swim beach parking area down an asphalt path to reach the west side of the swim beach—also where the state park rents canoes and kayaks if you need an extra boat. The paddle then curves past a large island and into a long embayment with many arms reaching into intimate coves. The scenic shoreline is wooded throughout; you will explore these coves, enjoying a quieter slice of Lake James. Stopping points are available. Along the way back, you will paddle alongside the Long Arm Peninsula. It offers three boat-in camping areas, if you are interested in such. Otherwise, your return trip loops back into the main lake and to the busy swim beach area.

River/Lake Overview

Lake James is a historic, large impoundment where the Catawba River, Paddy's Creek, and Linville River were dammed a century back. These three waterways drain a significant part of western North Carolina's high country east of the Blue Ridge, including fabled Linville Gorge. Lake James sits at the base of the Blue Ridge, where expansive mountain panoramas open from its waters. When Lake James was established in 1923 after seven years of work on its dams, not many people cared about living near mountains for the views or paddling the open waters under their mantle. James B. Duke, founder of Duke Power Company, was establishing hydropower for use in a growing Carolina market. The upper-most lake on the Catawba River, Lake James, named for Duke, stands at 1,200 feet elevation. More than 10 square miles of water surface—6,812 acres to be exact—stretch out beneath the hills and highlands. Around 150 miles of curving shoreline rise along the impoundment. The majority of shoreline is private, but there are public lands, such as the park shore of Lake James State Park, where this paddle takes place.

Unleashed below Lake James, the Catawba River takes an easterly tack through the foothills before turning southeasterly, making its way through the Charlotte-Gastonia metro complex, and is dammed numerous times. The

Launching from the Paddy's Creek Area of Lake James State Park

Catawba River enters South Carolina then reaches Lake Wateree, where it becomes the Wateree River, is dammed a final time, then flows 80 miles to meet the Congaree River southeast of Columbia, where the two waters merge to create the Santee River.

The Paddling

The carry from the parking area to the swim beach along an asphalt path stretches for about 60 yards. You pass a fishing pier along the way. Do not attempt to launch from there. After the carry, reach the west end of the swim beach and a great place from which to launch. The Paddy's Creek arm of Lake James extends to your right (west). You can see the Canal Bridge and the canal linking the Linville River Area (where you are) of Lake James to the Catawba River Area to your south.

Our paddling adventure heads east, keeping outside the buoys of the swim area. At 0.2 mile come along the picnic shelters overlooking the lake. This is a popular spot for lake lovers. Pass a deep embayment to your left at 0.3 mile and keep east, paddling around a point to turn northeast. Ahead you will see a narrow and shallow channel extending between the park to your left and a lake island owned by Duke Energy to your right. Take the channel. This shallow spot is avoided by motorboats due to the lack of depth. When the lake is drawn down in winter, the channel can become impassable. A beach on the island just after crossing the shallow is a popular stopping spot. However, no camping is allowed on this island.

By 0.8 mile you are in the main channel of the embayment lying between the park facilities to your left and Long Arm Peninsula to your right. The entire shoreline ahead is Lake James State Park and delivers a natural, unspoiled setting for the paddler. Linville Mountain rises in the distance and frames the attractive setting before you. Hardwoods line the shoreline along with pine— this would make an excellent autumn-color paddling trip. Work your way around or over fallen trees, now lying in the water at the shoreline's edge.

At 1.8 miles the embayment narrows and you pass through a water gate of sorts. In the distance, the rock cliffs of Shortoff Mountain stand out. Once through the water pass, the embayment widens and splits into two arms. At this point, head left and start cruising around this left-side embayment, itself a narrow water passage fingering into wooded hills. The narrowness of the embayment and the surrounding knolls lessen wind considerations. Curve your way into the fingers of the tarn, where small streams feed cool water and cool air to the lake during the warm-weather paddling season. These spots where stream meets lake can be very shallow. Keep apprised of the water depth as you paddle. Watch for fishing darting away as you paddle near.

At 3.0 miles you have cruised through both arms of this left-side embayment and are now curving north. The waters remain narrow and the shoreline alluring woodland, rich with sweetgum trees. Look for deer along the hillsides. You can't miss the chattering squirrels and singing birds. On the water, scan for easily startled herons; overhead, ospreys will complain incessantly before flying away if you paddle in their vicinity.

The paddling experience is good up here, although don't be surprised if you see pontoon boats parked in one of these quiet coves. Their presence affirms the alluring nature of this piece of Lake James. Work around the shores of this larger embayment. Look for wood duck nesting boxes in places. Enter the uppermost point of this eastern embayment, where an unnamed stream flows perennially. Here, willows, grasses, and brush form a transitioning wetland.

You are at 3.8 miles—the farthest point from the put-in at the swim beach. Begin working your way back southbound, with Long Arm Peninsula to your left. Pass through the narrows a final time at 4.4 miles. Stay with the left-hand shoreline. The waters widen and the South Mountains stand in the distance as you continue southerly. This embayment seems very large compared to the closed-in lake arms you've been paddling.

Lake James: Paddy's Creek Area

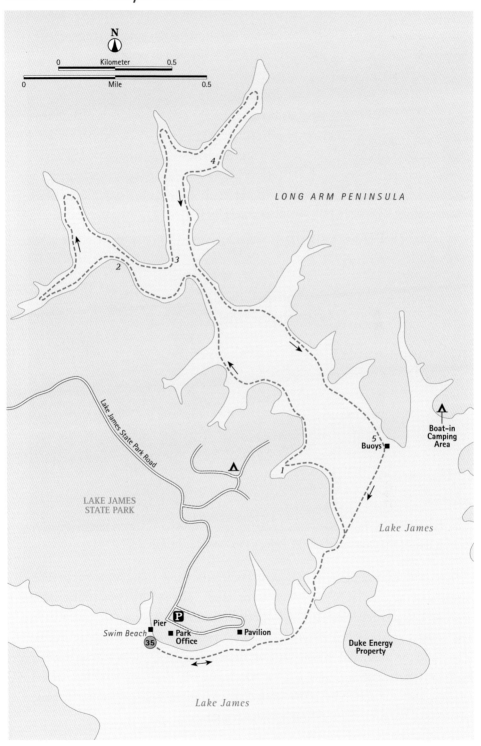

A kayaker plying Lake James with paddleboarders in the distance

Looking toward the swim beach at the Paddy's Creek paddler launch

At 5.1 miles, at a point of Long Arm Peninsula, come along some buoys indicating shallow waters. If you are camping at one of the three boat-in camping areas on Long Arm Peninsula, stay with the left-hand shoreline. Otherwise, turn southwest, crossing open waters to again cut between the Duke Energy–owned island and the mainland. If you want to add mileage, circle the island on the way back. Otherwise, from here it is a backtrack and you complete your loop at 6.1 miles. Additional activities in the immediate vicinity include swimming, fishing, picnicking, camping, hiking, and mountain biking.

36 French Broad River: Pisgah Forest to Blantyre

This rural float makes a gentle run through an agricultural section of the French Broad valley, a good river run for paddlers of all abilities.

Start: Pisgah Forest River Access

End: Blantyre Park

Length: 8.5 miles

Float time: About 4.2 hours

Difficulty rating: Easy

Rapids: Class I

River/Lake type: Medium-size agricultural river

Current: Gentle but steady

River gradient: 2.9 feet per mile

Water gauge: French Broad River at Blantyre (Check frenchbroadpaddle.com/gauges/ for runnability.)

Season: Mar through Oct

Land status: Private

Fees or permits: No fees or permits required

Nearest city/town: Pisgah Forest

Maps: USGS Horse Shoe NC; French Broad Paddling Trail

Boats used: Kayaks, canoes, johnboats

Organizations: French Broad River Paddling Trail; frenchbroadpaddle.com

Contacts/Outfitters: Lazy Otter Outfitters, 10 Banner Farm Rd., Mills River, NC 28759; (828) 756-1386; lazyotteroutfitters.com

Put-in/Takeout Information

To the takeout: From Asheville, take I-26 East to exit 40 (NC 280/Asheville Airport). Join NC 280 West and continue 7 miles. Turn left onto Ray Hill Road and follow it for 0.5 mile. Turn right onto Turnpike Road and continue for 2.8 miles. Turn right onto Brickyard Road and follow it for 0.3 mile. Turn left onto North Greenwood Forest and continue 0.5 mile. Turn right onto US 64 West and follow it for 1.6 miles. Turn left onto Grove Bridge Road and continue for 0.3 mile, bridging the French Broad River. After the bridge, turn left into the signed Blantyre Park river access. GPS: N35° 17' 56.8" / W82° 37' 23.2"

The French Broad is a smallish river near the town of Pisgah Forest.

To the put-in from the takeout: From Blantyre Park, backtrack across the Grove Bridge Road bridge to US 64. Turn left, joining US 64 West; continue for 3.5 miles. Turn left on Enon Road and follow it just a short piece. Turn right onto Old Hendersonville Highway. Stay with Old Hendersonville Highway for 3 miles then turn left onto Wilson Road, just after passing through a traffic light in the town of Pisgah Forest. Follow Wilson Road for 0.2 mile to the signed Pisgah Forest river access, on your left. GPS: N35° 15' 03.7" / W82° 41' 57.4"

Paddle Summary

This is a gentle float through a quiet agricultural area of the upper French Broad River valley. Despite its gentle nature, this section of the French Broad has a steady current flowing in a relatively narrow paddling area with standing trees on the shore and lots of tree snags in the water. Your biggest paddling challenge—and it isn't much—will be staying away from those tree snags. Mountain views come frequently as the Blue Ridge rises to the left of the river, with lesser mountains in the near. Although much of the surrounding region is level river valley, the waterway continually bumps against Shuford Mountain. Along the way the French Broad adds a major tributary in the Little River, flowing clear as it drains heralded DuPont State Forest among other upland terrain. Although the current is steady, allow plenty of time for the paddle so you can enjoy the scenery near and far.

River/Lake Overview

Purportedly the third-oldest river in the world (only the New River of the United States and Egypt's Nile River are older; these claims are not settled), the French Broad River is born in the high mountains of western North Carolina near the town of Rosman, where the forks of the French Broad come together. From there the waterway flows 116 miles in a wide arc through Asheville and the Tar Heel State to push through the crest of the Appalachians into Tennessee. An already big waterway by the time it crosses the Tennessee state line, the French Broad continues dropping in shoals and pools before being slowed as it enters Douglas Lake. It once again begins flowing below Douglas Dam and travels a little less than 40 miles to its end near Knoxville, for a total of 102 miles in the Volunteer State. Here the Holston and French Broad Rivers meet to form the Tennessee River, all part of the greater Mississippi River watershed.

The Paddling

The river starts out and remains much smaller than around Asheville. The tan waters stretch about 60 feet across at the Pisgah Forest put-in. The ramp here is small too, good for canoes and kayaks. The French Broad runs deeper here, its banks thick with trees and brush, including kudzu. Fallen trees effectively narrow the paddling lanes. Rocks are few along the banks and along the bottom. You are in a wide, still-bucolic agricultural valley, nestled between mountains gently rising from these agricultural lands.

After 0.25 mile you come to the first shoal; after flowing through the stony weir, you will realize it is a man-made erosion-stopping setup. Common throughout the upper river, these man-made shoals serve farmers and those downstream by preventing the banks from being washed away and the French Broad getting silted—with the added benefit of adding a little zing to paddlers floating the

French Broad River: Pisgah Forest to Blantyre

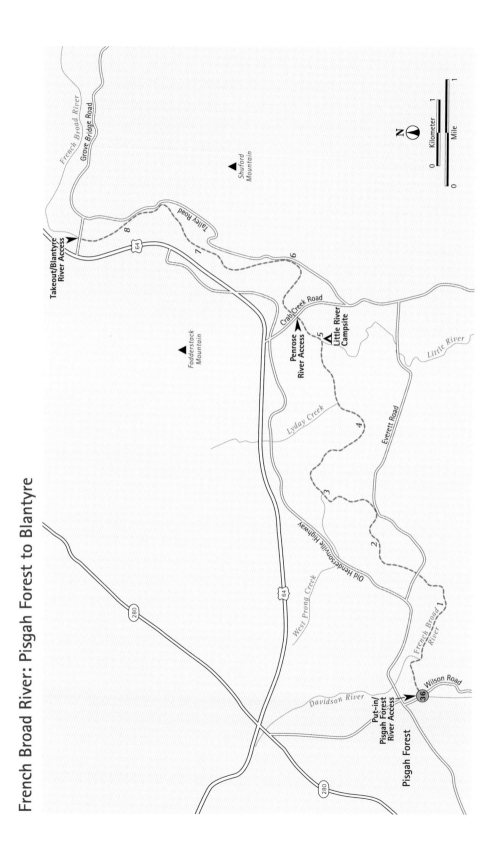

waterway. The routes are simple and straightforward through these rocks. At 0.4 mile the Davidson River enters on river left. This cool, clear, trouty watercourse drains mountains of the Pisgah National Forest ranging more than 1 mile high. You will soon bump into your first hill, a bluff where rhododendron overhangs the waterway, adding attractive blooms in early summer.

Simple riffles and easy man-made shoals keep the action going as you wind through the valley; at 1.5 miles float under Patton Bridge at Everett Road. Downstream, the French Broad meanders through flat farming country, yet a nearly continual line of trees border the waterway. Wooded ridges of Fodderstack and Shuford Mountains rise in the distance. At 3.0 miles West Prong Creek enters on your left; the French Broad then makes a major bend to the southeast.

At 4.4 miles Lyday Creek enters on river left near a large, conspicuous beech tree. The paddling remains easy and the current constant. Look for riprap along the banks, where farmers have stabilized the shoreline. At 5.0 miles the Little River enters on river right. The waterway drains wooded highlands, including waterfall-filled DuPont State Forest. The famed High Falls of DuPont is where the entirety of the Little River plummets from a huge granite face. It is hard to believe that the clear, quiet waterway at its confluence with the French Broad is the same river. The Little River campsite stands at the confluence of the French Broad and Little Rivers, directly at the confluence point. Stone steps just a little up the Little River provide access. The campsite includes a picnic table. *Note:* These campsites on the French Broad River Paddling Trail must be reserved in advance.

Surprisingly, the French Broad does not widen after the influx of the decent-size Little River, pushing on to reach the Crab Creek Road bridge at 5.4 miles. The Penrose river access is on river left just after the bridge. It offers a boat ramp and a small dock, and another spot to take a break. Below Penrose, trees partly canopy the river and the French Broad keeps a consistent steady flow. At 5.9 miles the river comes alongside the base of Shuford Mountain and turns north. From here on to Blantyre, the French Broad will continue to play tag with the ridge, running alongside where wooded bluffs rise and then pulling away toward more-level terrain. Woods rise along the river here and often form a near canopy. At 7.5 miles the river makes a hard bend to the left then enters a longish straightaway. You are nearly done with the trip. Enjoy the final easy, steady segment before floating under Grove Bridge Road to reach the Blantyre Park access, on river right at 8.5 miles. This access consists of concrete steps and a steep boat slide. It takes effort to pull your watercraft up the slide, so be prepared.

37 French Broad River: Rosman to Island Ford

This river adventure takes you down the uppermost French Broad River, running Class I shoals time and again.

Start: Champion Park River Access (Rosman)

End: Island Ford River Access

Length: 10.3 miles

Float time: About 5 hours

Difficulty rating: Easy

Rapids: Class I

River/Lake type: Small valley river bordered by mountains

Current: Steady to fast in places

River gradient: 5.4 feet per mile

Water gauge: French Broad River at Rosman (Check frenchbroadpaddle.com/ gauges/ for runnability.)

Season: Mar through Oct

Land status: Private

Fees or permits: No fees or permits required

Nearest city/town: Rosman

Maps: USGS Rosman NC; French Broad Paddling Trail

Boats used: Kayaks, canoes; tubes on some segments

Organizations: French Broad River Paddling Trail; frenchbroadpaddle.com

Contacts/Outfitters: Headwaters Outfitters, 25 Parkway Rd., Rosman, NC 28772; (828) 877-3106; headwatersoutfitters.com

Put-in/Takeout Information

To the takeout: From the intersection of US 276 and Broad Street in downtown Brevard, take Broad Street west for 0.5 mile to join US 64 West. Follow it for 2.5 miles and turn left on Pole Miller Road; continue 0.4 mile. Turn left on Island Ford Road and follow it 1.7 miles to the Island Ford river access, on your left just before bridging the French Broad River. GPS: N35° 10' 41.0" / W82° 45' 18.7"

To the put-in from the takeout: From Island Ford river access, backtrack on Island Ford Road and stay with it for 2.5 miles to US 64. Turn left, joining US 64 West.

Even the herons like this stretch of the French Broad River.

Stay with US 64 West for 4.9 miles. Turn left onto US 178 South and continue for 0.4 mile. Turn right on Old Turnpike Road and follow it a very short distance; turn left into the Champion Park river access, on your left. The put-in is down the hill a bit to a gravel bar on the French Broad River. GPS: N35° 08' 44.6" / W82° 49' 35.3"

Paddle Summary

This fun paddle on the uppermost French Broad is entirely different from the other three French Broad paddles in this guide (In fact, all four paddles on the French Broad in this guide differ greatly from one another). The paddle starts with a zing as you immediately enter the first of very many shallow Class I shoals on an intimate, literally cool waterway that keeps the action going. Float through the hamlet of Rosman, picking up two forks of the uppermost French Broad. Yet the waterway stays small and intimate, even as many a creek contributes its flow as you meander downstream. Wind your way northeasterly in a wide valley bordered by wooded bluffs, from which you are never far. Along the way, float beneath five bridges. The scenery is fine in the near, with wooded banks and overhanging trees forming a canopy on many stretches, as well as the far, with mountain vistas. The last part of the paddle curves around the northern half of Henry Mountain before ending at the Island Ford access. The run is served by a competent outfitter that makes this adventure even easier. Although the trip is more than 10 miles, the swift water and eye-pleasing scenery will leave even the most jaded paddlers satisfied.

River/Lake Overview

Purportedly the third-oldest river in the world (only the New River of the United States and Egypt's Nile River are older; these claims are not settled), the French Broad River is born in the high mountains of western North Carolina near the town of Rosman, where the forks of the French Broad come together. From there the waterway flows 116 miles in a wide arc through Asheville and the Tar Heel State to push through the crest of the Appalachians into Tennessee. An already big waterway by the time it crosses the Tennessee state line, the French Broad continues dropping in shoals and pools before being slowed as it enters Douglas Lake. It once again begins flowing below Douglas Dam and travels a little less than 40 miles to its end near Knoxville, for a total of 102 miles in the Volunteer State. Here the Holston and French Broad Rivers meet to form the Tennessee River, all part of the greater Mississippi River watershed.

The Paddling

Headwaters Outfitters is a first-class, locally owned outfit that services this run. I have used them and recommend them. Furthermore, I recommend this as a hot-weather paddle. You start at almost 2,200 feet; the water is cool, flowing off the mountains; and much of the run is partly canopied by trees. Champion Park is a small town greenspace with picnic tables and a gravel bar launch. Immediately enter a typical Class I shoal of the upper French Broad—fast, shallow, and fun. The rock-bottomed waterway is clear and clean. Brush, rhododendron, sycamore, willow, and maple line the banks of the small stream, barley big enough at this point to be called a river. You are literally floating through the town of Rosman. At 0.3 mile you paddle under the US 178 bridge and the USGS river gauging station. The town is left behind. Continue in fast riffles, floating by small Mill Creek, then a little bigger Middle Fork French Broad, then still bigger East Fork French Broad River, all by 1.3 miles.

Significant flow has been added to the river, which turns north after bumping into a bluff. Riffles continue, but you will also have man-made rapids where

French Broad River: Rosman to Island Ford

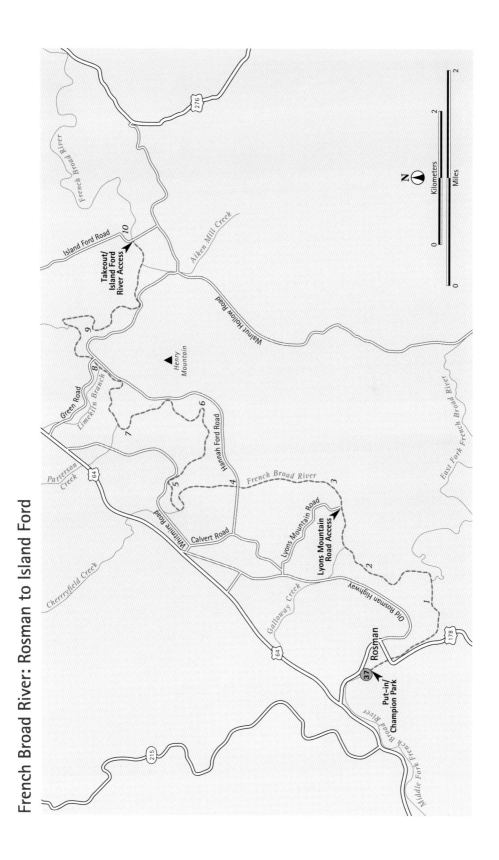

This uppermost part of the French Broad River features fun small shoals like this.

Mountain views are a regular feature of this river run.

farmers have placed rock along the French Broad to curb erosion. Trees overhang the waterway, keeping both the translucent water and paddlers cool in summer. Begin winding through an agricultural valley. Recurring, fun little shoals keep the action moving. Gravel bars are found along the shoals at lower water levels. At 2.4 miles you will see an old metal structure rising from the water, perhaps a former water intake station. Just beyond it, Galloway Creek comes in on the left via culvert. Beyond Galloway Creek, a hill rises on river right. You then float under the Lyons Mountain Road bridge and immediately come to the Lyons Mountain Road river access, on river left at 2.8 miles. Shoot a little rapid just after the bridge, then curve north as you run along a mountain to your right. Shoals continue. Watch for fallen trees that narrow the effective paddling lanes of the French Broad, which remains shallow and clear.

At 4.0 miles float under the Hannah Ford Road bridge. You are heading due north through agricultural flats, and the level terrain opens vistas of the majestic highlands of Pisgah National Forest rising ahead. At 4.5 miles the French Broad curves fast and sharp. A pair of creeks enter on river left as you turn right—first Morgan Mill Creek then Cherryfield Creek. At 5.1 miles another bump from a ridge sends the French Broad rushing southeast toward Henry Mountain, rising nearby. At 6.0 miles the French Broad makes another U-turn before curving back north; distant mountain views return.

The French Broad remains but 60 or so feet wide, smallish and clear, still moving along amid riffles and shoals. At 7.2 miles Patterson Creek enters on river left. Before long you have sidled alongside Henry Mountain again. Bluffs rise. The river is shallow, and you speedily pass modest Limekiln Creek before floating under the Green Road bridge at 8.0 miles. Watch here on the right as you float by a pair of accesses for Headwaters Outfitters camping area on your right. Riffles continue. At 8.6 miles big Catheys Creek enters on the left just before you curve sharply south at still another bluff.

The waterway continues its winding ways, bumping into Henry Mountain a final time at 9.6 miles. Rock and rhododendron complement the riverside forest. Tree cover is common on this stretch. At 10.0 miles Aiken Mill Creek adds its flow on river right. Paddle around a bend and there stands the Island Ford Road bridge. Float under it and reach the Island Ford river access on river left at 10.3 miles, ending the upriver paddling adventure. The access has a series of concrete steps rising steeply from the water.

38 Lake Adger

Wander through the wetlands and coves of this mountain-bordered lake. You'll even see a waterfall along the recommended loop paddle.

Start/End: Public boat ramp (old Red Barn Landing)

Length: 5.6 miles; could easily be longer

Float time: About 2.8 hours

Difficulty rating: Easy–moderate

Rapids: None

River/Lake type: Mountain impoundment

Current: None

River gradient: None

Water gauge: None

Season: May through Sept

Land status: Private

Fees or permits: No fees or permits required

Nearest city/town: Lake Lure

Maps: USGS Mill Springs NC

Boats used: Kayaks, canoes, motorboats, houseboats; no personal watercraft or waterskiing permitted

Organizations: North Carolina Wildlife Resources Commission, 1701 Mail Service Center, Raleigh, NC 27699-1700; ncwildlife.org

Contacts/Outfitters: Jim Smith & Associates, 2311 Hwy. 9, Mill Spring, NC 28756; (864) 583-8150; lakeadger.com

Put-in/Takeout Information

To the put-in/takeout: From Asheville take I-26 East for 31 miles to exit 59 (Saluda). Turn left and take Holbert Cove Road; continue for 9.4 miles. Turn left on Silver Creek Road and follow it for 2.2 miles; turn right at the signed Lake Adger public boat ramp. GPS: N35° 20' 12.0" / W82° 13' 51.0"

Paddle Summary

This paddle on the east side of the Blue Ridge takes place at Lake Adger, a pretty hill-framed lake beyond which rise regal mountain ranges. Here the Green River

Kayaker on a marshy part of Lake Adger

is slowed, and the clean, clear water spreads into hollows, forming exploration-worthy embayments. You'll leave the public boat ramp then enter the main lake on the north shore, curving into these wooded coves, then turn up long and slender Jackson Cove before returning via the south shore. Discover a delightful cascading cataract along this south shore while looking toward mountains rising ahead and the Green River marsh in the fore. The marshes present wildlife-viewing opportunities before you return to the point of origin. Overall, the smallish lake keeps the winds down, yet it is open enough to allow rich mountain views and big enough to paddle until your arms wear out, should you extend beyond the featured route.

River/Lake Overview

Lake Adger dams a portion of the Green River. The Green River is born in southern Henderson County, near the South Carolina state line. The Green flows northeasterly and is first dammed at Lake Summit, just south of Flat Rock. From there it is unleashed and cuts through a scenic gorge favored by whitewater paddlers as it passes under I-26. You can glimpse into the gorge and see the cliffs while on the interstate. Continuing on in Polk County, the Green River flows into Lake Adger.

This impoundment was dammed in 1925 by Blue Ridge Power, an early energy company. The location of the dam was Turner Shoals, and today the dam is still referred to as Turner Shoals Dam. The lake, named for the founder of Blue Ridge Power, John Adger Law, covers 438 acres of water surface and is bordered by more than 14 miles of shoreline. The land around the impoundment is all privately owned and is part of a low-density, environmentally sensitive development. However, the dam and the land under the water are owned by Polk County. The public boat ramp is managed by the North Carolina Wildlife Resources Commission. The hydroelectric operation of Turner Shoals Dam is managed by Northbrook Hydroelectric. Below Lake Adger, the Green River continues flowing easterly to meet its mother stream, the Broad River.

The Paddling

This less-known paddle near Lake Lure doesn't require a fee permit to paddle. Nor do you need to be a member of the homeowners association to use the lake. Just show up at the public boat ramp on Lake Adger and start paddling. Lake Adger is a paddler-friendly destination. Although motorboats are allowed, there are horsepower limits and, even more importantly, neither personal watercraft nor waterskiing is allowed on the lake. Although houses are in proximity to the tarn, they are often partly screened from the shore and, by covenant, have restrictions that keep the impoundment scenic.

North Carolina's mountains are dotted with private communities built around private lakes. Most don't have public boat ramps on them; Lake Adger does.

The lake is scenic and the housing development along the lake understated. And paddlers are welcome, especially considering that the ramp is operated by the North Carolina Wildlife Resources Commission and the lake itself is owned by Polk County. Before the land development, the current ramp location was known as Red Barn Landing. I guess that didn't sound highfalutin enough.

The public ramp has a single launch lane. Nearby, a floating dock is another possible launching spot. The public ramp is located next to the homeowners'

Lake Adger

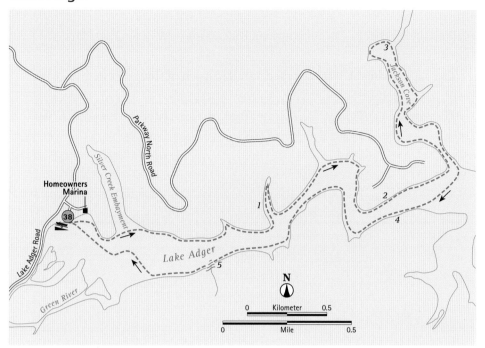

marina. As you look out to your right, the inflow of the Green River forms a marsh, with watery channels broken by vegetated areas. Paddlers can explore this area, making their way up the Green River. Under normal flows many of the channels are very shallow, but they do attract birdlife. Our paddle heads east, immediately passing the homeowners' marina, a small affair. To your right (south) White Oak Mountain stands out in bold relief. Beyond the marina, paddle around a point and pass the deep embayment of Silver Creek. Here look north toward Sugarloaf Mountain. Reach the main shoreline at 0.4 mile. Keep east along the slender east–west oriented lake, with more watery tentacles than an octopus.

The lake clarity reflects its mountain origins. The shoreline is generally hilly, with rich forests rising on the slopes. Rock outcrops add a scenic touch to the water's edge that can also be bluffs of soil. Amid nature, the low-density houses are decently integrated into the landscape, although you will pass many water-side docks. At 0.5 mile paddle past a notable rock outcrop on a point. At 0.7 mile turn into a steep-sided cove. By 0.9 mile you are back in the main body of the lake, yet the lake is never wide, keeping a small-water atmosphere. Soon turn into a very narrow, deep embayment, the head of which is a marshy wetland. Rejoin the main lake at 1.3 miles, keeping easterly along a shoreline of mixed

You can paddle right up to this waterfall on Lake Adger.

rock and soil. At 2.2 miles turn left (north) into Jackson Cove. This is one of the longest arms of Lake Adger and is fed by unpleasantly named Rotten Creek. Despite the moniker, the embayment and the stream are both pleasant prospects, leaving Jackson Cove worth visiting in your canoe or kayak.

At 3.0 miles come to where Rotten Creek feeds the lake. If you paddle close, you'll feel the cool air of the stream pushing into the warmer lake air on a Carolina summer day. This is also a marshy wetland of lush vegetation and shallow water. Curve by a private beach backed by a grassy hill before paddling

The scenery is fine while paddling Lake Adger.

back south, down Jackson Cove, and by 3.7 miles you are back at the channel of the Green River. Extra exploration possibilities extend to your left (southeast) toward Turner Shoals Dam. Otherwise, cross over to the south shoreline and begin heading west along Lake Adger. Extensive montane vistas open to the west. You can see McGraw Mountain and the cliffs of Cliffield Mountain forming sentinels 2,000 feet above the 910-foot pool elevation of Lake Adger. By the way, the lake varies no more than 5 feet from the 910-foot full pool and is usually at lower levels during the winter. The best time to paddle here is late spring through summer.

Continue along the south side of the impoundment (westbound), picking up new shoreline mileage, nearly all of which is wooded. At 4.7 miles you are aiming directly for Cliffield Mountain. In the lower foreground, the marshes of the Green River spread low. At 5.1 miles you are treated to a 25-foot stairstep cascading waterfall that flows directly into the impoundment. If paddling along the south shoreline, you can't miss it. This cataract can slow to a less-than-thrilling flow rate by autumn. Continue west toward the marshes of the Green River. Watch for shallows here, as well as herons and other birdlife. This is your best area for exploration should you seek wildlife. Scan northwest to spy out the marina and boat ramp, now in sight. Return to your point of origin, completing the paddling adventure at 5.6 miles.

39 Lake Oolenoy

Paddle this clear no-motors lake in the shadow of stunning Table Rock Mountain.

Start/End: State park boat ramp

Length: 2.9 miles

Float time: About 1.3 hours

Difficulty rating: Easy

Rapids: None

River/Lake type: Mountain impoundment

Current: None

River gradient: None

Water gauge: None

Season: Mar through Nov

Land status: Public

Fees or permits: Entrance fee required

Nearest city/town: Cleveland, South Carolina

Maps: USGS Table Rock SC–NC; Table Rock State Park

Boats used: Kayaks, canoes

Organizations: South Carolina Department of Natural Resources, Rembert C. Dennis Bldg., 1000 Assembly St., Columbia, SC 29201; (803) 734-9100; dnr.sc.gov

Contacts/Outfitters: Table Rock State Park, 158 Ellison Ln., Pickens, SC 29671; (864) 878-9813; southcarolinaparks.com

Put-in/Takeout Information

To the put-in/takeout: From Asheville take I-26 East to exit 54 (US 25 South/ Greenville) and follow US 25 South for 16 miles. Turn right onto SC 11 South and follow it for 4.3 miles. Turn right onto US 276 West/SC 11 South and continue for 5.4 miles, splitting left to stay with SC 11 for 6.8 miles. Note the first left turn into the Table Rock State Park Visitor Center. Continue over Lake Oolenoy and take the next left onto Sah Ka Na Ga View Road. Follow this road a short distance to a large parking area and long boat ramp descending into Lake Oolenoy, across the lake from the visitor center. Be considerate when using the ramp if others are waiting. GPS: N35° 01' 13.3" / W82° 41' 43.4"

Paddle Summary

This paddle circumnavigates Lake Oolenoy, a scenic impoundment lying at the base of Table Rock Mountain. Located at activity-filled Table Rock Mountain State Park, this aquatic adventure can be complemented with hiking and camping. Since Lake Oolenoy is at a lower elevation than many destinations in this guide, it offers an extended season. From the boat ramp you will circle the shoreline of no-gas-motors Lake Oolenoy, turning into wooded tapering coves before pulling out into the main lake. Here picture-postcard panoramas of Table Rock rise over the water. The paddle then turns into Reeds Run cove, where you paddle deep into an embayment, finding one of the sources of the lake. Finally, enjoy more mountain views, passing the park visitor center before entering the slim embayment of Carrick Creek, where nearer mountain vistas await. Explore up Carrick Creek as far as the depth will allow before circling back to the ramp.

Kayakers prepare to circumnavigate Lake Oolenoy.

River/Lake Overview

Lake Oolenoy is a 67-acre impoundment located within the boundaries of Table Rock State Park. Its headwaters include Carrick and Green Creeks, both of which flow from the south slope of 3,124-foot Table Rock Mountain. They first are slowed at 37-acre Pinnacle Lake, dammed upstream of Lake Oolenoy. Pinnacle Lake also presents first-rate mountain views from its waters; unfortunately, private boats are not allowed on the lake—you must rent a boat from the state park. Carrick Creek is released from the Pinnacle Lake dam then flows to fill Lake Oolenoy. Reeds Run also drains Table Rock Mountain and flows directly into Lake Oolenoy, creating one of its arms. Below the lake, Carrick Creek flows into Oolenoy River, which then flows into the south Saluda River above Greenville, South Carolina.

The Paddling

This watery adventure offers more than just paddling, with the setting being Table Rock State Park, one of South Carolina's finest preserves, within easy striking distance of Asheville/Hendersonville. The distinctive granite face of 3,124-foot Table Rock Mountain has attracted people to this scenic area since the days of the Cherokee, who believed the Great Spirit dined on the mountain's flat top, hence the name Table Rock. Later, this area was developed by the Civilian Conservation Corps (CCC) during the Great Depression. The CCC infrastructure handiwork was so well crafted that Table Rock Mountain State Park was placed on the National Register of Historic Places in 1989. Not that this park needed mankind's imprint to be special. Waterfalls, deep forests, and rock outcrops adorned the mountains long before the 3,083 acres became a state park in 1935. Therefore, especially since this is a shorter paddle, I recommend adding other state park activities onto your Lake Oolenoy adventure. Since this lake is at a lower elevation and farther south than the Asheville/Hendersonville area, the paddling season starts earlier in the spring and extends later in the fall. So when you get that paddling itch when March rolls around, the weather down here at Table Rock State Park may be just warm enough for you to enjoy a day on the water. And when fall colors in the North Carolina highlands have faded to brown, autumn's beauty will still show a cornucopia of hues on the trees here, complemented by the granite outcrops of Table Rock, allowing a last paddle before winter sets in.

Table Rock Mountain rises above Lake Oolenoy.

The boat ramp at the put-in is very long and steep. Set the parking brake on your vehicle when loading and unloading. The boat ramp parking area offers restrooms. You put in directly across from the worth-a-visit park visitor center. For now, head right, making a counterclockwise circuit around Lake Oolenoy. The wooded shoreline rises in hills of maple, oak, and pines, providing an agreeable contrast to the pure mountain waters of the impoundment; the scene as a whole is pleasing to the eye. Alder bushes rim the margin between land and water. At 0.3 mile a rock outcrop along the shore provides a good place to step out and regroup should you need to do so. Otherwise, continue cruising into a small embayment that becomes very shallow at its head, where a smallish stream drains the foothills below Table Rock before flowing into Lake Oolenoy.

Reach the head of the embayment and start turning toward the main part of the lake. Leave this first embayment at 0.6 mile. Here you can look north at your first watery views of Table Rock. Note the nearly sheer granite faces of the mountain, topped by tree cover. The knob to the right is The Stool. Stellar mountain views open as you head east along the south shore of Lake Oolenoy. The park visitor center and the bridge of SC 11 are visible to your north in the foreground across the lake. Reach the lake dam at 1.1 miles; here you turn into the bending arm of Reeds Run, another tributary of Lake Oolenoy. While paddling into the

Lake Oolenoy

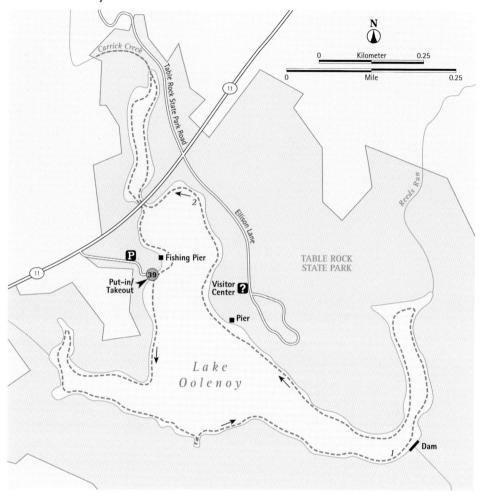

mouth of Reeds Run, feel the cool water flowing over sand before it enters the impoundment. Curving back out of the Reeds Run embayment, you will pass an observation pier and enjoy more mountain views while paddling past the park visitor center. You are coming closer to Table Rock, and the mountain rises and becomes more imposing.

Paddle the shoreline until reaching the narrow channel under the SC 11 bridge. Here you turn into the Carrick Creek arm of Lake Oolenoy. The arm is long and slender and bordered in places with big boulders. A direct view opens ahead. However, as the embayment shallows, you lose panoramas of Table Rock. Yet here you can work your way up the slender and shallow channel of flowing Carrick Creek. Wooded hills clothed in beech, rhododendron, and dog hobble—indicating

Paddlers here are rewarded with views like this.

a cooler microclimate—rise above. If fallen trees aren't blocking the way, you can paddle a good distance up Carrick Creek, but turning around can be a challenge. On your way back out, you will paddle over shallows at the mouth of Carrick Creek then paddle your way back under the SC 11 bridge at 2.7 miles. From here it is an easy cruise along the shore—just make sure to give the anglers on the park fishing pier wide berth as you pass them just before returning to the boat ramp at 2.9 miles, completing the paddling adventure at Table Rock State Park.

VIEW LAKE OOLENOY FROM ON HIGH

Want a top-down view of Lake Oolenoy? From the park's Carrick Nature Center, take the distinctive Table Rock National Recreation Trail, also developed during the Civilian Conservation Corps (CCC) era. It is 3.4 miles each way. See rock features aplenty en route, including rockhouses, huge boulders, and wide-open rock slabs from which incredible views emanate. The first part of the hike also passes several cataracts. Be apprised that the hike climbs nearly 2,000 feet from base to its high point. The first of the three primary views is from a CCC-era shelter, where to the northeast you can see Greenville and Paris Mountain. To the east and below are the state park's lakes. From there hike on to Panther Gap then along the top of the ridge, visiting Governors Rock and Table Rock itself. Parts of the hike traverse steps cut directly into the rock, enhancing the adventure at one of South Carolina's most prominent landmarks.

40 Bear Creek Lake

View a huge waterfall and lesser cascades while paddling this highland lake on the headwaters of the Tuckasegee River.

Start/End: Bear Creek Lake boat ramp

Length: 6.2 miles

Float time: About 3 hours

Difficulty rating: Moderate

Rapids: None

River/Lake type: Small mountain impoundment

Current: None

River gradient: None

Water gauge: None

Season: Apr through Oct

Land status: Private

Fees or permits: No fees or permits required

Nearest city/town: Cullowhee

Maps: USGS Big Ridge NC; Bear Creek Lake

Boats used: Kayaks, canoes, pontoon boats, speedboats

An angler tries his luck on Bear Creek Lake.

Organizations: North Carolina Wildlife Resources Commission, 1701 Mail Service
Center, Raleigh, NC 27699-1700; ncwildlife.org

Contacts/Outfitters: Bear Lake Reserve, 412 Lake Forest Dr., Tuckasegee, NC 28783;
(828) 293-3445; bearlakereserve.com

Put-in/Takeout Information

To the put-in/takeout: From Asheville take I-40 West to exit 27 (US 74/US 19).
Stay with US 74 for 22 miles to exit 85 (US 23 Business South) and drive for 1.3
miles. Turn left onto NC 107 South and continue for 12 miles then turn left on
NC 281 South. Follow NC 281 South for 4.1 miles and turn right onto NC 1137.
A sign here reads, "Bear Creek Lake Access Area, Open to the Public." Follow
gravel NC 1137 for 0.7 mile to dead-end at the public boat ramp. GPS: N35° 14'
38.6" / W83° 03' 50.5"

Paddle Summary

This paddle explores a large portion of Bear Creek Lake, a highland impoundment in the upper Tuckasegee River watershed. Although upscale homes are
scattered along the shore, the lake does have a public boat ramp you can use to
explore this mountain rimmed tarn, and even see a few waterfalls while you are
at it. Start in the northwest part of the lake and paddle southeast, bordered by
attractive shoreline upon which rise rugged wooded ridges. Make your way past
a few coves then curve to view the tall bluffs of the River Cliffs as well as Sols
Creek Falls, a 160-foot cataract. Paddle into the embayment of Sols Creek then
take the 0.25-mile trail up to this incredible cataract as it faucets over a rock rim.
From there, paddle beneath Eyelet Ridge, where another trail—albeit difficult—
leads to Flat Creek Falls, located within Nantahala National Forest. Back on the
water, turn into the embayment of Robinson Creek and explore this bouldering
cascade. Finally, make your way back to the public boat ramp, probably in a direct
line, since all this waterfall exploring adds mucho time to your paddle.

River/Lake Overview

Bear Creek Lake is one of four small impounds situated on the upper East
Fork Tuckasegee River. The other three are Tanasee Creek Lake, Wolf Creek Lake,

and Cedar Cliff Lake. The East Fork meets the West Fork Tuckasegee River just below Cedar Cliff Lake to form the Tuckasegee River. Flowing west from Tanasee Ridge, these upper forks of the Tuckasegee River flow northwest to meet the Oconaluftee River near Bryson City. From there the Tuckasegee flows into the Little Tennessee River and is dammed as Fontana Lake. That gorgeous impoundment borders much of the south side of Great Smoky Mountains National Park before cutting through a deep gorge and ending up on the west side of the Appalachians where the Little Tennessee flows to meet the Tennessee River.

The Paddling

Back in the 1920s, the mountains of western North Carolina were thinly populated and certainly not the recreation destination they are today. However, electricity had come to the Carolina high country, and residents wanted it. The Nantahala Power and Light Company needed a reliable energy source, and it seemed that the forks of the Tuckasegee River could be a viable source of hydropower. The West Fork was developed first, both for local power and for producing aluminum for aircraft manufacturing during World War II. In the 1950s a combination of the Korean War (more war-materiel demand) and increased local demand led to four smaller stairstep dams and lakes being built along the upper East Fork. Tanasee Creek Lake is the uppermost and comes in at 183 acres, while Wolf Creek Lake is but 49 acres. Bear Creek Lake is next and the largest, at 476 acres. The lowest impoundment is Cedar Cliff Lake, 121 acres big. Each of the impoundments is a worthy paddling destination. The upside of Bear Creek Lake is the waterfalls—also that its uppermost arms are on national forest property. But consider the others as potential paddling destinations as well.

Leave the North Carolina Department of Natural Resources public ramp and join Bear Creek Lake, elevation 2,552 feet, paddling southeast. Gladie Creek embayment, with docks and houses, stretches to your left; the large North Carolina Wildlife Resources Commission fishing dock is to your right. Join the main part of Bear Creek Lake, continuing southeast along the shoreline. Dodgen Ridge rises overhead as you paddle first into the Em Branch cove, reaching its head at 0.7 mile. Paddle close and you can see a modest waterfall tumbling into the lake.

The water reveals a high degree of clarity below while forests grow thick on the shore. Look for fish in the shallows. Gray rocks, rich with mosses and lichens, provide contrast to the wooded shore. Deed restrictions keep houses

The River Cliffs border Sols Creek Falls.

from getting thicker than the woods, yet you will pass plenty of docks and view houses. Occasional fallen trees reach from the shore into the water.

At 1.7 miles you have reached the head of Mill Cove. Though this stream does not have a waterfall, you can clearly hear the watercourse flowing down the heights of Dodgen Ridge, discharging into Bear Creek Lake. Stay with the shoreline, passing small beaches. Circle the ridge harboring the River Cliffs. Rocks and cliffs line the shore here, including one with a small cave at 2.4 miles. At 2.5 miles pass an island on your right. It is often used as a stopping spot. Here you turn left (north) and the River Cliffs rise to your left, an unmistakable line of stone amid the forest. Ahead, the sounds of Sols Creek Falls drift across the impoundment. And then you see the upper part of the falls, diving from a cliffline then into the woods, its base unseen.

At 3.0 miles you reach the head of the Sols Creek embayment. You can hear the cataract roaring, as well as other shoals. Paddlers can get into the shallow mouth of the creek and find a landing on the right. Here a well-beaten-down user-created trail leads up the right bank of Sols Creek, winding around rhododendron and amid trees and brush big and small. Make the base of Sols Creek Falls after 0.3 mile, and boy is the walk worth it. Here Sols Creek makes a reckless, narrow 160-foot faucet dive off the edge of a cliff, splashing onto rocks a bit at first then making a free fall into an open shallow pool from which spray bounces and wets everything about. In a word—wow!

Bear Creek Lake

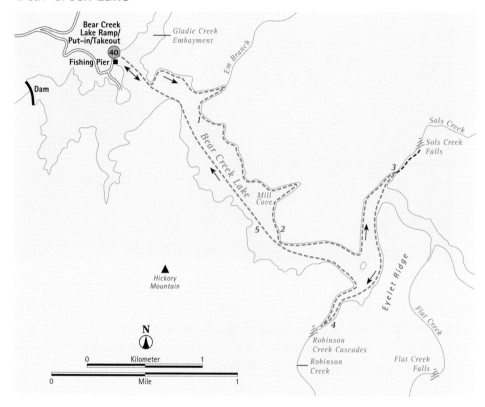

After hiking back to your watercraft, resume the paddle, leaving south from Sols Creek embayment to then cross the lake at a very narrow point. Work along the shoreline beneath Eyelet Ridge then come to the signed trailhead for Flat Creek Falls at 3.7 miles. This path works up Eyelet Ridge (on the top-ten all-time Southern Appalachian names list) then into Flat Creek up its valley. Flat Creek Falls is a 150-footer highlighted by an initial curtain drop followed by a long slide. It's not easy to reach. Old logging roads and user-created trails add to the challenge.

Resume paddling into the Robinson Creek embayment, reaching its mouth at 4.1 miles. Here modest cascades tumble over boulders into the lake. The creek mouth is often choked with logs, and frankly it is an afterthought compared to the two previous legendary spillers. From here, if you aren't worn out, your day is gone. Leave the embayment, turning back into the main lake at 4.4 miles. From here it is a little less than 2 miles as a straight shot to the ramp. Houses are spread along the west shore as you return, as is the development clubhouse.

Sols Creek Falls is but a short hike from Bear Creek Lake.

Hickory Mountain rises above this shoreline. If you want to explore more, and perhaps even camp out, paddle east from Sols Creek embayment to the upper reaches of Wolf Creek Lake, pitching your tent on national forest property.

CAMPING ADVENTURES AROUND ASHEVILLE

Camping is a wonderful way to enhance a paddling, hiking, or bicycling adventure, or it can simply be an adventure unto itself. The Asheville region has a variety of drive-up, auto-accessible campgrounds that serve as woodsy getaways for you and your family or a group of friends wanting to enjoy the great outdoors.

Some enduring scenes come to mind when I think of camping. Morning rays of sunlight piercing the trees, wood smoke gently curling upward from the flickering fire, riding bikes over gravel roads, the folly of erecting a brand new tent, friends and families enjoying supper together, all hands running for cover as an afternoon thunderstorm breaks loose, the smell of hamburgers wafting through the trees, an angler proudly displaying freshly caught fish while returning to camp, autumn's golden leaves drifting onto a cluttered picnic table.

To get you started on your camping adventures, here are five recommended frontcountry drive-up campgrounds for you to consider. All are within an hour's drive of Asheville and close to the hiking, bicycling, and paddling adventures detailed in this guide.

Mount Pisgah Campground: Looking out over the
Blue Ridge Parkway from near Mount Pisgah

Lake Powhatan

Nearest town: Asheville

Open: Mar through Dec

Individual sites: 97

Each site has: Picnic table, fire grate, tent pad, lantern post; Lakeside Loop also has electric, water, sewer

Site assignment: First-come, first-served and reservation

Facilities: Hot showers, water, flush toilets

Fee: Yes

Contact: fs.usda.gov/nfsnc

Very close to Asheville, Lake Powhatan Recreation Area offers a combination of quality camping for RVs and tents, with outdoor adventures accessible directly from your campsite. If you live in Asheville, it's a quick camping getaway; if visiting Lake Powhatan from afar, you can access city offerings as well as outdoor adventure opportunities. The well-maintained campground is divided into three loops stretched over rolling hills above Lake Powhatan. The Lakeside Loop, designed for RVs, with electric, water, and sewer, stands well above the water under preserved hemlocks. The Bent Creek Loop has large camps under tall forest. The Big John Loop lies in a pine-oak-hickory forest. Despite the hilly terrain, the campsites themselves are leveled with landscaping timbers. The Hard Times Loop is oldest and quietest if you like solitude. Water spigots and showers are convenient to all campers. For safety and security, campground hosts man the gates.

The campground also features twelve "glamping" canvas tents for overnight rental. Each tent includes a bed with linens, a bedside table, camp chairs, and a cooler in addition to a fire ring and outdoor picnic table. Lake Powhatan will fill on summer weekends. Ensure yourself a spot using the reservation system.

Recreation is immediate. Fish or swim at Lake Powhatan during the warm season. Boats aren't allowed on the impoundment. You can also angle on Bent Creek, vying for trout. Bent Creek Experimental Forest is a nationally rated mountain biking destination, with plenty of trails for all bicycler skill levels. Hikers also enjoy this network of pathways. The North Carolina Arboretum with an array of trees, trails, and interpretive information is a short distance away by auto. The city of Asheville, with its music, dining, and more, is close too, making Lake Powhatan a great base camp for outdoor—and indoor—adventures.

Access: From exit 33 on I-26 South in Asheville, take NC 191 south 2 miles to the signed right turn at a traffic light. Keep forward on Wesley Branch Road to dead-end at the campground. Campground address: 375 Wesley Branch Rd., Asheville, NC 28806. GPS: N35° 29' 17.0" / 82° 37' 45.3"

Mount Mitchell State Park Campground

Nearest town: Asheville
Open: May through Oct
Individual sites: 9
Each site has: Picnic table, picnic table, grill, bearproof food storage box
Site assignment: First-come, first-served and reservation
Facilities: Water spigots, flush toilets
Fee: Yes
Contact: ncparks.gov/mount-mitchell-state-park/camping

Asheville not only has the highest peak east of the Mississippi River in its backyard, it also has the highest campground east of the river as well, right here at Mount Mitchell State Park. Standing at 6,320 feet, this mountaintop getaway more closely resembles camping in northern New England than North Carolina. Yet another superlative: Mount Mitchell State Park is North Carolina's first and oldest state preserve.

The campground is set in a wind-sculpted, weather-stunted spruce-fir forest, found almost exclusively above 5,000 feet, along with mountain ash and a few hardwoods. The tent-only venues are strung along a gravel path, where campsites are separated by evergreens, delivering decent campsite privacy, despite the camps being fairly small and relatively close to one another. You'll find two water spigots and a bathroom with flush toilets along the campsite trail.

The intimate, quiet campground stays busy during summer, despite Mount Mitchell being cloaked in fog, rain, or snow 75 percent of the time. May and October can be downright chilly. Just be prepared, and you'll stay warm.

Hiking is the primary pastime at the state park, with auto touring on the Blue Ridge Parkway coming in a close second. Of course going to the high point of Mount Mitchell is a must, but a whole network of trails range through the high country here, including a great loop hike detailed in this guide. Even though the state park comes in at 1,860 acres, being surrounded by the Pisgah National

Forest and the Blue Ridge Parkway effectively increases the size of this special preserve, making hikes of all types and distances a possibility.

Access: From Asheville take the Blue Ridge Parkway north 34 miles to milepost 355. Turn left into Mount Mitchell State Park. The campground is 4 miles up the road on your right. Campground address: 2388 NC 128, Burnsville, NC 28714. GPS: N35° 45' 35.0" / W82° 16' 16.5"

Cataloochee Campground

Nearest town: Waynesville
Open: Mid–Apr through Oct
Individual sites: 27
Each site has: Picnic table, fire pit, lantern post
Site assignment: Reservation only
Facilities: Water spigots, flush toilets, hot showers
Fee: Yes
Contact: nps.gov/grsm/

Cataloochee Valley is one of the prettiest places in Great Smoky Mountains National Park. And that is saying a lot. Home to wild elk, bordered by mountains, striped with trout streams, and overlain with historical buildings, Cataloochee Campground can be your home base for exploring this special place. At 2,600 feet, Cataloochee Valley offers warm summer days and cool nights. The twenty-seven-site camp is set in a flat and bordered by Cataloochee Creek on one side. White pines tower over the camping area, adding another plus to this campground so popular—and remote—that reservations are required for an overnight stay.

The campsites are set in a flat on a basic loop; six are on Cataloochee Creek. A campground host greets you at the entrance, keeping things safe and sound. This is primarily the domain of tenters and small popups; the winding entrance road keeps most RVers away. No showers are available, but the camp does have flush toilets and water spigots.

Remember that reservations are required. Also, smart campers will factor in the winding dead-end road and natural attractions within Cataloochee, getting all their supplies before entering Great Smoky Mountains National Park.

Once settled in, you can relax in the campground, fish the streams, spyglass for elk, or do what most people do when they come here—hike. Make the historic hike to Little Cataloochee Church. Visit a valley with a remote dwelling then come to the venerated white house of worship, tracing old pioneer roads turned trails. The hike to Mount Sterling is within easy striking distance. Climb into spruce-fir forest and savor 360-degree vistas of the eastern end of the Smokies and beyond. See the giant tulip trees, Civil War graves, and homesites on Caldwell Fork Trail. Numerous footbridges add to the fun. Visit the Woody Place on Rough Fork Trail. Other historic structures can be seen via the scenic road through Cataloochee Valley. Just make sure to reserve your site, then make the most of your time in this special swath of the Smokies.

A Cataloochee Campground hiker stands near preserved Cook Cabin.

Access: From exit 20 on I-40 west of Asheville, drive west on NC 276. Follow it a short distance then turn right on Cove Creek Road, which you follow nearly 6 miles to enter the park. Two miles beyond the park boundary, turn left onto the paved Cataloochee Road, and follow it for 3 miles. The campground will be on your left. GPS: N35° 37' 52.0" / W83° 05' 10.4"

Mount Pisgah

Nearest town: Asheville
Open: Mid-May through Oct
Individual sites: 68 tent-only, 29 pop-ups and vans, 33 RVs
Each site has: Picnic table, fire grate, lantern post, bearproof food storage locker; some have tent pads
Site assignment: First-come, first-served and reservation
Facilities: Hot showers, water spigots, flush toilets
Fee: Yes
Contact: nps.gov/blri

Situated at almost 5,000 feet in elevation along the Blue Ridge Parkway, this campground offers sites for RVs, pop-ups, and tents, each in their own loops set among highland spruce, birch, and maple mixed with thickets of rhododendron. This is my favorite campground along the entire Blue Ridge Parkway. For starters, the campground makes the most of its highland setting, weaving the campsites into the stunning scenery.

The sites are well maintained and well groomed, adding to the already beautiful natural scenery. A campground host keeps your camping experience running smoothly. Since it has both reservable and first-come, first-served sites, you can usually get a site anytime you want, but reservations are recommended on major summer holiday weekends. Bears roam these parts, so keep your food in the food storage locker or in your car at all times. Additionally, be prepared for cool conditions at this nearly mile-high camp.

Adventures aplenty are within easy striking distance of the campground. Head to the top of Mount Pisgah or the observation tower atop Frying Pan Mountain. Additional nature trails are strung all along the Parkway hereabouts. You can visit Shining Rock area or Yellowstone Falls and Graveyard Fields. Hikes to these places are detailed in this guide. For watery fun, visit Sliding Rock on US

276 south of the Parkway, a water feature on Looking Glass Creek where kids of all ages shoot down a natural water slide into a pool (fee in season).

For convenience's sake, a camp store and the Pisgah Inn are located just across the Parkway from the campground. You can even walk to breakfast, lunch, or dinner from your campsite. Just don't post your fancy meal on the Internet—you want your friends to think you're roughing it.

> Access: From Asheville take I-26 South to exit 33 (NC 191) and take NC 191 South to the Blue Ridge Parkway and milepost 393.6. Turn south on the Parkway and continue to milepost 408. The campground will be on your right. GPS: N35° 24' 09.7" / W82° 45' 23.0"

North Mills River Campground

Nearest town: Mills River
Open: Year-round; limited services Nov–Mar
Individual sites: 31 tent and trailer sites
Each site has: Tent pad, picnic table, fire ring; one site has full hookups
Site assignment: First-come, first-served and reservation
Facilities: Water spigots, flush and waterless toilets, hot showers
Fee: Yes
Contact: fs.usda.gov/nfsnc

Set in Pisgah National Forest not far from Asheville, North Mills Campground presents an attractively wooded, relaxed campground. Set in a flat along the mountain stream that is North Mills River, the camp is staffed by camp hosts, keeping it safe and sound. Equipped with hot showers except during winter, this camp makes a good midway point between attractions of Pisgah National Forest and downtown Asheville, just 30 minutes away.

A bridge leads across North Mills River to the main campground, with a mix of deeply wooded and open sites—your choice. And with only thirty-one sites, it won't seem too big or overcrowded. You will find your fellow campers local families and active groups. A picnic area occupies another stretch of the riverside flat. One way to check out adventure opportunities is to drive FR 1206, leaving from the campground, coming out near the Pink Beds, a highland mountain vale with a nearby visitor center on US 276 where you can learn about the history of

North Mills Campground: Looking Glass Falls is just part of an auto tour emanating from North Mills Campground.

American forestry. From there you can drive to Sliding Rock, a natural waterslide along Looking Glass Creek. You'll also drive by Looking Glass Falls, yet another cataract in this land of waterfalls. Make your way down to Brevard before returning to your escape camp at North Mills River. A sizable trail network is within easy access of the campground. This is where a map of the Pisgah District of Pisgah National Forest comes in handy. Walk or mountain bike atop ridges and along streams, enjoying the vast woodlands protecting the Blue Ridge, then return to your convenient and scenic refuge.

Access: From exit 40 on I-26 South of Asheville, take NC 280 for 3.8 miles. Turn right onto North Mills River Road (NC 1345). Turn right at the campground sign and follow North Mills River Road for 5 miles, intersecting the North Mills River Campground. The park address is 5289 North Mills River Rd., Mills River, NC 28742. GPS: N35° 24' 23.7" / W82° 38' 35.9"

About the Author

Johnny Molloy is a writer and adventurer based in Johnson City, Tennessee. His outdoor passion started on a backpacking trip in Great Smoky Mountains National Park while attending the University of Tennessee. That first foray unleashed a love of the outdoors that has led Johnny to spend most of his time hiking, backpacking, canoe camping, and tent camping for the past four decades. Friends enjoyed his outdoor adventure stories; one even suggested he write a book. He pursued his friend's idea and soon parlayed his love of the outdoors into an occupation. The results of his efforts are more than seventy-five books. His writings include hiking, camping, and paddling guidebooks; comprehensive guidebooks covering a specific area; and true outdoor adventure books covering all or parts of twenty-six states.

Johnny continues writing and traveling extensively throughout the United States, engaging in a variety of outdoor pursuits. His non-outdoor endeavors include serving the Lord as a Gideon, world history, and University of Tennessee sports. For the latest on Johnny, please visit johnnymolloy.com.